THE
CITY GARDENER'S
HANDBOOK

A London balcony garden, Circa 1877 *Courtesy, Library, Massachusetts Horticultural Society*

THE
CITY GARDENER'S HANDBOOK

The Definitive Guide to Small-Space Gardening

Linda Yang

Line drawings by
Stephen K-M. Tim

Garden plans rendered by
Sharon Bradley Papp

Book design by
Martin Moskof

STOREY
BOOKS

North Adams, Massachusetts

The mission of Storey Publishing is to serve our customers by publishing practical information that encourages personal independence in harmony with the environment.

Cover design by Cynthia N. McFarland
Cover photographs by Valerie W. Gerry

The information in this book is true and complete to the best of our knowledge. All recommendations are made without guarantee on the part of the author or Storey Publishing. The author and publisher disclaim any liability in connection with the use of this information. For additional information please contact Storey Books, 210 MASS MoCA Way, North Adams, MA 01247.

Storey Books are available for special premium and promotional uses and for customized editions. For further information, please call Storey's Custom Publishing Department at 1-800-793-9396.

Grateful acknowledgment is made to the following for permission to reprint previously published material:

J.M. DENT & SONS, LIMITED: Excerpt from *The Book of Garden Ornament* by Peter Hunt (1974). Reprinted by permission of J.M. Dent & Sons, Limited.

DOUBLEDAY, A DIVISION OF BANTAM, DOUBLEDAY, DELL PUBLISHING GROUP, INC.: Excerpt(s) from *Are You Your Garden's Worst Pest?* by Cynthia Westcott. Copyright © 1961 by Cynthia Westcott. Used by permission of Doubleday, a Division of Bantam, Doubleday, Dell Publishing Group, Inc.

DUKE UNIVERSITY PRESS: Excerpt from *Gardening For Love: The Market Bulletins* by Elizabeth Lawrence, edited by Allen Lacy. Copyright © 1987, 1988 by Duke University Press. Reprinted by permission of Duke University Press.

DAVID R. GODINE, PUBLISHER, INCORPORATED: Excerpt from *The Opinionated Gardener* by Geoffrey B. Charlesworth. Copyright © 1988 by Geoffrey B. Charlesworth. Reprinted by permission of David R. Godine, Publisher.

NORTHEASTERN UNIVERSITY PRESS: Excerpt from *To Dwell Is to Garden: A History of Boston's Community Garden* by Sam Bass Warner, photographs by Hansi Durlach. Copyright © 1987 by Sam Bass Warner, Jr. Photographs copyright © by Hansi Durlach. Reprinted by permission of Northeastern University Press.

RODALE PRESS, INC.: Excerpt from *Pay Dirt* by J. I. Rodale. Copyright 1945 by J. I. Rodale. Reprinted by permission of Rodale Press, Inc., Emmaus, PA 18098.

Acknowledgments of garden owners, designers and landscapers are on page 301.

Printed in the United States by Vicks Lithograph & Printing
10   9   8   7   6   5   4   3   2   1

Library of Congress Cataloging-in-Publication Data

Yang, Linda.
    The city gardener's handbook : the definitive guide to small-space gardening / by Linda Yang.
        p. cm.
    Includes bibliographical references (p.) and index.
    ISBN 1-58017-449-3 (alk. paper)
    1. Gardening. 2. Container Gardening. 3. Title.

SB453 .Y29 2002
635.9'67—dc21

2001057618

For Naomi and David

the next generation of gardeners,

and John, for the garden we'll continue making

Contents

Foreword to the New Edition

Katherine Powis
Librarian, The Horticultural Society of New York

City gardeners are up against it: the concrete and grit, the lack of light, the cramped spaces, and sun-scorched, wind-burned rooftops. And that's just what this book is about. For in spite of the challenges, plants and gardens do manage to appear in the most unlikely places—from annuals in colorful tree pits and artistic window boxes, to herbs in flourishing streetside community spaces, to shrubs and trees in lavish, secret private retreats—all softening the hardscape and breathing nature's colors and life into the urban scene.

The perception that gardens and gardening offer sanctuary speaks to the critical role that plants play in the urban environment. Thriving greenery tempts—even beguiles—city folk, sets them dreaming, and often brings them right to the gardener's door. So when hopeful gardeners come to our library door to ask me how to get started or how to cope with the many demands of planting, I put *The City Gardener's Handbook* into their hands. It's just the best book on the subject I know.

Here at The Horticultural Society of New York, we are committed to improving the quality of city life through horticulture. Our staff bring garden know-how to children in public schools, to communities around public libraries, and to prison inmates on Rikers Island. And our midtown-Manhattan library, often referred to as the heart and soul of the organization, welcomes all with an interest in plants and gardens to browse, read, research, enquire, learn, and grow.

It's here in our reading room that questions posed sometimes sprout into conversations, as those eager to share engage with those eager to know, discussing books like this one, which provides answers to the problems at hand. Gardeners are like that; they just can't help themselves. The informality and spontaneity of these exchanges keeps my job fun. City gardeners resemble information seekers everywhere. Because they are nurturing a passion, they need to know—not everything on the subject, of course, and certainly not all at once.

Beginners often look for help only as the need arises. When the bulbs arrive, they want to know which end goes up. After perusing the catalogs, they wonder what a hardy annual is. Seasoned gardeners, on the other hand, are always seeking to expand their inventory of perennials and shrubs to take their gardening to the next level.

Whether you're just setting out in your small landscape or are already immersed in its joys, you'll quickly discover *The City Gardener's Handbook* has much to offer. In plain-spoken language, it covers gardening, from the basics to some of the most advanced techniques—with a focus on the full range of conditions unique to city habitats. Its accessible format makes it easy to refer to, but its captivating style will likely draw you into sitting down and reading all the way through.

A garden in the city, regardless of its size, is a precious thing. If you're fortunate enough to have outdoor space in town, consider yourself doubly blessed, for in Linda Yang you have a good neighbor as well. Not the kind who leans on the fence regaling you with her own garden successes, nor the kind who frowns on you for what you don't know. Linda is someone who's been there, done that—both upstairs (a balcony and rooftop terrace) and downstairs (front and back yards), someone with an expert hand extended, coaxing you along as needed.

City gardeners can now take heart. After a brief hiatus, *The City Gardener's Handbook* is back in print once more.

Home gardeners in Robert Buist's city nursery, Philadelphia 1846. *Courtesy, Library Company of Philadelphia.*

*. . . the sort of garden as very likely was laid out in Philadelphia
in the early years, [was] enclosed, rectilinear in design, practical
in use, and informal in planting.*
—Elizabeth McLean, *British and American Gardens in the Eighteenth Century,* 1984

Foreword

Jane G. Pepper
President, Pennsylvania Horticultural Society

The demand for practical information by the city gardener has grown
steadily, making it truly a pleasure to welcome *The City and Town Gardener.*

It is 15 years since Linda Yang first treated us to the joys of *The Terrace
Gardener's Handbook.* Here, finally was a gardener who spoke directly
to the unusual challenges city gardeners face. She understood firsthand
the frustration of trying to fit a whole botanic garden on a balcony, of trying to beat conditions few country gardeners face, and there were lists of
plants the author could recommend because she had grown most of
them herself. The copies of this book in our library at the Pennsylvania
Horticultural Society are well thumbed, and the rear flyleaf shows they
have circulated more per year than many other volumes.

This successor book seems especially valuable in Philadelphia, where for
more than two centuries gardening has been a prime activity—some
might say a passion. William Penn's plan for the city, which he projected
as a "greene Country Towne," made provision for gardens throughout
the townscape that would please the eye and produce vegetables, fruits
and herbs "for the economy of the household." In 1759 a traveler to
Philadelphia described the city as being well endowed with "villas, gar-

dens and luxuriant orchards." Notable too was the home of Edward Shippen, the mayor of the newly established city, whose "Orchards and Gardens adjoyning to his Great House [included an] extraordinary fine and large Garden abounding with Tulips, Pinks, Carnations, Roses, Lilies . . ."

Such keen gardeners eagerly sought new introductions and developed firm friendships with local botanists like James Logan and John Bartram. And by the middle of the nineteenth century Philadelphia had produced such outstanding seedsmen as David Landreth and Johnson & Stokes, and nurserymen like Thomas Meehan and Bernard M'Mahon.

In 1827 the Pennsylvania Horticultural Society was formed to address the needs of the burgeoning group of gardeners. Today the society continues to serve its city in many ways—not the least of which is the annual Philadelphia Flower Show, host to nearly a quarter million visitors. The show allows the society to further William Penn's notion of a "greene" Philadelphia by generating revenues to assist residents in the planting of vegetable gardens, street trees, windowboxes and small parks, which sparkle with color and add to the ambience of the neighborhoods. The society's annual City Gardens Contest also recognizes the challenges these gardeners face. The judges—several hundred each year—never fail to marvel at the ingenuity and dedication with which the urban plant enthusiasts tackle their tough assignments.

As Ms. Yang says, "we city gardeners must learn to disregard the discouraging, then proceed to confound the cynical." Gardening in town is not easy and city gardeners across the nation deserve the very best information. They deserve Ms. Yang's smooth chapter on getting started and her introduction to the plants to choose. They deserve the lists that are sure to help them as they develop their own roster of reliable resources. The city gardener also deserves Ms. Yang's cheerful, optimistic approach. She tells of those she's met whose triumphs over adversity will encourage others to do what good gardeners everywhere do—give it a try. She's eager, too, to help others learn through her own mistakes, and the book is full of practical, hard-won, nitty-gritty advice.

Since Ms. Yang produced her first book we've been treated to her articles on city gardening in a variety of publications, and in particular her regular column in The Home Section of Thursday's *New York Times.* As you benefit from the author's experiences, know that others, in turn, will benefit from your endeavors. It's a special treat to walk by a colorful front yard on a busy street, or to peek through a gate and enjoy a glimpse of a carefully tended patio or balcony terrace. There's nothing quite like a flourishing garden in a sea of concrete and glass.

Brooklyn gardens overlooking New York harbor, Circa 1860 *Courtesy, The New-York Historical Society*

This [garden] place is dedicated to the honorable pleasures of
rejoicing the eye, refreshing the nose, and renewing the spirit.
—Erasmus, *Convivium Religiosum,* circa 1500

Preface

No, I am *not* a frustrated country transplant. I was born in Brooklyn, attended college in Philadelphia, and grew two children in various Manhattan sites. I harbor not one whit of hankering for any greener pasture.

I can't recall the first time I found myself fielding questions about how I gardened on a balcony, and later on a rooftop terrace. Nor do I remember when I began answering in more detail than any listener expected. But those responses led to my writing *The Terrace Gardener's Handbook,* which was originally published in 1975 and reissued in 1982. That book focused on gardens "upstairs"—balconies, terraces, rooftops, penthouses and patios—where plants grow *above* the ground, in containers.

With the wealth of new garden information and more city gardeners than ever, an update seemed appropriate. So did an expansion to include gardens "downstairs"—front or back yards where plants grow *in* the ground. It seemed logical to use as a starting point some of the original information, and those familiar with *The Terrace Gardener's Handbook* may detect, here and there, a voice from that earlier work. That book grew out of firsthand experiences "upstairs"; this successor has grown out of firsthand experiences "downstairs," thanks to my relocation to a city house with a yard.

Life leads along many strange paths, and I consider it the purest of good luck that after several years of practicing architecture I slipped off the road the University of Pennsylvania had prepared me for and into the garden. In retrospect, this rerouting into horticulture was inevitable for the five-year-old who never forgot her bewilderment at watching city workers chop down the "illegal" street tree her father had nurtured.

In 1979 I was asked to inaugurate a city garden column for a new section of Thursday's *New York Times* called The Home Section. Conceived during the administration of Executive Editor A. M. Rosenthal, The Home Section and my garden column evolved under the discerning eye of two gifted journalists: former Living/Style senior editor Nancy Newhouse and the late Home Section editor Dona Guimaraes. I am grateful that I had nearly a decade of Dona Guimaraes's truly inspired guidance. I am grateful too, that her successors, Jane Traulsen, and now Stephen Drucker, have continued to give me a legitimate excuse to do exactly what I have come to enjoy most: visit, photograph, learn from and then write about my fellow city gardeners.

No garden book can possibly come into being without the kindness of friends, and many have been more than generous with their contributions. I am particularly beholden to Richard Abel, publisher of Timber Press, who reissued *The Terrace Gardener's Handbook* and encouraged me with kindness and expertise through much of this work, and Barbara Anderman, not only for exemplary counsel but for being the first editor to try to convince me I had another garden book tucked inside.

Horticultural mentors from the earliest years include Elizabeth Scholtz, now director emeritus of the Brooklyn Botanic Garden, and two who did not live to see this book completed: Harriet K. Morse, a gifted author and the very model of sensitivity and intellect, and Elizabeth C. Hall, the doyenne of horticultural librarians, whose string of credits barely hint at the good-humored services she provided generations of gardeners.

More than a little psychological support, pithy horticultural insights or good garden leads were provided through the years by many treasured friends—several of whom even waded through portions of this manuscript. For varied contributions, special mention must be made of Jean Byrne, Ken Druse, Nicolas H. Ekstrom, Patti Hagan, Elvin McDonald, Dr. Peter K. Nelson, Evelyn Jacobs, David Harrington, Allen Lacy, Pamela Lord,

Ted Marston, Deborah Peterson, Helen Pratt, Dr. Ann F. Rhoads, Lalitte Scott, Arthur Sheppard, Lawrence B. Thomas and Julia Winpenny.

At Random House, I am grateful in particular to editor Jason Epstein, publisher Joni Evans, production editor Dennis Ambrose, production manager Linda Kaye, and editorial assistant extraordinaire Jamie Weisman.

More personal thanks are due my mother, Esther Freden Gureasko. My husband John's suggestions were not always received with grace, but were it not for him, none of this could ever have been—and that includes the two best things I ever grew: Naomi and David.

As with all things addictive, there should probably be a warning label on this book. The innocent must be counseled before tasting of the pleasures a city garden brings: a refuge from a world of troubles, an oasis where waters truly heal. Paradise is, after all, a garden—from the ancient Persian cum Greek *paradeisos,* or private park of kings, where there was peace and beauty amid fruiting trees and flowers.

And what better paradise than a city refuge where tender foliage offers comfort from harsh concrete, brick and steel?

Linda Yang
New York City, 1990

Postscript to this new edition

Just as a garden needs periodic renewing, so does a garden book . . . and that includes this one. So I'm grateful to John Storey and Storey Publishing for giving me a chance to do just that—create this new edition with its updates throughout.

I must register gratitude, too, for the astonishingly patient and extraordinarily caring staff at Storey Publishing—in particular Gwen W. Steege, Carey Boucher, Rebecca Ryall, the art department and production team, and the ever-gracious Jean Melillo and Tina Parent, who answer the Storey phones.

Linda Yang
New York City, 2002

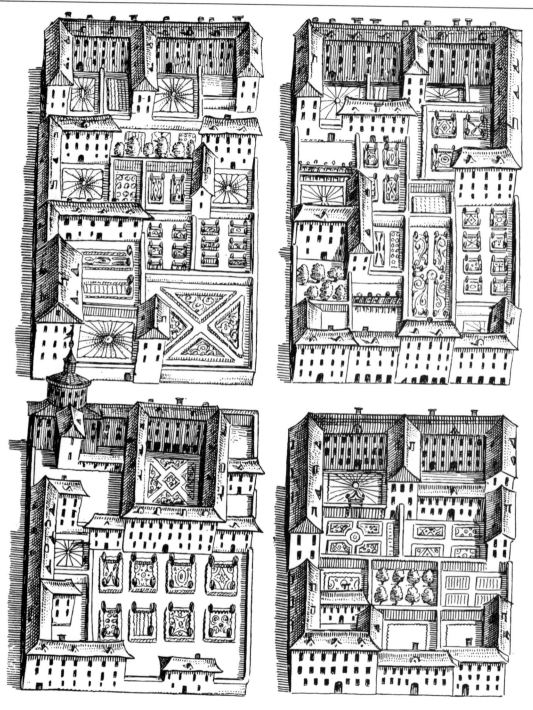

Townhouses and gardens in Turin, Italy. Circa 1662

Throughout most of history human beings have built their cities with gardens and open spaces . . . our old word "to dwell" fused two older words that had two distinct meanings: to build and to cultivate the land.
—Sam Bass Warner, Jr., *To Dwell Is to Garden,* 1987

1. Getting Started

"You're doing *what?*" the taxi driver shrieked as we careened along Manhattan's avenues. "Starting my garden," I repeated meekly, hoping my second reply would end his mirrored stare backward so he'd watch the oncoming trucks instead. At the next red light he turned his head the half circle needed for a clearer view of yet another eccentric rider—this one grappling with a bag of cow manure—and I braced myself for that now familiar observation: "That's crazy—you can't *really* garden in the city!" I know that "city gardener" sounds like a contradiction. But *really* garden is what I really try to do.

a backward glance With the arrogance reserved for native New Yorkers, I assumed we were the world's first city gardeners. Historical documentation is meager—a paragraph here, a letter there—but a backward glance suggested I was only off several millennia; the earliest "urban" plots appear to have been in the ancient towns that evolved from market sites for farmers. Not the sumptuous pleasure groves of emperors and kings, these were practical patches that provided their owners with foods, flavorings, dyes and cures —and other satisfactions, I'm sure.

from market to We know, for example, about first-century Rome, an authentic mini-
metropolis metropolis where cramped villas were surrounded on four sides by

streets. In his vast horticultural encyclopaedia of 77 A.D., Pliny the Elder described flower gardens perched on balconylike ledges in front of townhouse windows. The blossoms colored the narrow fronts, he wrote, "so that every day the eyes might feast on this copy of a garden, as though it were a work of nature." Flat rooftops too, were used for plant-filled boxes, or as Lucius Seneca wrote, "on high towers were planted fruit trees and shrubberies with roots where their tops ought to be." In their open central courtyards, the fashionable had a garnish of vases, fountains and statues, along with frescoed walls of birds and flowers to add an illusion of space.

The city gardener is a determined soul who must sow where there are more obstacles and inhabitants than soil.

getting to know your place

The modern urban site comes in an assortment of sizes, shapes and character traits from the expansive rooftop, with its sweeping vistas and sunny skies, to the secluded backyard, which has more wall than view. No matter if yours is "upstairs," where plant roots are confined to containers— or "downstairs," where plants spread freely in Earth—the key to success lies in how well you know your place.

So try to resist the temptation of jumping in and buying the first bright bloomer that beckons. You'll reduce your sum of expensive blunders if you take time, *in the beginning,* for a conscientious survey outside.

the basic statistics

However tiny your space (or inept you feel wielding a pencil), it's best to start by drawing a *simple* outline of your property's shape. Use a soft, dark-leaded pencil and draw on something that's sturdy, comfortably portable, convenient to lean on—and that won't flap in the wind. For this I'm a shirt-cardboard fan, but you might prefer the back of a large pad, a shoebox top, or anything else that is apt to survive countless trips to nurseries (and years of changing your mind).

With luck you'll find your space is an easily sketched rectangle or square, a "U" shape or "L"—but there are trapezoids and curved corners too. Don't panic if you don't have a simple outline, because all you're after is its general form. Once your silhouette is in place, it's easy to measure and record a few vital statistics: the length of each major portion and each area's widest and narrowest parts.

If yours is an unusually large or complex space and you feel shaky about your ability to draw, transfer your measured plan to graph paper.

views, good and bad

Now take a slow look around you. City views may include grand "borrowed scenes" of breathtaking skyscapes or spires. But more common, and more important, are the ugly intrusions you must plan to disguise. You might find a chain-link fence, a neighbor's rotting shed, a cadaverous-looking plastic balcony divider, a forest of roof pipes, a water tower or an oppressive brick wall. Take note of what you find and where you find it—the vistas, both good and bad.

upstairs windows For upstairs gardeners in particular, this includes window scenes of your own terrace as seen from indoors. All-season perspectives are crucial since for much of the year the view is through glass. Your observations can be added right onto your sketch, but if erasures unnerve you this is the time to add a tracing paper overlay.

existing plants If your place is a previously planted yard or rooftop terrace, inventory the plants you find. There may be one or more splendid specimen shrubs or trees worthy of note, perhaps hidden beneath a much-needed pruning. If what you find is not worth saving, don't agonize over methods of making new plans from old. Fighting an existing plan or trying to resuscitate sickly plants is not the way to enjoy a garden. It takes an experienced gardener to deal with wholesale slaughter, so plan on relocating your inherited species—preferably to someone else's garden.

the search for sun In every site there are unique local environmental factors called *microclimates* that profoundly affect the planting and the plan. But a knowledge of astronomy and an understanding of the compass are useless since city microclimates often defy all rules.

To begin with, there's the search for sunlight.

Just because the realtor told you your garden "faces south," don't expect to be blinded by sunbeams all day, or even any part of the day. If any structure comes between your patch and the sun for any significant length of time, the light you actually have does not qualify as the "full sun" that garden manuals glorify.

And "structure" doesn't mean only tall buildings.

You may find a tall fence, a dense canopy of trees, a corner of a neighbor's house or even a chunk of yours. What you have to determine by observation—and record on your cardboard plan—are the sunlit areas you *actually* have. Mark where the direct rays touch, their approximate duration, and the time of day, using either written notes, a light pencil shading or shorthand initials like FS for full sun, if there are more than 7 hours daily (see sun conditions, page 66).

a seasonal watch The time of year also affects the light in the city garden. The vernal equinox, which falls around March 21, marks the "official" beginning of spring. The sun is poised above the Equator, and day length equals night. From mid-March until the end of June, daylight hours noticeably lengthen as the sun continues its climb in the sky (above most city obstructions). At this time too, the sun is on a more northerly course. This means that gardeners with an open northern exposure can expect several hours more of direct sun.

a balcony ceiling Unfortunately, summer's sunny days are not guaranteed for all. If your space is one of a series of tiered balconies stacked each above the other like open drawers, you will look up and find a ceiling instead of sky. A roof poses problems if you pretend it isn't there, so measure and record your ceiling's height. It is the most important aspect of this uniquely modern space.

Contrary to what you might expect, a roof doesn't mean you can't have a "real" garden. A ceiling is useful for hanging flowering baskets from, and

Summer hyacinth
Galtonia candicans

(I like to believe) the reason that small weeping trees are propagated. What a roof does mean is that as spring progresses and the sun travels higher in the sky, your space will be covered by your upstairs neighbor's shadow.

reflections No city gardener can be choosy about light, and making the most of limited balcony sun means finding and using reflections. In the summer, for example, several hours after the midday sun has dropped behind the buildings that surround me, my plants shimmer in a brilliant, occasionally eerie glow. It is indeed the afternoon sun—but *reflected* into my shady space by helpful neighboring structures. Reflections from the city's myriad shiny windows and bright or glazed walls hardly equal the sun, but they do yield precious moments of extra, useful light.
Determine your natural reflections now, and later you can devise artificial means for increasing them (like mirrors and paint, see pages 42, 45).

And what if your hidden yard or tiered balcony seems to receive sunlight "by appointment only"? I promise you a plant for *every* condition (see Chapter 4), but first you must appraise the light you find. If yours is truly a shady spot, you can forget right now about ripe tomatoes or radiant roses. But since a consoling sample seems in order immediately, rest assured your seasonal plants can include crocus in spring, the puckered, oval foliage of hosta in summer, fresh mint in fall and evergreen yews in winter.

assessing your pollutants Depending on their location, some city gardens may be plagued by soot or pollutants. A majority of plants do manage to survive, but it's best to note on the margin of your cardboard plan what kind of dirty environment prevails. So look around to see if you find spewing chimneys. Or perhaps you'll find torpid air that's trapped deep within city canyons (this is a guaranteed headache if you're determined to grow mildew-prone species like some varieties of lilacs, roses, and phlox).

the soil Few new gardeners even notice their soil. New container gardeners have no problem, since they have no soil. But if you've just taken over an *old* terrace garden, or are about to *replant* an existing yard, it's best to know now something about the planting medium you find.
soil structure Soils are discussed in Chapter 6, but at this time it's sufficient to determine if yours seems to be naturally more sandy or claylike. The ideal structure is something in between and is easy to turn and work with a trowel. Neglected city soil more typically resembles concrete. Dig in and

study the condition you find. If you don't know what to make of it, plan on collecting a small bagged sample and taking it with you on your first nursery visit.

toxic soils　While a cursory glance may help determine soil structure, toxic soil is less easily discerned. If you expect to concentrate only on ornamentals (that means flowers, shrubs and trees) you don't have to worry. But if edibles (fruit, vegetables and herbs) are a must, toxic conditions must be confronted. They must also be dealt with if you have young children who enjoy playing in dirt.

lead　Of particular concern is the presence of heavy metals like cadmium and
and cadmium　lead. Gardens within 50 feet of a busy thoroughfare, for example, are most likely to contain particles of lead from automobile emissions. Or there may be lead-based paint chips from old or demolished structures.

soil testing　If you suspect toxic conditions, by all means have your soil tested. You can do this either through your state college's Cooperative Extension Service, which is a division of your state's agricultural school (the telephone number and address are usually under the government listings in your telephone directory) or through a private soil testing company (see list page 292).

hot surprises　Although it's generally known that some plants won't survive intermittent gusts of icy air, random blasts of *hot* air (from the heaving machines we've learned to ignore) can be equally lethal. It took me the longest time to figure out why everything I planted in what seemed to be an ideal spot in my garden shriveled up and died. What I didn't understand was that the plants were in direct line with a clothes dryer exhaust (it was a simple matter to install a plastic baffle to redirect the air). Other potentially damaging hot air sources to watch for are stove or oven fans and air conditioner exhausts.

radiant heat　Unfortunately difficult to detect, but potentially just as harmful are microclimates of radiant heat. Experiments by Dr. Nina Bassuk of Cornell University showed that on a broad mid-Manhattan avenue in summer, the daily temperatures at street locations on the sunny side ranged from 20° to 30° higher than those in the shade—the result of a buildup of heat on the metal surfaces of parked cars and heat radiated from the asphalt street. Temperatures often reached well over 100F° and created desertlike conditions for trees that were supposedly growing in a temperate zone. (Extra watering was the solution.)

subsurface problems　Subsurface steam or hot-water pipes are just as insidious. Typically hidden in apartment building cellar ceilings or sidewalks, they're difficult to detect. Hot pipes that extend under plantings prevent soil from cooling properly in winter and encourage overheating in summer. Since you may not find them now, keep this in mind if yard plantings regularly expire from no other apparent cause.

Portulaca
Portulaca grandiflora

on rooftops   Hot spots can also occur on a penthouse or rooftop terrace, where air warmed by the sun is trapped by parapet walls of stone. Warm building air from the rooms below may also filter up into a rooftop garden. This condition is aggravated by inadequate roofing insulation. If this causes a problem, it can be ameliorated with a raised, open-slat wood deck (and this is easier to effect than new roofing).

coping with wind   Then there are those who will find they have to cope with wind. While you can't change your exposure, a strategically positioned barrier (wood fencing, tempered glass or a wall of hedges) may help convert a tumultuous gust to a tolerable breeze.

The problem is that it's not so easy to predict wind strength and location. And its direction may ever be a surprise, as I learned one summer—as usual, the hard way.

Predictions were for a hurricane from the west. Since my terrace was shielded on its western side by a wood fence, a tall hedge and another building, I assumed I was well protected, until the next day when I discovered my children's vinyl pool had vanished. Peering over that western fence, I saw the pool settled on the ground nineteen stories below. It had been deposited there by a microclimate that had caused the winds to reverse.

the travel route   If the crucial connection between your rooftop garden and the street is a stairwell, elevator or narrow terrace door, take time to measure it before you buy a large container or plant. Also, plan on being around to supervise its travel along the route. I wasn't and came to regret it.

A magnificient tree from a country nursery was delivered when I was out. The building's superintendent took one look at it, decided it wouldn't fit in the elevator, and insisted that the nurserymen take it back.

the elevator   I did indeed make unprintable remarks upon my return, for I knew the tree would fit. I had measured the elevator and found its *diagonal* dimension was greater than its vertical one. I had also assumed that even if my appraisal were off, I could take advantage of the small emergency panel that opens a portion of every service elevator ceiling; hauling a tree to the nineteenth floor obviously is a bona fide emergency.

beginning thoughts on design   Unlike André Le Nôtre, the landscape architect of Versailles, we city gardeners have neither vast tracts of land to alter nor forests of trees to carve. But this is not to say there is no need to think ahead about design.

It's true some folk are determined to map out every inch of space with military precision. But given the limited area within which we toil, it's rarely productive to try to plot each corner in minute detail and then rigidly adhere to this plan.

flexibility first   Better, instead, to develop a flexible outlook and accept in advance that a small city landscape must be allowed to change and grow through the seasons and the years—just as plants and people do.

Ah, you mutter, but what if, in my ignorance, I make a grotesque design decision or embarrassing selection of plants? Well, since that's how most of us learn, it's nice that plants aren't puppies—plants can be abandoned without guilt.

That being said, it's appropriate to ponder some basics of landscape design, in particular the two fundamentally different approaches that designers employ.

the formal approach
At one extreme is the formal composition, a tightly controlled organization. It is distinguished by symmetry and a crisply mathematical order in the placing of plantings, walks, furnishings and containers. Axes and geometric lines predominate, and plants and architectural features or ornaments are chosen with an eye to their contribution to neat patterns and classic form. Plants are fastidiously groomed, with many selected for their amenability to repeated pruning and shaping.
The formal design is best exemplified by the Renaissance gardens of Italy, and those of seventeenth-century France. The style is believed to have originated in Egypt, where 3,000 years ago orderly grid systems of canals irrigated symmetrical lines of trees.
I have seen meticulously "formal" gardens in town.

a naturalistic view
In marked contrast is the "naturalistic" composition, with a seemingly random, asymmetrical placing of plants, paths, furnishings and planters. Irregular masses are used to define a variety of spaces, and curved or gently flowing lines predominate. Nature's outlines serve as inspiration for plant pruning and maintenance. While scale and proportion remain important considerations, plant outlines are not balanced by mirror images.
The naturalistic design is best exemplified by the English mid-eighteenth-century "landskip." Those undulating, picturesque parklands are believed to have been inspired by the landscapes of China.
And I have seen wildly "naturalistic" gardens in town.

space with style
Design differences notwithstanding, a successful city garden reflects not only its owner's personal taste but a pragmatic response to the city's challenging environment—in particular, to its peculiar constraints of space. And this is a good place to start, even before you begin your quest for specific plants.

an upstairs experience
Upstairs gardeners, for example, are frequently faced with a rooftop terrace, penthouse or balcony that is long and narrow in the extreme. When I gardened in that space—a slender "L" shape that was wrapped around a

Weigela
Weigela florida

nineteenth-floor apartment—a somewhat naturalistic design evolved from my determination to create an illusion of width.

After considering the "givens" on my cardboard outline, I decided to experiment first by plotting out areas in chalk, drawing right on the terrace floor (an act inspired by my children's play). Large circles and rectangles represented clusters of various-sized plants and containers. Instead of lining them up like soldiers against a wall, I distributed them in groups at varying distances to create a kind of serpentine walk.

Some clusters were close against the building, near windows, to assure year-round views from inside. Since I was blessed with a fine rooftop panorama, other plants were grouped against the outer railing, where they would serve as a frame. Varying heights and textures of evergreen and deciduous trees and shrubs contrasted with flowers and vines to transform my erstwhile bowling alley into a meandering, "naturalistic" cottage-garden path.

then downstairs   More than a decade later, my family and I moved to a townhouse with a typical rectangular backyard. My husband declared that this time he needed space to stroll "without bushwhacking through a jungle," and I too was ready for change (having become addicted to jamming in more plants than any city gardener has room for). The time seemed right to make neater, more formal planting spaces within which I could play.

First I made an orderly stone walk extending halfway up into the center of the yard and then outlining the remaining portion. Off this promenade I made planting areas of various sizes delineated by evergreen and deciduous trees and shrubs in loosely symmetrical massings. These plants provide the structural backdrop to savor from indoors all year.
Within the spaces created by the shrubs and trees are the seemingly serendipitous mix of whatever I currently find captivating. Here are "plant collections"—roses, herbs, perennials, grasses, bulbs and annuals—grouped in the spirit (I tell myself) of the "controlled abandon" of the American-born British garden designer Lanning Roper. (He subsequently altered his witty phrase to "careless rapture," which doesn't suit me at all.)
Sculptured rocks, multiple levels, steps, low mounds and even a small free-form pool now contribute texture and a change of topography to this formerly flat domain.

to each his own   City gardens serve their owners in a variety of ways, and if you've room enough for choice, only you can choose the most sensible spot for dining, entertaining, reading, repotting, a fine sculpture or a children's play space. If there's one thing I've learned in years of visits to fellow city gardeners, it's that there's no single "right" way to plan or plant. I continue to be amazed at the vastly different designs and plant combinations I see in sites that are physically identical to mine.

copies to dream on   At this point your cardboard outline contains the observations that are the beginning of your city garden's history. Arm yourself with a stack of photocopies of your drawing and you'll have scores of plans on which to doodle, dream, change your mind and record new plants. As you amble through the next few chapters, these copies should help smooth your route to a gratifying plan.

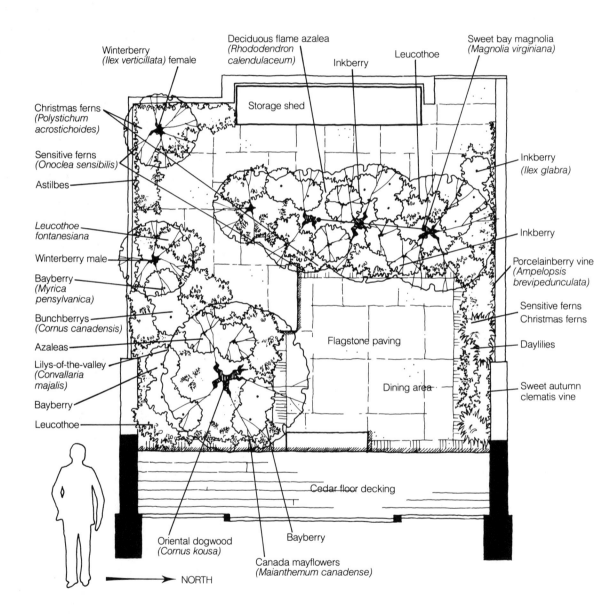

Winterberry
(*Ilex verticillata*) female

Deciduous flame azalea
(*Rhododendron
calendulaceum*)

Inkberry

Leucothoe

Sweet bay magnolia
(*Magnolia virginiana*)

Christmas ferns
(*Polystichum
acrostichoides*)

Sensitive ferns
(*Onoclea sensibilis*)

Astilbes

*Leucothoe
fontanesiana*

Winterberry male

Bayberry
(*Myrica
pensylvanica*)

Bunchberrys
(*Cornus canadensis*)

Azaleas

Lilys-of-the-valley
(*Convallaria
majalis*)

Bayberry

Leucothoe

Storage shed

Inkberry
(*Ilex glabra*)

Inkberry

Porcelainberry vine
(*Ampelopsis
brevipedunculata*)

Sensitive ferns
Christmas ferns

Daylilies

Flagstone paving

Dining area

Sweet autumn
clematis vine

Cedar floor decking

Oriental dogwood
(*Cornus kousa*)

Bayberry

Canada mayflowers
(*Maianthemum canadense*)

→ NORTH

Plantings are arranged perpendicular to the side wall to create diagonal movement and visually divide a small Philadelphia garden. Large paving stones and a change of level add an illusion of space to the 16- by 20-foot site. Rainwater, collected in sunken perforated borders around the paving edges, is directed into the soil.
Andropogon Associates, Ltd.

Plan for this garden is shown on opposite page.

PLANTS TRANSFORM
BARREN SITES

The zigzag arrangement of containers creates a serpentine path through an 8- by 40-foot rooftop terrace. Crabapple trees, blueberry and hydrangea shrubs, an autumn flowering cherry tree *(Prunus subhirtella 'Autumnalis')* and roses ('Gene Boerner' and climbing 'Don Juan') share their tubs with annual bloomers that include ageratum, petunia, periwinkle and marigold. Ripening tomatoes and rosemary are in smaller containers.

The pendulous limbs of a weeping Higan cherry tree *(Prunus subhirtella* 'Pendula'*)* provide shelter for a snug seating area and a screen for neighboring buildings.

Potted houseplants, hanging baskets and flower-filled window boxes convert a 6-foot-wide balcony into a garden. A single large tub with a small weeping flowering cherry tree ensures a multi-seasonal view.

A dense cascade of hardy English ivy obscures the planters that form a curved path on a penthouse terrace. The garden's green and white theme includes white bark birches, white flowering azaleas, andromeda, crabapples and cutleaf Japanese maples.
Johnny Appleseed Landscaping

A homemade trellis marks the entry to a 21- by 50-foot yard. The curved bluestone path leads to a shady seating area defined by a circle of five closely spaced honey locusts. Underfoot are sweet alyssum, ajuga and creeping Jenny *(Lysimachia clethroides)*. The walk passes along an exuberant plant mix that includes a yellow moth mullein *(Verbascum blattaria)*, Siberian iris, lacecap hydrangea, *Corydalis lutea,* hosta, coral bells *(Heuchera sanguinea), Sedum spectabile,* astilbe, staghorn sumac and a white rambler rose.

Ken Druse, Garden Design

Clump white birches and a weeping cherry tree obscure a grim rear yard view. The raised brick planting beds add a third dimension and permit the addition of a foot of improved soil. A small recirculating fountain helps mask traffic sounds from a nearby street.

Signe Nielsen,
Landscape Architect

LATTICEWORK, GAZEBOS, STORAGE AND SEATS

It's never too early to begin construction. The latticework for a 30- by 30-foot rooftop terrace is fire-treated pine painted white and topped with playful circles. The natural cedar tubs have small seating ledges. Plantings include weeping birches, weeping cherries, junipers, daylilies and impatiens.

Corlett Horticultural Design

A mail-order gazebo, painted to match its Victorian San Francisco home, is the terminus of a curved hedge of boxwood *(Buxus sempervirens 'Suffruticosa')* that surrounds silvery-leaved santolina and rose topiaries. Nearby are white marguerites *(Chrysanthemum frutescens)* and pink peony tulips. A mature Norfolk Island pine *(Araucaria heterophylla)* overhangs a corner of the garden.

Josephine Zeitlin,
Landscapes

A custom-designed gazebo of weathered cedar is the airy focus of a small backyard. A brick path outlines a grassy square planted with a checkerboard of red and white tulips.
Conklin Rossant Architects

White wisteria wraps itself around a redwood gazebo providing sheltered seating on a sunny rooftop. The dense planting includes an American mountain ash *(Sorbus americana)*, crabapple and Japanese white pine *(Pinus parviflora)* trees, along with roses and blueberry shrubs.

A Parisian rooftop is enclosed in painted trelliswork that provides support for honeysuckle vines and a perforated backdrop for mounds of lavender and white marguerites.

An evergreen euonymus *(Euonymus japonica)* espalier is a glossy wallcover behind billowing cheddar pinks *(Dianthus gratianopolitanus),* blue and white perennial flax *(Linum perenne)* and a dwarf blue spruce.

Trompe l'oeil trellis-work and mirrors cover an entire wall and bring depth and light to a small, dark backyard. Gurgling fountains add sound; daffodils, tulips and caladium add spring color.

Luther Greene,
Garden Design

A lattice *trompe l'oeil* perspective inspired by an eighteenth-century French drawing adds elegance and depth to a lifeless, flat wall. The classic theme extends to the clipped English holly *(Ilex aquifolium)* and potted topiary myrtle. A Korean snowball bush *(Viburnum carlesii compactum)* adds fragrant white floral highlights.

Painted latticework and a round mirror make a rooftop chimney disappear. The garden seen in the circle is a reflection.

Cream-colored latticework used like wallpaper decorates a brick wall and disguises a storage closet. Plants include rhododendrons, cotoneasters, a multi-stemmed shadbush *(Amelanchier canadensis)* and pink impatiens.
Daniel D. Stewart,
Stewart Associates

A hollow, cushioned seat doubles as generously proportioned storage space.
Johnny Appleseed Landscaping

Trelliswork is used to support climbing roses and to visually unify containers and seats. Plants include lamb's ear, lavender 'Hidcote,' chrysanthemum, sedum 'Autumn Joy,' moor grass *(Molinia caerula)*, fountain grass *(Pennisetum alopecuroides)*, blue fescue, shore juniper *(Juniperus conferta)* and Mugo pine.
Donald J. Walsh, Landscape Architect

Despite the rain, dining al fresco is inviting in the cozy space created by tubbed birch trees, junipers and a table awning. Azaleas, geraniums and caladiums add color.
John Mayer,
Landscape Gardener

Snow gives a garden bench a change of face.

A gently curved gravel path gracefully obliterates the shape of a 17-by 19-foot penthouse terrace. An oval pond and four large planters with trees and shrubs are surrounded by pachysandra. The ground cover grows in a 3-inch-deep, soilless mix that rests on top of heavy plastic sheeting.

John Mayer,
Landscape Gardener

Plan for this garden
is shown on
opposite page.

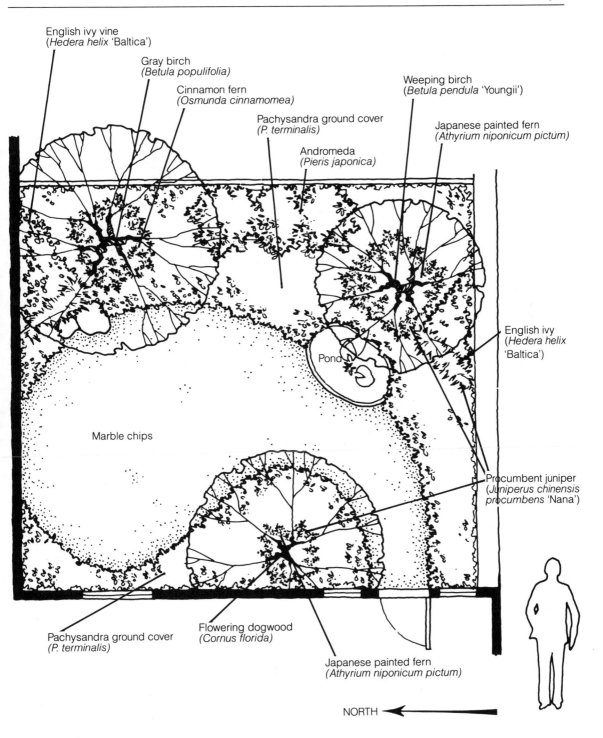

English ivy vine
(*Hedera helix* 'Baltica')

Gray birch
(*Betula populifolia*)

Cinnamon fern
(*Osmunda cinnamomea*)

Pachysandra ground cover
(*P. terminalis*)

Andromeda
(*Pieris japonica*)

Weeping birch
(*Betula pendula* 'Youngii')

Japanese painted fern
(*Athyrium niponicum pictum*)

English ivy
(*Hedera helix*
'Baltica')

Pond

Marble chips

Procumbent juniper
(*Juniperus chinensis
procumbens* 'Nana')

Pachysandra ground cover
(*P. terminalis*)

Flowering dogwood
(*Cornus florida*)

Japanese painted fern
(*Athyrium niponicum pictum*)

NORTH ←

Thornless Honey Locust
Gleditsia triacanthos 'Inermis'

The human race has a desire—as powerful in the aboriginal as it is in the 20th century . . . not to leave well alone but to add decoration; and the meaning of the verb "to decorate" . . . is "to adorn or beautify."
—Peter Hunt, *The Book of Garden Ornament,* 1974

2. Nonplant Considerations

Once upon a time, less long ago than I care to admit, I believed that nothing but plants were worthy of consideration when it came to my city garden. The "invegetate ornaments"—as John Worlidge called them in 1677 —only got in the way of my horticultural enthusiasm and determination to discredit the myth that greenery cannot survive an urban setting. But as the number of city gardens I visited multiplied, my botanical myopia was displaced by an appreciation of the garden as a place for people too. I came to see that, as with any inhabited space, the comfort level is improved by decorative as well as practical architectural elements—some of which are best considered even before plants are in place. So now, as a certified believer in the benefits, pleasures (and in some cases necessities) of nonplant considerations, my mission is to proclaim this truth to others.

what goes on outside Some aspects of nonplant planning may be less an artistic consideration than a practical balance between available space and the owner's needs. This was made clear to me one day in the townhouse yard of the conductor of an internationally known symphony orchestra. His wife, the Serious Horticulturist, was lamenting her sparse collection of peripheral plantings. And naturally I sympathized. But no sooner had she finished her lengthy apologia, than it became obvious that for this couple, the most important aspect of the garden was *not* a floral border but their large central space. And it was completely paved. Her husband's position made it imperative that they host regular cocktail parties for a variety of groups—not the least of which was the entire ninety-member orchestra.

Moor Grass
Molina caerulea
'Variegata'

what's underfoot   So while a first step in garden planning is deciding how you wish to use your space, you may first need to know what's under your foot. Asphalt roofing and chipped tiles are often the lot of the rooftop gardener. Mud or concrete seem to adorn the yard.

Fortunately, there's no law that says you must live with the surface you find, and from the formal to the informal there's a range of covers to suit every gardener's toes.

a rooftop "path"   One of the more intriguing topside changes I've seen was on a small rooftop terrace where the owner created a natural looking "path" of gravel and stones that curved through a green carpet of pachysandra plants. Both plants and stones had been placed directly on the building's asphalt roofing after the surface was protected with heavy polyethylene sheets. This green ground cover clearly was content with its 3-inch layer of lightweight soil, which rested on top of the sheeting.

quarry tile or plastic Assuming you've decided your rooftop surface warrants an architectural change, you have several options. A good grade of quarry tile, for example, dresses up any space, and with the many new patterns and tones you no longer have to settle for a basic brown square. But quarry tile can be expensive, too heavy in weight and possibly more permanent than is appropriate. One of several handsome alternatives is a plastic floor tile called Mateflex. Originally designed in France and planned as a resilient surface for sports, this system of interlocking modules has an open honeycomb grid pattern. It comes in various colors and is lightweight and easily installed without adhesive.

advantages Another useful disguise is the raised wooden deck. Even a slightly ele-
of a raise vated surface adds a refreshing three-dimensional change of pace to an otherwise flat expanse. But more important, a wood deck is a superb structural device for distributing the weight of planting tubs over a broader area.
Although typically cut in rectangles or 2-foot squares, wood decking can be fabricated in various sizes and shapes, making it versatile enough to fit odd spaces on terraces with peculiar profiles. You can alternate pieces to produce different patterns—like a simple checkerboard—or run diagonal slats in opposite directions.

portable floors Wood decks should be built in portable-size sections so that they can be easily carried through the building lobby and living room, upstairs and in elevators. Manageable sizes facilitate the initial installation as well as partial or total removal later for tasks like sweeping collected debris or autumn leaves. They also make the deck's removal easy should there be roofing problems later.
And "roofing problems" is the rooftop gardener's euphemism for *leaks*.

coping with leaks Leaks are an unfortunate fact of upstairs garden life, and something that must never, *never* be forgotten. As one friend put it, a rooftop terrace is like a balloon—you can't ever be sure it won't be punctured and leak. So before starting *any* work on a new rooftop or balcony garden, determine whether any necessary repairs are still outstanding. Repair procedures always drag on interminably, and your garden plans will have to wait. But mending a roof usually means removing the entire surface, so you're better off with no valuable plants or expensive planters to be shifted, or new furnishings to be ruined. Contractors also work faster when no objects impede their progress.

waterproofing in Babylon

Leaky rooftop terraces, by the way, are hardly a modern phenomenon. Water seepage has plagued the upstairs gardener since the Hanging Gardens of Babylon—and that dates at least from the sixth century B.C. Although not technically an "urban" retreat, this 3-acre structure had seven landscaped levels that rose to a height of 75 feet. Leaks were controlled with an elaborate waterproofing membrane that included layers of papyrus mixed with asphalt. Several centuries later in Rome, the flat roofs and colonnaded balconies of townhouses were built with an understructure that kept moisture from seeping into the rooms below.

don't blame the plants

So let's keep one thing straight. Contrary to what building managers say, *plants do not cause leaks.*
Of course, neither do they prevent them. That's up to you.
Precautions include using a deck to distribute the weight of heavy planter loads over a broader area and keeping soil weight minimal (see page 155). Also, monitor your plants' roots so they don't escape from the container's bottom to search for water in your building's joints.

water problem origins

Where do water troubles really come from? While no one can answer for sure (and be suspicious of anyone who insists he can), most leaks do seem to originate within the roofing or parapet walls, a result of poor workmanship at the time of the roofing installation, poor-quality roofing materials, or improperly installed weatherproofing compounds or flashing. Other culprits include the elements—alternate freezing and thawing —and the passage of time.
Then too, structural or material weaknesses may permit rain or snow to enter directly into a parapet or retaining wall. While repointing or reflashing may be all that's needed, building managers are capable of some pretty hideous alternatives. Particularly dreadful is the aluminum cover or "cap" for the top parapet stone, which is called the coping. A dubious solution at best, this approach ignores the fact that rain and snow are also driven laterally.
In one case, a coping cap could not be avoided, but the wall's original appearance was saved simply by inserting the aluminum membrane between the top course of bricks and below the coping stone.

footing the bill   If you're a co-op or condominium gardener, you may now be wondering who is responsible for resurfacing your outdoor rooftop or balcony floor (assuming no leak is involved). Unfortunately, this is an area of continuing controversy, so it's not for me to say. But if you didn't check at the time of purchase, do so before sending your management a bill. You're sure to find it's simpler to pay for a flooring change yourself, and if you plan a major architectural alteration, get permission first—in writing.

drains or puddles   Before adding a deck, plastic tiles or any other new terrace cover, note the location of drains and the slope of the floor. Test to see if and where puddles develop after a hosing or rain. It's not smart to impede the drift of water in its gravity flow toward the drain, so be sure you don't obstruct it. Be sure too, that whatever cover you use is removable for cleanups.

Chaste tree
Vitex agnus-castus

If the drain appears to be missing, keep looking. You will probably find it's located on your next-door neighbor's terrace.

versatility downstairs Drainage problems can also plague the downstairs gardener when the patio surface has not been pitched to slope *away* from the house and toward a drain—preferably one in working order. On the other hand, the downstairs gardener, unburdened by problems of weight, has a limitless choice of surface covers.

paving surfaces While garden paths can be traced in pulpy or loose materials like bark chips, shredded root or gravel, dining patios are better with a firmer surface. Clever patterns for patios or paths can be created with rocks, slate, bluestones, millstones, cobbles, bricks and variously shaped precast concrete pads. Use a combination for a decorative textural effect. Local sources of stones can be found in the yellow pages of your telephone directory under building materials, brick or masonry supplies.

respect your roots If you are lucky enough to find mature shrubs or large trees adjacent to your future patio, take care not to cover their soil with a solid sheet of concrete. That is exactly what new neighbors of mine did after moving into their townhouse, only to watch mystified as a fine old white mulberry tree died; the new patio floor created a heavy and impervious barrier over the tree's roots, and air, water and nutrients could no longer reach them.
Newly poured patio concrete and footings also leach limestone and alter the soil chemistry. This can be harmful to woodland plants (see page 141).

coping with cracks In yards with existing plantings use paving stones set on a bed of sand. A heavy hosing may make for some messy washing-away at first, but you can minimize this by filling the larger openings with stones, rocks or shells or a small amount of concrete. For minimal patchwork a convenient product is Sakcrete, an instant compound that's sold at hardware stores.

horticultural fillers You can solve the problem of open floor joints at the same time you enrich your horticultural content by filling them with small plants. A good "crack filler"—as my husband calls them—is any dense, low growing ground cover like maiden pink or thyme (see list page 184).

something to sit on "How much of the day do you sit out here?" a visitor once asked as we

sipped iced tea with freshly harvested mint al fresco. Since we were parked at a recently refurbished table, on newly cushioned chairs, the question shouldn't have embarrassed me. But I assumed everyone accepted my self-image as *Gardener:* one who ceaselessly bends, kneels and sweats over treasured plants. And certainly never rests.
However, I hereby admit to an occasional pause—and when I do, I like a comfy place to tarry.

We modern city folk take for granted our versatile outdoor furnishings, yet comfortable seats are a relatively recent amenity. Medieval ladies and their amorous lads lounged on turf-covered mounds (their passion, no doubt, kept them warm, considering their seat's damp chill). Later, ornate marble and stone garden benches served more as terminal features for vistas than as cozy spots to unwind. How fortunate that we are limited only by mundane considerations like durability, rust resistance, appropriateness of style, "cleanability" and sufficient space to ensure a good fit.

from minimum practical

My earliest balcony was quite small and my young children needed a clear space to play. A lightweight folding aluminum table with matching chairs from a nearby dime store proved indispensable, indestructible and economical. Gussied up with a fancy cloth and seat pads, this practical selection even assumed a certain minimal elegance for "company" dining (or so in my youthful haze I wished to believe).
An enticing assortment of garden furniture is available by mail (see page 290) as well as from department stores. If your budget is tight and you can bear to delay, wait for bargains in mid or late summer, when major stores clear out "old" stock with reductions and sales.

to endless choice

Some gardeners feel it's imperative to coordinate their indoor and outdoor furniture styles. Others see no need for a connection at all. Whichever approach suits you, you can be sure that the possibilities for indecision will be enhanced by a dizzying assortment (traditional, rustic and modern) as well as materials (teak, oak, redwood, twigs, stone, wrought iron, plastic, wicker and rattan).

and color

Then there's the choice of paint or fabric color.
In what can only be regarded as an example of genuine optimism, white holds a special appeal for many a city slicker. Sure, it looks great in the store, but in a small or shady garden white must be used with care. In addition to endless cleaning, white furnishings can mean a jumble of strident arms and legs. If white furniture is a must, at least add some

architectural or horticultural balance—a white trellis, perhaps, or white blossoms or silver-leaved plants.

And be careful too with furnishings that are green.

Gertrude Jekyll, the illustrious British gardener, neatly summarized the problem when she called green a "doubtful colour . . . likely to quarrel with the varied natural greens which are near it."

Subtle colors work most harmoniously in the small garden—a natural or dark earthy bronze or brown. Muted tones won't overwhelm the area, conflict visually with anything that grows, or readily reveal the inevitable blanket of town grime. In any case, don't be afraid to experiment—a can of enamel spray paint facilitates matters most economically whenever you feel inspired to change.

neighborly fences   That good fences make good neighbors is obvious in urban sites, where privacy helps ensure sanity. Fences are also useful for blocking unsightly views and tempering the wind. The simplest fencing is a solid wall of vertical or horizontal wood strips or alternating wide and narrow pieces. I'm partial to the stockade style of wired cedar stakes, whose unobtrusive tenor and delicate scale blend so naturally in a small space.

Rooftop gardeners in multi-story apartment buildings may have to use wood treated with a fire retardant to satisfy local municipal codes—a rule where rooftops also serve as emergency exits.

Forget-me-not
Myosotis scorpioides

for safety's sake The upstairs terrace must be made safe for climbing children—and adults with a fear of heights. But you must save that view. Materials for see-through fencing include sheets of clear plastic, tempered or safety glass, or wood pickets, which are good wind barriers too. If Cyclone fencing makes you more secure, use the thin-gauge, coated kind, which is less unsightly then the schoolyard style.

a cheap screen Some unlikely materials make surprisingly useful screens. On my first balcony, inexpensive bamboo shades turned on their side and tied to the parapet enclosure were a tidy, elegant, easily installed fence. Even if they aren't windproof or long lived, they are a cheap cover-up for a multitude of city needs.

latticework For a truly classic cover, nothing beats a lattice—the humble wood slats once known as "carpenterswork" whose history of garden service is documented in medieval manuscripts and paintings at Pompeii. Ever changing in sunlight and shadow, latticework evokes romantic images of grand country estates. But don't underestimate its versatility in town. Even a pint-sized arbor or trellis gracefully tempers the sun's overhead rays, supports fruiting or flowering vines, shrubs or trees, and separates or defines areas of disparate use.

as disguise Artfully applied like wallpaper, a lattice veneer is also the perfect cover for an imperfect backyard wall or balcony rooftop. Used alone or backed with fabric or vinyl, a latticework screen veils grim vistas, camouflages messy workspaces and tactfully obscures the view of prying neighbors. A lattice veneer may also be applied to containers, storage units or other objects in need of visual unification. And nothing organizes a disorderly rooftop panorama like a neat latticework frame.

patterns Latticework patterns include horizontal and vertical grids, diagonal or diamond motifs, or a plaid of double slats. For a more "finished" appearance, use a heavier piece of wood to top off all edges.

and size Slat widths can be varied from 1 to 2 inches, thicknesses from ¼ to ½ inch. Open distances between the slats can range from ¾ inch to a foot. The greater these openings, the airier the lattice appears—and the cheaper its cost.

materials Redwood, cedar, teak and cypress are among the rot-resistant woods used for outdoor trellises that need no preservative, and these can be allowed to weather naturally. Easier on the budget but equally serviceable are woods like pine, which does need a protective primer of exterior-quality paint or stain before construction. Another coat of paint or stain should be added for longevity after the trellis is assembled, and there should be regular recoating every few years.

ready-mades But if your talents don't lie in the area of construction, you can also buy prefabricated arbor or trellis panels at large garden centers, lumber yards, hardware stores and even by mail. Standard sections are typically 2 or 4 feet wide by 8 feet tall, and there are different patterns to be mixed or matched.

trompe l'oeil The most inventive garden application of latticework is the false perspective known as *trompe l'oeil* (literally, "fool the eye"). The secret of *trompe l'oeil* spatial illusion lies in the diagonal lines that radiate from an imaginary vanishing point (the classic example is a picture of railroad tracks). The technique dates at least from the eighteenth century, when artisans fashioned for the French royal court elaborate designs known as treillage. With *trompe l'oeil* treillage, theatrical illusion moved from the confines of the indoor stage to the outdoor landscape, and we are the better for it. Artfully deployed, even a small *trompe l'oeil* treillage adds considerably to the illusion of depth.

garden mirrors When it comes to adding depth and making small spaces brighter, there's nothing like a mirror. I was introduced to outdoor mirrors by the late Luther Greene, a master of illusion in garden design. He told me he discovered their advantage when he positioned one *diagonally* at the far end of a narrow balcony and was astonished at how it opened up the view. Later, he improved the mood of a dark and claustrophobic yard by coating the entire two-story rear property wall with mirrors. Further depth and illusion were provided by the addition of a white wood *trompe l'oeil* perspective.

a secret garden In fact, any number of mirror *and* trellis marriages are possible. One gardener, whose densely planted terrace was not improved by an intrusive brick chimney, covered it with a lattice of painted galvanized metal. An oval mirror in the center gives the impression of peeking into a secret garden—but the thicket you see is the terrace behind you. Weatherproofing of mirrors is ensured by gluing them to marine-grade plywood and sealing the edges with silicone caulking.

Having paid for fancy trelliswork, you may not wish to cover it over with messy plants and obscure your expensive artwork. And there is sufficient

Zinnia
Zinnia elegans

historical precedent for this approach. But if you believe that a trellis is only as good as the plants that accompany it, you must use plants that are *removable* and therefore compatible with long-term maintenance needs. (see espaliers, page 231).

hiding space   If you think that jamming furniture into your garden space is not suffi-ciently challenging, then you're ready to grapple with finding a hideaway for the fertilizers, tools, pots, pesticides, and other objects that mysteri-ously multiply with the seasons. Forget that kitchen cabinet. At best it's in-convenient, at worst it's dangerous. Garden centers and mail-order catalogues often feature "miniature" toolsheds. These are swell if you have space. But it takes an inventive soul to reduce their bulk to make them fit unobtrusively into a tiny plot. A narrow prefabricated "closet" fits in more easily.

a seating bonus   Even better is the storage unit that serves more than one purpose. A relatively inexpensive product, available at large lumberyards or hard-ware shops, is an unfinished deacon's bench, an enormous chest with a hinged top and a simple backrest. For many years I used one of plywood pine. Never intended for the outdoors, its longevity was ensured with several applications of outdoor stain and a cheerful, weatherproof vinyl-covered seat.

made to fit I subsequently came across clever variations on this theme, storage units in the form of rows of wood chests with hinged tops. In one small rooftop terrace, the units were custom made to enclose the entire space. Built to a width of about 15 inches and a comfortable seating height of about 16 inches, they were covered with plump (washable) cushions, providing an extraordinary amount of outdoor seating. Where they were not cushioned, the storage chest tops served as platforms for a changing summer exhibit of flowers.

Hosta or Plantain-lily
Hosta plantaginea

gazebos From the gold cloth pavilion of Cleopatra to the painted teahouses of China, garden shelters have served as airy edifices for al fresco dining with grace. To the French they were "pavillions," to the Italians "loggias" and to the English Victorians "gazebos" (which is believed to be a pig-Latinized version of the phrase "I shall gaze about"). Whatever its name, a gazebo shrunk to manageable proportions adds a focal point to any city space. And before you assume you have no space to spare, check the dimensions in the suppliers' catalogues (see list page 291).

awnings A gaily patterned fabric awning adds a cheerful swath of color to either a rooftop or a yard. It also provides glorious shelter from the overhead summer sun and the overhead gaze of neighbors. You can attach your awning directly to a building wall or, for a winsome touch (especially on a balcony), use the kind that mushrooms up from the center of a circular table.

To extend an awning's life, wait until it's dry before rolling or folding it closed. And if you can safely reach its top, periodically brush off the soot and wash the surface with soap and water.

on windy rooftops On rooftops where fierce winds prevail, a secure awning installation is imperative. On my nineteenth-floor terrace, summer gusts occasionally resembled autumn hurricanes, so for additional wind control I used anchor chains to secure the corners of the awning's frame to the parapet railing. Rips caused by winter winds are irritating and expensive but also avoidable if in autumn you take the time to wrap the unit in a protective blanket of burlap.

concrete skytops A lot more secure, if a lot less romantic, are the concrete roofs of apartment balconies built one above the other in tiers. When I was a balcony gardener with an overhead roof, I found I could increase the reflected light by painting the ceiling's underside white. (Yes, it's risky if you climb a ladder to do the job, but with a roller and long extension handle instead it's not unnerving at all.)

Other effective toppings for balcony gardens include wood lattice or a quietly patterned swath of canvas or vinyl. A *faux* canopy, secured to the ceiling front and rear with nails and slightly draped in the center, can be made to resemble a real awning—and obliterate the truth.

statues, sundials or wind chimes The variety of nonplant ornaments you can add to your garden is limited only by your imagination, budget and space—sundials (for either floor or wall), exotic lava stones, birdhouses, birdbaths, wind chimes, fountains, wall plaques and scaled-to-size outdoor statuary or sculpture.

I'm not wild about pink flamingos or plastic elves, but I'm sure there are those who hate my assortment of strange seashells and stones. Whatever your preference, you can be sure the ornaments of your dreams will not be found quickly. So be patient during your quest; like everything else in horticulture, the pursuit of perfection never ends. Once you have them, place the nonplant embellishments you wish to see where you'll really see them. And this means through the window all year long.

let there be light A garden illuminated at night sparkles with green silhouettes in summer and shimmers with snowflakes in winter. Plant textures, forms and tones can induce extraordinary peace when the garden day is done. Thanks to a proliferation of easily installed weatherproof gadgets, outdoor lighting is now easier, safer and within every budget range. There are illuminating lamps in both traditional and contemporary styles, and the choice of materials includes aluminum, copper, bronze or wood.

But overillumination is a mistake. Your goal should be a subtle mood— on the order of gentle moonlight, not imitation sunlight. For as many a wise woman has found, semidarkness cloaks imperfections leaving only the pleasure of mystery and romance.

planning your scene In the garden, at least, this is achieved most easily by illuminating trees and shrubs from the *bottom up,* not the other way around. Use light to accent sculptured limbs and unusual specimens by placing the fixtures close to the soil and directing the beams skyward. Also effective is backlighting; place the light source behind the plant, and the outline becomes a silhouette. Light may be used too, to strengthen shadows on architectural accents like *trompe l'oeil* latticework or fountains, or to give sculpture depth. Use colored lights sparingly—or better still, not at all—and hide your light source. This way, you (and your neighbors) see only the effect, not the glare.

chores versus drama Utilitarian downlights can be used to extend garden chores or outdoor cooking into the evening hours. As with any good stage lighting, though, keep these practical lights on a separate circuit; you don't need them interfering with the effect of your evening spectacle.

some systems and circuits Exterior lighting circuits are now designed to be just that—heavy gauge and weatherproof. Originally, 110-volt fixtures fed directly off the household line, so a professional electrician was compulsory. Now low-voltage systems with transformers reduce (or "step down") the voltage. You can buy these in kits that are safe, easily managed and ready to install.

do-it-yourself kits So unless you're an electronics whiz, stick to one of these packaged sets. You'll find them at large lighting centers, well-equipped hardware shops and some garden centers. Kits usually include the basic items you'll need: a transformer to reduce the household system of 115/125 volts to 12 volts, a 50- or 100-foot weatherproof cable and a timer to operate the outdoor lamps on a 24-hour clock. If the timer is separate it's well worth whatever extra you pay, especially if the controls are outside. One rooftop gardener I know installed an elaborate lighting system she rarely uses because it's such a chore to throw a switch on a cold or rainy night.

locating controls If there's an outdoor, weatherproof outlet to plug into, that's fine, so long as the transformer and timer are weatherproof too. To bring your conduit in to an indoor socket, drill a small opening through the corner of a window sash and snake the line through. The transformer (and timer) can also be plugged into the nearest room socket, which for safety's sake should also be one with a ground.

hide that cable Yard gardeners can conceal electric conduits by sinking them just below the surface of the soil. Upstairs gardeners, however, must be more inventive. If there's no raised surface to hide them beneath, clip the cables just below the parapet coping, or snake them discreetly behind planters.

Should you have any misgivings about a lighting venture, hire a licensed electrician. And if you feel the need for an excuse to justify this expense, remember that aside from keeping your guests from tripping (and suing), lights deter burglars. And this may be the most important nonplant consideration you have.

Daylily
Hemerocallis sp.

*Gardening is about cheating, about persuading unlikely plants
to survive in unlikely places and when that trick is well accom-
plished the results can be highly satisfying.*
—David Wheeler, *Hortus,*1987

3. Meet Nature's Dramatis Personae

Before all else, we city gardeners must learn to disregard the discouraging, then proceed to confound the cynical. Country cousins with quantities of land would have us believe that only very few or very boring
plants can endure a city—or, worse, that no "good" plant deserves this
fate.

no negatives Yet it seems whenever I hear of a species that "won't survive" an urban
site, that plant is the pride of the next city garden I visit—from arugula to
water lilies, and beach plum too.

Certainly it's self-defeating to invite into a tiny space plants with questionable habits—like super-rapid root growth (the specialty of weeping willows) or grossly oversized leaves (a monster called *Gunnera* with
elephantine foliage). And many a city gardener must live with sun-starved
specimens that won't warrant a flower-show prize. Yet so long as human
beings can live, breathe and revel in the congestion that's a city, plants
will manage too.

Just as unnerving is the lament "I have no room for plants." Well, if its possible to walk outside and turn around (no matter on a balcony, terrace,
doorstep or yard), it's possible to grow not only a blaze of summer blossoms, but a small tree or shrub as well. I refuse to accept a plea of "no

room" from anyone. (Laziness, perhaps, is closer to the truth.) That being said, it's appropriate now to consider the kinds of plants you will meet—not only on the following pages, but in any other garden book you use.

all the garden's a stage

More than once I've heard landscape designers compare the creation of a garden to the production of a theatrical play. Onstage, actors with certain traits are indispensible to certain scenes; in the garden, plants with certain traits are essential for certain effects. Plants—like actors—are grouped within a number of broad categories. Their roles, in this case, are assigned them by botanists and nurserymen. An understanding of these groupings makes it easier to take advantage of the range of characters that comprise nature's dramatis personae.

the leading players

The leading players in the landscape are trees and shrubs. They establish and define garden structure and ensure a year-round view. Even a single tree or shrub is an important design element. It plays this role whether

Baby's Breath
Gypsophila paniculata

it's grown in a container on a high-rise balcony or in the backyard of a historic townhouse.

the woody ones Trees and shrubs make up the horticultural category known as *woody* plants, an allusion to the solid texture of their trunk or stem. Some trees and shrubs—like birches or crabapples—are *deciduous,* which means they drop their leaves in winter. Deciduous woody plants are treasured for their fine summer foliage or glorious blooms, but they're not the plants to use if a multiseasonal coverup is your goal. For this, there are *evergreens*—the plants that sport their covering of foliage all year. Evergreens are divided into two major groups that are neatly distinguished by their leaves. One category includes plants like junipers, yews and pines, whose leaves are narrow, and these are called *needle* evergreens. The other group includes plants like rhododendrons, azaleas and hollies, whose leaves are wide, and these are called *broad-leaved* evergreens.

a versatile palette Nature—and the horticultural breeder—have created deciduous and evergreen woody species in a broad palette of shapes, sizes, tones and textures, so you can use your plants to achieve many special effects. You might, for example, use an evergreen, prostrate Chinese juniper to soften the edge of a large planter or carpet a slope. Bend the flexible limbs of a Japanese holly to frame a view, or edge a parapet wall or outline a boundary with a row of red-leaved dwarf Japanese barberries. You can also use four weeping, flowering cherries to form a mini-*allée* or two pendulous birches to imply a woodsy mode. (The list of leading players—trees and shrubs—begins on page 68).

the supporting cast Trees and shrubs are onstage through four seasonal acts. But it takes a broad supporting cast to make the city garden's drama complete. From spring through autumn other horticultural characters provide a kaleidoscope of tones, textures, scents, shapes and sounds. These are the non-woody players—perennials, annual flowers, vegetables, bulbs, herbs, vines and even tropical houseplants. The true stars of the summer garden, these characters are a particularly versatile lot. Plant them either directly in the ground or in containers; mass them along a railing, doorstep or fence, or hang them in baskets from a balcony, awning frame or porch or secured to a building wall.
Their potential is limited only by your space and growing conditions and your energy, imagination and funds.

perennials One of the most important members of the supporting cast is the group called perennials. My tattered old copy of Norman Taylor's *Encyclopedia of Gardening* (a treasured "bible"), defines a perennial as a "nearly ever-living plant." Now technically this includes trees, shrubs and tropical houseplants. But when gardeners boast about their "perennial borders," the plants they're extolling are the *herbaceous* species—like astilbe, core-opsis or hosta—those whose stems are soft, not woody like the trunks of shrubs or trees.

hardy and herbaceous Perennials that tolerate local winters are known as *hardy*. Hardy, herba-ceous perennials disappear in autumn, when their tops die to the soil. But underground, their roots survive and support the life that will re-emerge in spring. Since many perennials return in increased numbers, they can be divided and shared with friends or transplanted to empty cor-ners. And since most can be counted on to reappear for years, gone is the seasonal effort and expense of annuals.

For this reason, there are those who think of perennials as "low-mainte-nance" plants—and to this extent, they are. But in fact, unless you also dis-count weeding, watering, feeding, pruning, dividing and staking, the low-maintenance concept is only a dream.

flowering perennials The classic perennial border—a profusion of flower color and con-trasting foliage and form—is most closely associated with the grand En-glish estates of the late nineteenth and early twentieth centuries. Popularized by writers and gardeners like William Robinson and Ger-trude Jekyll, those glorious plantings owed their existence primarily to abundant cheap labor. By the middle of the twentieth century hired help was a luxury, garden size had diminished, and in America a mobile popu-lation lacked the patience perennials demand.

Their renewed popularity—for some an obsession—is a result, in part, of the efforts of enthusiastic nurserymen who have developed so many new, easily grown hybrids. These are now propagated in the same light-weight containers and soil in which they are later sold—usually in full leaf and frequently in flower.

perennial liabilities But nothing is without a price. And in city yards or rooftop containers where growing room is at a premium, perennials must be chosen with care since many flower for a limited time only. It's not so easy to orches-trate a lengthy sequence of bloom in a small space. It is particularly diffi-cult—even impossible—when there is more shade than sun. Subtle combinations of textures and foliage are sure to excite the horticulturally

Ribbon Grass
Phalaris arundinacea picta

sophisticated. But if *your* personal goal is spring to fall, nonstop, easy-care color, an English cottage garden with wall-to-wall perennials may not be for you.

for foliage   In any case, colorful flowers aren't the only important perennials. Foliage plants like woodland ferns and ornamental grasses also play a supporting role.

ferns   Fernlike plants predate dinosaurs. In the modern garden they impart woodland magic beneath shrubs and trees or where little else can be counted on. Unlike flowering plants, which multiply by seeds, ferns are propagated by single cell spores borne in clusters called sori that line the leaves or fronds. Medieval gardeners, unable to understand how ferns reproduced, regarded them with fear; modern gardeners should not mistake the seed capsules for insects.

ornamental grasses Ornamental grasses include many handsome plants with colors that range from wine red to gold and silvery blue. Heights vary from several inches to several dozen feet. Their beauty lies not in their tiny, individual flowers, but in lithesome leaves and long-lasting, feathery plumes. Ornamental grasses are thus distinguished from their mundane green cousins, whose sole reason for being is to serve underfoot. But more important, while lawn grasses are highly demanding of water, fertilizer and the gardener's time, most ornamental grasses are satisfied with something akin to neglect.

annuals And then there are *annuals.*
Summer's exuberance lies with the glorious blooms of petunias, marigolds, cosmos, morning glories, sunflowers and zinnias, a group that is sometimes referred to as "bedding plants." Annuals also include a majority of vegetables—tomatoes, cucumbers, radishes and beans—the plants of historic kitchen gardens and the raison d'être of the earliest city plots. Unlike perennial flowers, which strut their stuff only for days or weeks at a time, annual flowers purchased in spring can be expected to blossom more or less nonstop, straight through to autumn. Annuals differ from perennials in that their total lifetime (seed, flowers, fruit and death) is all in one year.

color everywhere Annuals comprise a colorful, versatile group that rarely fails to add worry-free, pleasurable hours. Jam them into a pot, hanging basket or window box, plop them midseason into a spot where something else has expired, use them to surround street trees or fill otherwise unproductive corners of even the tiniest balcony, terrace or yard. (The list of supporting players begins on page 78.)

the zone map Early in this century horticulturists began classifying trees, shrubs and herbaceous perennials according to their tolerance of frost in order to create an orderly system of hardy plants. The most workable scheme, and the standard for much that followed, was a map devised by Alfred Rehder. Published in 1927, it linked similar conditions of frost in wide swaths later called "zones." Zone maps soon made an appearance in garden books, and later in mail-order catalogues.
In wide use now is a variation on Rehder's map. Developed by the U.S. Department of Agriculture (USDA), it too divides the United States

and Canada into zones. The coldest is 1, the warmest is 10. Recently, the letters A and B were added to reflect further variations within each zone, and some nurseries now also add letters of their own. When reading a catalogue or book, you must check the system being used (and in this book I've used the early USDA code, see page 67).

it's not just the cold The problem of hardiness, however, is further complicated by the fact that plant survival is affected not only by cold but by wind, light exposure, snow cover, soil composition and proximity to a body of water. Drought is a factor in the demise of some plants, while for others it's heat (which is why tulips don't naturally brighten Miami. Recognizing this, The American Horticultural Society recently developed a map with 12 heat zones—and the quest for accuracy continues. Since in any case it's rarely possible to predict the behavior or tolerance of any living thing—either plant or planter—experienced gardeners use hardiness classifications only as a guide.

defying the rules Along these lines, I'd always believed that when in doubt about winter tolerance, it was best to use species considered safe for a colder zone. I loudly proclaimed this view to rooftop gardeners, in particular, until one politely told me this simply wasn't so. For years, he insisted, he had maintained, on his eighteenth-floor terrace, a large stand of dusty miller, a gray-leaved perennial that according to the canons of zone maps won't tolerate New York cold. When I studied his site, I realized he wasn't succumbing to hyperbole. His south-facing terrace was an exemplary microclimate of winter warmth; high masonry parapet walls virtually eliminated the wind, provided shelter for the tubs, and helped retain the radiant heat from the building's brick surfaces and the floor below. So now I rephrase my erstwhile sage advice: on exposed city rooftops or sites where winter winds are fierce, you're *probably* better off with species that are hardy in colder zones.

tender perennials Perennials that are not hardy—those whose roots cannot survive certain levels of frost—are called *tender*. Tender perennials in my zone typically include not only dusty miller but rosemary, lantana, coleus and the popular windowbox geranium. Here, where frost prevails, tender perennials are normally used in the garden only from spring through fall.

houseplants outside Included in the category of tender perennials are *tropical* species or houseplants. Whether grouped in freestanding pots, transplanted into window boxes or hanging baskets, or tucked into soil under large shrubs, tropical houseplants are superb outdoors in the summer garden.

Rosemary
Rosmarinus
officinalis

Some, like the begonia, fuchsia or streptocarpus, are favored for their flowers; others, like coleus or croton, are treasured for colorful leaves. Asparagus fern, creeping fig and grape ivy have graceful, cascading foliage that is good for hanging baskets, while dracaena and ficus are good summertime trees.

don't rush the season But take your time when introducing your houseplants to the great outdoors. Rare are the city slickers—new gardeners especially—who are not tempted by the first balmy spring day to rush the season and make their place green in a hurry. Which is precisely how I lost a huge, grown-from-seed avocado one cool April, the first year of my balcony garden. With the demise of this treasure, my shady, barren space remained so until midsummer, when an upstairs neighbor requested that I "plant-sit" while she went away. My reward for lugging her large collection of houseplants downstairs was the instant Eden I dreamed of.

When you do finally move your houseplants outdoors, shield them at first from the bright sun and strong winds they aren't used to. In autumn, take them back in well before the firing of your winter furnace. Again, they need time to readjust—in this case, to weaker light and stuffy air.

tender perennials treated as annuals In what can only be regarded as a conspiracy to confuse amateur gardeners, true annuals and tender perennials are lumped together by garden centers, making them difficult to distinguish. And that can produce some surprises.

The head of the garden committee at a neighboring co-op apartment building was meticulous each autumn about ridding the front-door garden of fading annuals. One year, for reasons unknown, she didn't get around to her usual task and through much of that winter greeted me with complaints about the wizened red salvias that tarnished her pristine snow.

Imagine her amazement (and mine) the following summer when the salvias not only reappeared, but were back in full bloom. "Annual" salvias are not really annuals at all, but tender perennials. And, thanks to an unusually mild winter, hers had survived. (Naturally she declared she would *never again* bother to pull out summer flowers, and the next year, after a more typical winter, all the plants died.)

For this reason some garden periodicals and catalogues now use a phrase like "grow as an annual" when depicting tender herbaceous perennials like impatiens or snapdragons or tender shrubs like lantana or verbena. (And these suppliers deserve a blue ribbon for promoting horticultural accuracy.)

biennials Another, less well known category of fine summer plants are the *biennials*. Although this group comprises far fewer species than either annuals or perennials, included are such outstanding flowers as Canterbury bells, hollyhock and sweet William. Biennials, as the name implies, take two years to complete their life cycle, with the flowers appearing the second year. But it is not unusual to find, tucked in among garden shop offerings, two-year-old potted biennials, in full bud and ready to bloom.

bulbs and their cousins *Bulbs* are such fail-safe gems they're worth every bit of space you can spare. Because the flower bud is already in place at the time of purchase, no matter how dim your light, the first year's bloom is guaranteed (assuming you've purchased mature bulbs from a reputable source). Tulips, daffodils and alliums are true bulbs. Crocuses are close cousins (technically called *corms*). Where sunlight is minimal, plant only shorter species; tall growers need sun to develop stems that are strong enough to remain vertical.

beyond the tulip Tulips have become synonymous with spring but city gardeners should take advantage not only of the many other bulbs that flower in spring, but the many bulbs that flower in *other* seasons. Bulbs are planted the season before the one in which they bloom—and this does take some planning.
Late spring is the time to plant the summer-flowering bulbs like summer hyacinth.
Late summer is the time to plant the autumn-flowering bulbs like autumn crocus.
Autumn is the time to plant winter bloomers like winter aconite. And for convenience, autumn is the time when spring bloomers are planted too.

bulbs treated as annuals Strictly speaking, bulbs (and corms) are herbaceous perennials in that they're long-lived plants whose leaves die to the soil at the end of their growing season. For this reason, some gardeners leave hardy bulbs in the ground and grow other plants above or around them—a fine idea where there's room. The problem in a small garden is that every growing inch counts.
Other gardeners dig up their tender bulbs after the leaves have died (having therefore made and stored the food that ensures next year's flowers). They then store them away until it's time to replant. This too is a fine idea if you have storage space to spare. However, neither method will ensure new flowers if you have conditions that are less than ideal: inadequate sunshine, poor soil or too much or too little moisture. And where container space is minimal, it's preferable to save the space for other seasonal plants.
Furthermore, many spectacular bulbs—tulips especially—are the result of intensive hybridizing. If left in the ground, they revert to a much less colorful form.

The bottom line for city gardeners is that often it's easier and better to treat bulbs as if they were annuals and discard them after they bloom.

herbal delights Some old-fashioned gardeners are feeling quietly smug these days. It seems that everyone else has finally discovered what they have known for ages: the true magic of herbs lies not in dusty medieval folklore, but in their use and delight. Those who don't live in town may insist that the small city garden, with its pressing walls and restricted space, is reminiscent of a medieval monastery cloister. But they seem to forget that no

Basil
Ocimum basilicum

monk looked out of his cell at a multistory condominium. This unromantic attitude, however, should not deter you from reaping a bountiful harvest of thyme for your stew, mint for your tea, lavender for potpourri or globe thistle for dried arrangements.

the "b" of herbaceous The botanical definition of *herb* varies considerably, as does the word's pronunciation. Traditionalists, like me, sound the "h" like the British; others cling to the Old French "erbe."
Theoretically, at least, "herb" is short for herbaceous (a plant that does not produce a woody stem). Yet those in the know subscribe to the sixteenth-century view of herbs as "plants in the use of Man." This means

not for cooking only, but for fragrance, dyes, cosmetics, medicine, magic —or a combination of all.

a touch of lore Lore attesting to the magic of herbal cures dates from earliest times and exists in every culture. In Europe it proliferated thanks to the Herbal Doctrine of Signatures, which was promulgated by the sixteenth-century physician Paracelsus. The belief was that a plant's resemblance to a part of the body was a clue to its use. So a plant like lungwort *(Pulminaria),* which has spotted oval leaves, was the herb to cure ailing lungs. Since it was up to the lady of the castle, or the monk in the cloister, to determine which plants were good for what, many a remedy was dreamed up after the fact; if the patient survived, the herb was the right one to use. A good imagination was probably a useful prerequisite.

a limitless repertoire Questionable properties notwithstanding, the sixteenth-century view of herbs was conveniently broad and thus ensures a virtually limitless repertoire. So alongside the dill, parsley and sage a modern city herbalist may legitimately grow vegetables like cabbage, hardy shrubs like Chinese witch hazel, tender shrubs like rosemary, hardy herbaceous perennials like snakeroot, ground covers like sweet woodruff and bulbs like lilies.

vines and climbers Vines have been called nature's drapery, and there's no better way to clothe a naked city wall or shroud an immovable object. Vines also frame views, and give shelter to birds and cooling shade for city buildings (with reduced air conditioning costs inside).
But not all vines climb the same way.
To ensure that your selection succeeds in getting up in the world, you must give it the surface it wants—as I learned from the many times I failed to impose my will on species more stubborn than I.

aerial rootlets Some vines climb by tiny, suction cup–like discs or small *aerial rootlets* along their stems. This group, which includes hardy vines like Boston ivy, is good for broad or flat walls of brick, stone or concrete. Vines with aerial rootlets should not be grown on wooden structures or surfaces where restaining or painting is needed.

twiners *Twiners* won't grow on a wall since they must have something to wrap around. This group, which includes hardy vines like honeysuckle and annuals like morning glory, is good for balcony railings, water tower legs, chain-link fences and lattices. Since they're not selective about what they embrace, twiners are also fond of telephone poles and television cables (although they are not appreciated by either industry). They must also be kept off trees and shrubs, which they eventually strangle. Twiners are also very specific about direction—clockwise or counterclockwise, depending on the species. And don't even think about trying to change them.

tendrils   A variation on the twining vine theme is plants that move with the help of *tendrils,* or slender side shoots that look like curly hairs. This group includes hardy vines like clematis and grapes. The tiny appendages, despite their delicate appearance, hold securely onto anything narrow enough to encircle—chains, ropes or latticework. They also cling to the stems of other plants. But unlike twiners, vines with tendrils have manners and don't kill their support.

Cotoneaster
Cotoneaster dammeri

using leaners   Since many vines strenuously object to being removed, you may not wish to use them on trelliswork or garden structures that need regular repainting. The plants to consider instead are *leaners.* These are plants like climbing roses, whose name notwithstanding do not adhere to their supporting surface. As a result, they are easily dislodged.

and espaliers   Among the most distinguished of the leaners are the trees and shrubs that have been *espaliered,* that is, trained to grow flat against a wall or lattice. The word "espalier" is from the French—*epaule* or shoulder—an

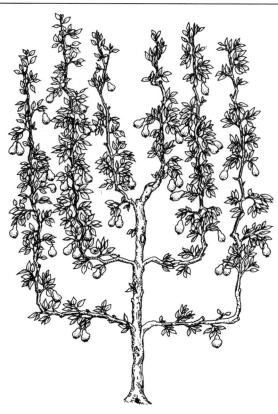

Espaliered pear tree
Pyrus communis

allusion to limbs that are trained to grow at right angles to the trunk, traditionally in a symmetrical pattern. The espalier technique is generally associated with ancient Rome, but the method is now believed to date from ancient Egypt.

ready-mades For centuries, professional gardeners took pains (and years) to create their own espaliers using fruiting species like apple, pear or quince. But in these days of instant everything, you can find nursery-trained espaliers on inexpensive forms waiting to be picked up, toted home and plopped in wherever you need one. An espaliered shrub or tree is a striking addition to any garden, but its flatness makes it particularly valuable where growing space is restricted. For plants to espalier yourself see page 231.

topiary whimsies Gardeners love messing with Mother Nature. And like the espalier, the *topiary*—a plant sheared into a fanciful shape—has enjoyed renewed popularity in town. The name originated in ancient Rome, where elaborate ornamental gardens or *topia* were tended by slaves known as *topiarii*. A seemingly limitless range of outlines has since evolved and, as with the espalier, you can now buy for a reasonable sum topiary triangles, cubes, spirals, spheres, tiered globes and even small animals and birds.

place them with care Adding topiary is like adding sculpture. Pair two to flank a formal entry or line several in a row to define a path or edge a stairs. A single can serve as an impressive focal point whether grown in a rooftop container or as a specimen centerpiece in a yard.

harmonious tones Compatible foliage tones and flower colors are an important part of the small city garden's design. Overpowering shades—brilliant orange or blazing red—can be difficult to handle. They're also harder to combine than quiet pastels. If you like vivid hues, you can soften their bluster with a foil of white flowers or plants with silver-gray leaves. You can also group them with plants in the next closest tone—for example, a bright orange butterfly weed near pale yellow marigolds. Purples and blues tend to recede. Back these flowers with plants with lighter tones or place them in front of the garden. Otherwise their dark blossoms may not even be seen.

working with color In a small space, the scattershot or confetti look—a red begonia here, a yellow marigold there—can really be a mess. You can avoid this by planting clusters of at least three, five or seven of the same plant. Or, for truly painless planning, stick to a single color theme.

go with the spectrum On the color wheel used by artists, the spectrum is divided into opposite sides. If you think of it as a compass, you could say that north is green and south is red. East is yellow and west is blue. Harmonious combinations of flower colors are most easily built by using flower tones from one side only—say a range of purples and blues. Accent plants can then be added from the opposite side (in this case, yellow), with artistry and restraint.

the trick is in the combinations In the next chapter you will find an introduction to several hundred members of nature's dramatis personae. The key to success lies in how you use this cast of characters to create a multiseasonal blend of complementary outlines and colors, and contrasting textures and tones.

Dill
Anethum graveolens

If you want to identify plants expertly, you should spend a lot of time surreptitiously reading labels.
—Geoffrey B. Charlesworth, *The Opinionated Gardener,* 1988

4. Narrowing the Choices: Some City Plants I've Known

where to begin

At this point, you've spent a respectable length of time observing your space and meeting some of nature's dramatis personae. Still, you may think you don't know quite where to begin or which plants to buy. New gardeners in particular may feel horticulturally insecure, so you may be surprised to discover you know more than you suspect about the plants you need.

answering your own plant questions

Begin by returning to a copy of your cardboard plan, that original sketch you made of your space (see page 4). For each area you should now be able to answer the following questions and jot your thoughts on a tracing paper overlay or photocopy:

- ❧ Will the design for this area be served best by:
    A deciduous or evergreen, shrub or tree?
    Perennials, annuals, ground covers or edibles?
    A vine, espalier or nonplant cover?
- ❧ What light tolerance will plants require here?
- ❧ What height or width of plant is most practical here?
- ❧ Which season(s) of interest does this area need?
- ❧ Does this space demand a specimen plant or one with unusual form?
- ❧ Are wind-, heat-, moisture- or drought-tolerant plants needed?

the crossword puzzle Narrowing your plant possibilities is a little like doing a crossword puz-
approach zle: you start with a lengthy list of required traits, then work toward finding a single "word." The required traits, in this case, consist of your
answers to the questions above; the single word is the name—or names
—of plants that fit. And you can be sure there will be many more than
one.

about the lists Groups of plants are listed throughout this book, but I've tried to orga-
nize the collection that follows to help you get started. All plants included
may be grown outside, either *in* the ground in a yard or *on top of the
ground* in a container. (Pruning is the secret to keeping city plants under
control, and this is covered in Chapter 11; winter conditions for plants in
containers are in Chapter 7.) Space has limited this list to a mere several
hundred plants—admittedly, a *personal* selection—and these are arranged in three major categories:

The leading players: Splendid shrubs and terrific trees
The supporting cast: Favorites for flowers, foliage, fragrance or
flavor
Creative covers: Climbers for walls and fences

signs of light The left-hand column indicates the minimum sunlight needed during the
growing season. All green plants need light to thrive (only mushrooms
grow in the dark, and they're not green), but there are always surprises. If
a plant appeals but you aren't sure it will thrive—experiment. When in
doubt, try it out.
The light conditions are divided as follows:

FS = **Full Sun** = no less than about 7 hours daily
SS = **Strong Sun** = midday, or total of at least 5 hours
WS = **Weak Sun** = early or late day, total of at least 3 hours
NS = **No Sun** = less than 3 hours or bright reflected light

nomenclature The plants are listed alphabetically by common name (where popular
ones exist) with the scientific name following. This order may horrify
some of my garden friends who insist that Americans be "more British"
and converse only in botanical Latin. But there are those for whom flu-
ency in the language of horticulture lags behind the ability to garden, and
I feel these lists will serve everyone better this way.

size, shape and other useful qualities Each plant listed includes notes on approximate size, shape and seasonal interest along with a brief paragraph on growing requirements and notable species or hybrids.

and hardiness In some cases, there is also a hardiness zone rating. For this, I have used the map of the U.S. Department of Agriculture. Find and then memorize the zone number appropriate to your condition:

USDA ZONE NUMBER	MINIMUM WINTER TEMPERATURE
Zone 3	− 40° to − 30° F
Zone 4	− 30° to − 20° F
Zone 5	− 20° to − 10° F
Zone 6	− 10° to 0° F
Zone 7	0° to 10° F
Zone 8	10° to 20° F
Zone 9	20° to 30° F
Zone 10	30° to 40° F

maneuvering the budget A final word—about money.

Quality plants are expensive, and setting up a garden is hardest, financially, on beginners. New rooftop, balcony and terrace owners especially, face enormous initial outlays, since soil components as well as containers must be built or bought. The first warm day in spring can inspire a terrific frenzy—but every plant does not have to be in place on the Fourth of July, or even by Labor Day. Take it easy, be patient (that's supposedly the gardener's golden rule) and let your garden grow and change—just as the plants do—over the seasons and years.

Gentian
Gentiana sino-ornata

THE LEADING PLAYERS: SPLENDID SHRUBS AND TERRIFIC TREES

Sun Conditions				
FS	SS	WS	NS	

FS	SS	WS	NS	
x	x			**ABELIA** *(Abelia grandiflora)* Shrub; moderately rapid grower with rounded form, to 4 feet, Zone 5 Summer: mid to late pink flowers often continuing into fall Autumn: purple-bronze foliage Winter: broad-leaved evergreen or semievergreen I was first smitten by this glossy, dark green shrub when I saw it covered with blooms on a small rooftop. Like its cousins in the honeysuckle family, it is completely undemanding, easily controlled with pruning, and freely bears trumpet-shaped flowers. On windy or unprotected sites it may die back to the soil line in winter. Notable cultivars include 'Prostrata' and 'Francis Mason.'
x	x			**AMERICAN ARBORVITAE** *(Thuja occidentalis)* Shrub or tree; moderately slow grower in globular, pyramidal or columnar shapes, to over 40 feet, Zone 2 Winter: scaly-looking needle evergreen The arborvitae on a neighbor's penthouse terrace survived both burning sun and vicious winds. Reputed to prefer moist soil, this one never noticed when its owner forgot to water. Hybrids vary in tone from deep green to bronze and bright gold, and the flat, fan-shaped foliage contrasts well with other evergreens.
x	x	x	x	**ANDROMEDA or JAPANESE ANDROMEDA** *(Pieris japonica)* Shrub; moderately slow grower, broad cylindrical form, to 8 feet, Zone 6 Spring: white, pale pink or light red flowers Early summer: red-bronze new foliage Winter: broad-leaved evergreen, prominent white flower buds These dark green, willow-shaped leaves are a glistening backdrop for bright spring bloomers. Moist, acid soil with some shelter from afternoon sun is best. Notable cultivars include: 'Dorothy Wycoff' (dark red flower buds open to pink), 'White Cascade,' 'Red Mill' (hardy to Zone 5, bright red spring foliage).
x	x	x		**AUTUMN COLOR** *Plants of special interest in fall. See page 211.*
x	x	x	x	**AZALEA** *Azaleas are now officially classified with rhododendrons. See page 75.*
x	x	x	x	**BIRCH** *(Betula spp.)* Tree; slow to medium grower, mostly narrow form, some pendulous species, to over 40 feet, Zone 3 Spring: chartreuse catkins Autumn: golden foliage Winter: bark color, prominent gray-brown catkins "Ladies of the woods" are how these graceful trees were described by the horticul-

THE LEADING PLAYERS: SPLENDID SHRUBS AND TERRIFIC TREES

Sun Conditions

FS   SS   WS   NS

turist T. H. Everett. My first birch was a single tree in a rooftop container; I now have a backyard "grove" of four. Most species of birch adapt well to nearly any soil and site and also tolerate wind. Bark tones range from white *(B. papyrifera)* through chalky gray *(B. populifolia)* and reddish brown *(B. lenta).*

x   *x*

BLUEBERRY *(Vaccinium corymbosum)*
Shrub; medium slow grower with somewhat rounded form, to 10 feet, Zone 4
Spring through summer: cream-colored flowers followed by edible purple-blue berries
Autumn: crimson foliage
Winter: jagged silhouette, crimson twigs, prominent flower buds
You can't beat highbush blueberries for year-round interest and sublime edible fruit. Two plants with overlapping bloom sequences are needed for pollination—but don't rely on neighbors, grow them yourself. Rich, acid, somewhat moist soil is best. My own two shrubs bloomed prolifically for years in a single 24-inch-wide tub. Notable cultivars, in order of flower appearance include, 'Earliblue,' 'Patriot,' 'Blueray,' 'Bluecrop,' Berkeley,' 'Herbert' and 'Coville.'

x   *x*

BLUE SPIREA or BLUE-MIST SHRUB *(Caryopteris clandonensis)*
Shrub; medium grower, slightly rounded form, arching branches, to 3 feet, Zone 7
Summer: late blue flowers
Wandering in a nursery late one August, I couldn't resist purchasing this small shrub with its silvery foliage and blue flowers. For sturdy growth, cut the stems back severely in spring. Rich, well-drained soil is best.

x   *x*

BUTTERFLY BUSH or SUMMER LILAC *(Buddleia davidii)*
Tree or shrub; moderately rapid grower, vase shaped, to 9 feet, Zone 6
Summer: mid to late purple, pink, white or red flowers
Butterflies do indeed enjoy the spiky, extremely fragrant flowers, which should be removed as they fade to encourage repeat bloom. A severe trimming very early in spring is also good. Notable cultivars include 'Charming' (pink), 'Fascination' (orchid pink) and 'Dubonnet' (purple).

x   *x*

CALLERY PEAR *(Pyrus calleryana)*
Tree; moderately rapid grower with oval outline, to 40 feet, Zone 5
Spring: white flowers
Autumn: crimson foliage
This easily grown tree is approaching overuse for street planting, but it's hard to resist a plant with so many seasons of beauty that is also so willing to tolerate drought and neglect. Notable cultivars include 'Bradford,' 'Redspire' (more pyramidal in form) and 'Aristocrat' (more horizontal branching with wavy-edged leaves).

THE LEADING PLAYERS: SPLENDID SHRUBS AND TERRIFIC TREES

Sun Conditions			
FS	SS	WS	NS

x	x	x		**CHERRY** *(Prunus* spp.*)*

Tree; slow to medium grower round, vaselike and pendulous shapes, to 30 feet.
Spring: white, pale pink, purple or crimson flowers
Summer: some species have edible fruit
Autumn: golden or bronze-red foliage

The species and cultivars of cherries number in the hundreds, including many delicate-flowered ornamentals (plants that do not bear edible fruit). Notable species include the Oriental or Japanese cherries *(P. serrulata).* The autumn-flowering cherry *(P. subhirtella* 'Autumnalis'*)* flowers in both spring and fall. (The first October mine bloomed, a surprised neighbor called to alert me that my tree was "confused.") The edible sweet cherry *(P. avium)* requires two varieties for pollination; it's easier to grow the self-fruitful sour cherry *(P. cerasus).* Unfortunately, all members of the genus *Prunus* are subject to more than their fair share of diseases and pests. Nursery labels are often confused, so to be sure you get the flower color, size and shape you want, buy trees when they're in bloom.

x	x	x	x	**CHOKEBERRY** *(Aronia arbutifolia)*

Shrub; slow grower with upright form, to 8 feet, Zone 5
Spring: white flowers
Summer: glossy red fruit through fall
Autumn: scarlet foliage

The red chokeberry is an easily grown (some say "weedy") American native that is not fussy about growing conditions; it's superb for dense shade. A proven cultivar is 'Brilliantissima.'

x	x	x		**CORKSCREW WILLOW** *(Salix matsudana* 'Tortuosa'*)*

Shrub or tree; rapid grower with narrow outline, to 40 feet, Zone 4
Winter: twisted spiral twigs

Twisted spiral twigs make this plant a favorite in the winter garden and with flower arrangers. The slender brown-gray branches and pale green leaves are a fast-growing, bright green, bushy screen. The willow is easily maintained and tolerant of neglect, but its rapid root growth makes it a most demanding container plant.

x	x	x	x	**COTONEASTER** *(Cotoneaster* spp.*)*

Shrubs; medium slow to rapid growers; height and zone vary with species
Spring: white or pink flowers followed by red or black berries that linger through fall
Autumn: berries and red foliage in some species
Winter: some evergreen or semievergreen

This enormous genus includes many easily grown, handsome species. The rock-spray cotoneaster *(C. horizontalis)* grows to 3 feet, is semievergreen and has a hori-

THE LEADING PLAYERS: SPLENDID SHRUBS AND TERRIFIC TREES

Sun Conditions			
FS	SS	WS	NS

zontal branching pattern good for training against a wall. The bearberry cotoneaster *(C. dammeri)* is 1 foot tall and a good evergreen ground cover. The small-leaved cotoneaster *(C. microphyllus)* has glossy, fine-textured evergreen leaves.

x   x   x   x **CRABAPPLE** *(Malus* spp.*)*
Tree; moderately rapid grower, rounded, vaselike and pendulous shapes, to 30 feet
Spring: white, pink or crimson flowers
Summer: red, yellow or green edible fruit through fall
Autumn: red or golden foliage
Crabapple species and cultivars number in the tens of hundreds. Most are extraordinarily tolerant and cheerfully survive unspeakable neglect on rooftops and yards. New cultivars appear with overwhelming regularity, but among the tried and true are 'Adams' (pale pink flowers), 'Red Jade' (white with pendulous branches), 'Pink Spires' (lavender flowers) and 'Donald Wyman' (pink-white flowers). Rampant crossbreeding and inaccurate labeling mean you will very likely never know the real name of the plant you buy. To be sure of the color, purchase plants in bloom.

x   x   x   x **DOGWOOD** *(Cornus* spp.*)*
Shrubs or trees; slow growers with broadly round or upright narrow forms and
varying height depending on species.
Spring or early summer: white or pale pink flowers, followed by berries in some
species, that linger through fall
Autumn: red or gold foliage
Winter: red twigs (some species)
The many exquisite shrubs and trees that make up this genus prefer moist, well-drained, acid soil and some wind protection, as befits their natural edge-of-woodland home. The early blooming American native tree *C. florida* is vulnerable to many problems and is much overplanted. I prefer the trouble-free Kousa or Japanese dogwood *(C. kousa)* with its upright branching to about 25 feet tall. Mine flourished for years in a tub with a northern exposure, just beyond a window where I could enjoy its many seasonal changes. Treasured too are the shrubby red osier *(C. sericea)* and tartarian dogwoods *(C. alba)*, whose slender stems (to about 6 feet) are a striking crimson in winter if they have good sunlight. *C. alba* 'Elegantissima' has handsome gray-green leaves edged in white.

x   x   x **DROUGHT-TOLERANT PLANTS**
Plants that tolerate minimal moisture. See page 195.

x   x   x **DWARF SHRUBS**
Plants that remain small. See page 237.

THE LEADING PLAYERS: SPLENDID SHRUBS AND TERRIFIC TREES

Sun Conditions				
FS	SS	WS	NS	

FS	SS	WS	NS	
x	*x*	*x*	*x*	**ESPALIERS** *Plants to train flat against a wall. See page 231.*
x	*x*	*x*		FORSYTHIA *(Forsythia* spp.*)* Shrub; rapid grower with upright, arching limbs, to 15 feet Spring: yellow flowers Winter: gold-green speckled twigs Forsythias are easily grown and tolerate both drought and neglect. The degree of flowering is in proportion to the amount of sunlight. Notable cultivars include the compact 'Bronxensis' (1½ feet tall), the pendulous 'Sieboldii,' and the upright 'Lynwood.'
x	*x*	*x*	*x*	GINKGO or MAIDENHAIR TREE *(Ginkgo biloba)* Tree; slow grower with narrow asymmetrical silhouette, to over 70 feet, Zone 4 Autumn: golden foliage This handsome relic dates from the age of dinosaurs. Its beautiful, fan-shaped leaves are pest free and thrive despite impossible sites. A slender outline and slow growth makes it a favorite tree for narrow sidewalks or wherever space is minimal. Mature female plants bear seeds that are particularly malodorous; plant males only. 'Sentry' is a columnar cultivar.
	x	*x*	*x*	GOLD DUST PLANT or AUCUBA *(Aucuba japonica* variegata*)* Shrub; moderately slow grower with bushy, rounded form, to 15 feet, Zone 7 Autumn: scarlet fruit on female plants Winter: broad-leaved evergreen I admit this is not one of my favorites, but neighbors swear by its tropical gold-flecked leaves for brightening dense shade. An extremely easy plant to grow, but male and female plants are both needed for the brilliant fruit.
x	*x*			GOLDENRAIN TREE or VARNISH TREE *(Koelreuteria paniculata)* Tree; moderately fast grower, narrow oval outline, to 35 feet, Zone 5 Summer: yellow flowers followed by clusters of pale green seed pods Autumn: golden foliage This is one of the few summer-blooming trees, and one of the fewer still with yellow flowers. It is easily grown in well-drained soil. Notable cultivars include 'Fastigiata,' which is narrowly upright, and 'September,' which flowers late.
x	*x*	*x*	*x*	**HEDGES** *Plants for hedges, borders or other dividers. See page 226.*
x	*x*	*x*	*x*	HOLLY *(Ilex* spp.*)* Shrub or tree; moderately fast grower; height and zone vary with species Spring: small, pale yellow flowers

THE LEADING PLAYERS: SPLENDID SHRUBS AND TERRIFIC TREES

Sun Conditions

FS   SS   WS   NS

Autumn: black or red berries that linger through winter
Winter: Some broad-leaved evergreens

Most holly species require both male and female plants to ensure a bountiful crop of berries. Japanese holly *(I. crenata)* has small, shiny oval evergreen leaves, grows to 20 feet and is hardy to Zone 6. I use the dwarf 'Compacta' as a carefree boxwood substitute in my herb garden. The evergreen American holly *(I. opaca)* has spiny leaves and grows to 40 feet. The slightly less hardy English holly *(I. aquifolium)* is taller. Inkberry *(I. glabra)* may reach 15 feet, is hardy to Zone 4 and is aptly named for its handsome black fruit. Expecially notable are the blue-green Meserve hybrids 'Blue Maid,' 'Blue Princess' and 'Blue Angel.' 'Blue Stallion' is a reliable pollinator for the ladies.

x   x   x   **HONEY LOCUST *(Gleditsia triacanthos)***
Tree; moderately fast grower, loosely asymmetrical shape, to over 50 feet, Zone 5
Summer: cascading podlike fruit on some cultivars, lingering through winter
Autumn: golden foliage

The honey locust is easily grown, tolerates both drought and neglect, and has a graceful open silhouette with delicate foliage for the barest of shade. I especially like the curly seedpods that dangle until they darken and drop in autumn, when neighborhood children collect them. The oldest and best of the thornless cultivars is 'Moraine.' Other notables include 'Sunburst,' whose young leaves are golden-yellow, and 'Skyline,' which is more pyramidal in shape.

x   x   x   **HYDRANGEA *(Hydrangea spp.)***
Shrub or tree; medium-fast grower, height and zone vary with species
Summer: flowers that linger through fall (some species)
Autumn: colored foliage some species

Don't confuse the tender hothouse hydrangeas with the many hardy garden plants. The bigleaf hydrangea *(H. macrophylla)* grows to 6 feet with good sun but tolerates shade. Its large, globular flowers change from blue to pink depending on the acidity in the soil (an excellent soil tester for blueberrries and other species that must have an acid reaction; see page 141). The oak-leafed hydrangea *(H. quercifolia)* is a slow grower to 6 feet, has white summer blooms and oak-shaped leaves that bronze in autumn and tolerate shade. The peegee or panicle hydrangea *(H. paniculata* 'Grandiflora'*)* is a quick grower to 25 feet with large white late-summer flowers that turn purple-pink in autumn and make good dried arrangements.

x   x   x   **JAPANESE BARBERRY *(Berberis thunbergii)***
Shrub; medium-fast grower, oval to rounded form, to 6 feet, Zone 5
Spring: yellow flowers
Autumn: red berries and bronze-red foliage

THE LEADING PLAYERS: SPLENDID SHRUBS AND TERRIFIC TREES

Sun Conditions			
FS	SS	WS	NS

Winter: may be semievergreen

This easily grown thorny shrub is also pest and disease free. One neighbor uses a clipped row as a border to keep passersby from sitting on his large frontyard planter. *B.t.* 'atropurpurea' has red-purple foliage in full sun. Notable cultivars include the compact 'Red Bird,' the dwarf 'Crimson Pygmy,' and 'Aurea,' which has striking golden foliage and grows to about 4 feet.

x	*x*	*x*	

JUNIPER *(Juniperus spp.)*

Shrubs or trees; moderately fast growers, some pendulous forms; height and zone vary with species

Autumn: blue berry-like cones on female plants

Winter: needle evergreen

The hundreds of fine junipers with their sharp, scalelike evergreen needles range considerably in size. The creeping juniper *(J. horizontalis)* is a good ground cover; *J.h.* 'Blue Rug' is steel blue in color and grows flat. The Chinese junipers *(J. chinensis)* include versatile cultivars like 'Columnaris,' a narrow silver-green column, and 'Pfitzeriana Aurea,' which is golden yellow. Another popular narrow, upright plant is the eastern red-cedar *(J. virginiana)* 'Skyrocket.'

x	*x*	*x*	*x*

LEUCOTHOE *(Leucothoe fontanesiana)*

Shrub; slow grower, to 6 feet, Zone 4

Spring: white or pale pink flowers

Autumn: bronze foliage that lasts though winter

Winter: broad-leaved evergreen

These graceful arching stems and leathery leaves combine well with other woodland plants. Several variegated forms have leaves that are pink and white.

x	*x*	*x*	

JAPANESE MAPLE *(Acer palmatum)*

Shrub or tree; moderately slow grower, rounded form, to 20 feet, Zone 5

Spring: new growth is pink, pale green or red

Autumn: reddish foliage

The many kinds of Japanese maples generally require well-drained, rich soil but tolerate part shade. Some, like 'Atropurpureum,' which has red leaves, retain their color all season. Others gradually turn green. The leaves vary from those cut into five parts to those with eleven. The most lacy and delicate is the threadleaf maple *(A.p. dissectum),* which also has graceful pendent limbs.

x	*x*	*x*	*x*

MOISTURE-TOLERANT PLANTS
Plants that tolerate wet soils. See page 194.

x	*x*	*x*	*x*

MOUNTAIN LAUREL *(Kalmia latifolia)*

Shrub or tree; moderately slow grower with somewhat rounded form, to 15 feet, Zone 4

THE LEADING PLAYERS: SPLENDID SHRUBS AND TERRIFIC TREES

Sun Conditions
FS   SS   WS   NS

Early summer: pale pink, white or spotted red flowers
Winter: broad-leaved evergreen, prominent flower buds
This native woodlander is surprisingly at home in town and, like its relative the rhododendron, needs moist, acid, well-drained soil. But unlike its cousin, its dark green leaves do not curl on frosty mornings. Buy in spring when the plant flowers to be sure your selection is mature enough to bloom. Notable cultivars include 'Bullseye,' 'Yankee Doodle,' 'Sarah,' and 'Ostbo Red.'

x   x   **PINE *(Pinus* spp.*)***
Shrubs or trees; some pendulous forms; height, rate of growth and zone vary with
    species
Winter: needle evergreen
The hundreds of pine species and cultivars offer a glorious assortment of choices including the mugo pine *(P. mugo mugo),* a dense, globular slow-growing shrub, the Japanese black pine *(P. thunbergiana),* which tolerates extreme wind and is superb for rooftops, the dragon's-eye pine *(P. densiflora* 'Oculus-draconis'*),* a slow grower with yellow markings, and the dwarf white pine *(P. strobus* 'Nana'*),* which spreads slowly in a gray-green mound.

x   x   **QUINCE *(Chaenomeles speciosa)* and *(Cydonia oblonga)***
Shrub or tree; moderately slow grower, to 8 feet or 20 feet respectively, Zone 4
Spring: pink, salmon, red or white flowers followed by fruit
This is a good example of the confusion that occurs when only common names are used. *Chaenomeles* is a rounded, somewhat thorny shrub, useful for hedges, with pink to scarlet spring flowers and yellow-green bitter fruit. *Cydonia* is a graceful tree that is easily espaliered, with white or pink spring flowers and sweet, golden, pear-shaped fruit. In their own ways, both quinces are superb.

x   x   x   x   **RHODODENDRON and AZALEA *(Rhododendron* spp.*)***
Shrubs or trees; size and zone vary with species
Spring to early summer: white, lilac, purple, red, pink or yellow flowers
Winter: broad-leaved evergreen (some deciduous species), prominent flower buds
Rhododendrons and azaleas are now officially classified as members of the same genus, adding to a beginner's dismay at finding several thousand species, varieties and hybrids to choose from. The group includes something for any condition or design: big leaves and small, evergreen and deciduous, tall trees and ground-hugging bushes, and flowers in virtually every color and shade. Most garden species prefer some shelter from sun and wind and a rich, acid, well-drained soil that is evenly moist. But their tolerance is great, I discovered, when for years I watched a lilac-colored catawba *(R. catawbiense)* on a terrace below me thrive despite blazing sun and total neglect. To be sure of getting the flower size and color you want, visit nurseries in spring and buy plants in bloom.

THE LEADING PLAYERS: SPLENDID SHRUBS AND TERRIFIC TREES

Sun Conditions			
FS	SS	WS	NS

FS	SS	WS	NS	
x	x			**ROSE** *(Rosa* spp.*)*

Shrubs; moderately rapid growers, narrow bushy form, to 5 feet; zone varies with species and hybrid
Summer: white, yellow, pink, red, orange or purple flowers
Autumn: colored foliage (some species)
Winter: prominent seedpods (called hips)

Roses are truly versatile city plants for use as single specimens, clustered in groups, or as hedges. The nearly fifty classifications are not easily defined, but among the most popular shrub roses are the floribundas (bushy plants with clusters of flowers that are good repeat bloomers), hybrid teas (taller plants with one flower to a stem, often with less reliable repeat bloom), grandifloras (a combination of hybrid teas and floribundas), miniatures or minis (diminutive bushes usually under 2 feet with flowers smaller than a quarter) and the heritage or old roses (plants in existence prior to the last quarter of the nineteenth century, many of which rarely repeat bloom after an early-summer flush). Outstanding hybrids are selected yearly by All American Rose Selections, Inc. (AARS), and these are marked with small metal tags. Some of my favorite repeat bloomers are 'Cherish' (pale pink), 'Chicago Peace' (pink blend), 'Europeana' (dark red), 'French Lace' (white), 'Iceberg' (white), 'Saratoga' (white) and 'Spartan' (coral). Two that manage to flower even with barely 4 hours of sun are 'Betty Prior' (pink) and 'The Fairy' (pink).

FS	SS	WS	NS	
x	x	x	x	**SHADBUSH, SERVICEBERRY or JUNE BERRY** *(Amelanchier canadensis)*

Shrub or tree; moderate grower with somewhat rounded form to 25 feet, Zone 5
Spring: white flowers followed by purple-red berries
Autumn: golden-red foliage

The exquisite cloud of white spring flowers (that appear when the shad are running) is always much too brief. This is an easily grown plant better for a shady backyard than a windy rooftop.

FS	SS	WS	NS	
x	x	x		**SOURWOOD, SORREL TREE or LILY-OF-THE-VALLEY TREE** *(Oxydendrum arboreum)*

Tree; moderately slow grower with rounded head, to 40 feet, Zone 5
Late spring or early summer: white flowers
Autumn: scarlet crimson foliage
Winter: spidery-looking seedpods

Among the treasured memories of my nineteenth-floor terrace is the sourwood's crimson autumn foliage set ablaze by a setting sun. A distant relative of the rhododendron, the sourwood prefers moist, rich, acid soil and some shelter from wind. This tree truly gives year-round pleasure. Just don't let its habit of leafing out late in spring scare you into thinking it's expired.

THE LEADING PLAYERS: SPLENDID SHRUBS AND TERRIFIC TREES

Sun Conditions				
FS	SS	WS	NS	

x	x	x		**THORNY PLANTS** *Plants with defensive thorns or briars. See page 187.*
x	x			**UMBRELLA PINE** *(Sciadopitys verticillata)* Tree; slow grower, somewhat oval in shape, to 30 feet, Zone 6 Winter: needle evergreen The long, bright green needles on this handsome plant are arranged in large whorls like an umbrella's ribs. It contrasts well with broad-leaved evergreens. Good drainage is important and so is a wind-protected spot.
x	x	x		**WASHINGTON HAWTHORN** *(Crataegus phaenopyrum)* Shrub or tree; moderately fast grower, broadly oval shape, to 30 feet, Zone 5 Spring: white flowers Autumn: orange-crimson foliage and scarlet berries that linger through winter This North American native is a compact, thorny tree that makes a fine single specimen or hedge and is appealing through many seasons. Members of this genus tend to be vulnerable to many diseases and pests.
x	x	x		**WEEPING TREES** *Trees with pendulous outline. See page 229.*
x	x	x		**WIND-TOLERANT PLANTS** *Trees and shrubs for windy locations. See page 216.*
x	x	x		**WINGED EUONYMUS or SPINDLE TREE** *(Euonymus alata)* Shrub; moderately slow grower, to 9 feet, Zone 3 Spring: small green flowers Autumn: scarlet foliage Winter: corky "wings" or ridges on twigs I have long been partial to this handsome plant with its rigid, vaselike shape, probably because it was the pride of my first balcony. It is easily grown in sun or shade, tolerates neglect, and is useful either as a hedge or single specimen. 'Compacta' is smaller and more rounded.
x	x	x	x	**WITCH HAZEL** *(Hamamelis spp.)* Shrub or tree; moderate grower with rounded outline, to 25 feet, Zone 4 Autumn: flowers (some species) and golden foliage Winter: flowers (some species) In my garden winter's end is heralded by the spectacular yellow ribbonlike blooms of the Chinese witch hazel *(H. mollis)*. It shrugs off February's snow and puts later-blooming forsythias to shame. This easily grown shrub is a cousin of the native witch hazel *(H. virginiana),* whose golden, spidery blooms appear in autumn. The vernal witch hazel *(H. vernalis)* also blooms late in winter. The small flowers are either

THE LEADING PLAYERS: SPLENDID SHRUBS AND TERRIFIC TREES

Sun Conditions
FS   SS   WS   NS

FS	SS	WS	NS	
				yellow or slightly red. Witch hazels enjoy the company of broad-leaved evergreens, which are admirable backdrops for their golden display.
x	x	x	x	**YEW** *(Taxus* **spp.***)* **Shrub or tree; medium-fast grower; shape, height and zone vary with species** **Autumn: red seeds (female plants)** **Winter: needle evergreen** Yews are invaluable, extremely versatile city evergreens that tolerate poor soil, shade and neglect as well as severe shearing into hedges, topiary or whatever else you wish. The new spring growth is pale green, but the needles darken with age. Natural shapes of cultivars vary from prostrate, rounded, globe-shaped, somewhat pendulous, treelike and columnar. The English yew *(T. baccata)* is hardy to Zone 7; the Japanese yew *(T. cuspidata)* to Zone 5. The intermediate yew *(T. media)* is a cross between the two with some of the best qualities of each.

(handwritten margin note: ? column one for shade side ? container ?)

THE SUPPORTING CAST: FAVORITES FOR FLOWERS, FOLIAGE, FRAGRANCE OR FLAVOR

Sun Conditions
FS   SS   WS   NS

FS	SS	WS	NS	
x	x	x		**AGERATUM** *(Ageratum houstonianum)* **Annual; to 12 inches** **Flowers: purple, white or pink, all summer** This easily grown, virtually fail-safe flower bears bunches of fluffy blooms from early spring until frost.
x	x	x	x	**AJUGA or BUGLEWEED** *(Ajuga reptans)* **Hardy perennial; to 6 inches, Zone 2** **Flowers: purple-blue or white, spring** A vigorous ground cover for difficult spots, ajugas have oval-shaped leaves that are nearly evergreen in mild winters. Notable cultivars include 'Atropurpurea' with bronze leaves, 'Rubra' with deep purple leaves, 'Variegata' with variegated leaves and 'Metallica Crispa' with silvery, ruffled foliage.

THE SUPPORTING CAST: FAVORITES FOR FLOWERS, FOLIAGE, FRAGRANCE OR FLAVOR

Sun Conditions
FS   SS   WS   NS

FS	SS	WS	NS	
x	x			

ALYSSUM, also BASKET-OF-GOLD *(Alyssum* spp.*)*
Hardy and tender perennials
Flowers: spring and/or summer
Plants called alyssum include flowering species like basket-of-gold (may be listed as *A. saxtile* or *Aurinia saxtalis),* which has brilliant golden spring blooms and does best in sunny, exposed spots, and mountain alyssum *(A. montanum),* which is smaller, longer lived and more fragrant. Another gem is sweet alyssum *(Lobularia maritima),* a 2–3-inch-high tender perennial that tolerates some shade, self-sows easily, and freely bears white, pink or purple flowers from spring until frost.

	x	x	x	

ASTILBE *(Astilbe,* spp.*)*
Hardy perennial; Zone 5
Flowers: spring or summer
Count me among those who swear by these ferny-leaved plants for brightening shade. Give them rich, moist soil and protection from wind, and they'll produce graceful flower spikes in white, pink, red or purple that range from 8 inches up to several feet. With the countless hybrids it's hard to choose, but my favorite is *A. chinensis* 'Pumila,' whose 10-inch-high, lavender-colored flowers and dense, low foliage make it a good ground cover. Astilbes are easily divided and easily moved. Other handsome cultivars include 'Europa' (pink flowers), 'Fanal' (red) and 'Bridal Veil' (white).

x	x	x		

AUTUMN COLOR
Perennials with autumn color. See page 211.

x	x			

BALLOON FLOWER *(Platycodon grandiflorus)*
Hardy perennial; to 15 inches, Zone 4
Flowers: purple-blue, white or pink, early summer
Moderately rich soil and a minimum of a half day of sun will ensure a profusion of the single or double 2–3-inch flowers that more closely resemble bell-shaped stars than balloons.

x	x	x		

BASIL *(Ocimum basilicum)*
Annual; to about 15 inches
Flowers: late summer
Basil is easily grown and easily sown. A pot on the window was once a sign that the lady expected her suitor, but a more modern association is with garlic in pesto. I also like to add it to spinach, green beans, zucchini, tomato sauces, and salads. Tasty hybrids include the pungent lettuce–leaf basil 'Crispum' and the somewhat sweeter-flavored, smaller-leaved bush basil 'Minimum.' For a colorful garnish use 'Purple Ruffles,' whose name accurately describes its foliage. Make seedlings bushy by pinching the center bud after the plants produce their second set of leaves.

THE SUPPORTING CAST: FAVORITES FOR FLOWERS, FOLIAGE, FRAGRANCE OR FLAVOR

Sun Conditions

FS	SS	WS	NS	
x	*x*	*x*		**BEGONIA** *(Begonia spp.)* Tender perennial Flowers: pink, white or red, all summer to frost The countless species and cultivars of these tropical plants are superb for many city conditions. The two most popular species are the flowering wax begonias *(B. semperflorens),* which are reliable bedding plants and good around street trees, and the angel wings *(B. coccinea),* which are most effective cascading over a window box or rooftop tub. Look for hybrids with unusual foliage tones.
x	*x*	*x*	*x*	**BERGENIA** *(Bergenia cordifolia)* Hardy perennial; to 12 inches, Zone 2 Flowers: pink, spring This plant's large, oval-shaped leaves are a good backdrop for finer foliage species like ferns, snakeroot or bleeding hearts. A native of Siberia, bergenia's foliage turns bronze in early autumn and often remains attractive well into winter. Bergenias are happiest in moist, well-drained soil, but are forgiving if neglected. A notable cultivar is the tall, purple-toned 'Purpurea,' which has dark pink blooms.
	x	*x*	*x*	**BLEEDING HEART** or **DUTCHMAN'S BREECHES** *(Dicentra spp.)* Hardy perennial; to 12 inches, Zone 3 Flowers: pink or white, spring and/or summer It was always a shock when my old fashioned *D. spectabilis* went dormant and disappeared, leaving a big midsummer gap. Now I plant the *eximia* hybrids, whose fine-textured, blue-gray foliage lasts until frost. Except in deepest shade there are also nearly nonstop blooms. Dicentras need rich, moist soil and a wind-sheltered spot and make a fine understory for evergreens. Divide when they get crowded. Notable cultivars include 'Luxuriant,' a free-flowering pink-red, and 'Alba,' which is white but flowers less freely.
x	*x*	*x*		**BROWALLIA** *(Browallia spp.)* Annual; to 12 inches Flowers: blue-purple or white, all summer to frost A star-shaped flower with a graceful habit of cascading over the side of containers or baskets. It does get straggly with too much shade.
x	*x*	*x*	*x*	**BULBS** *Summer-flowering bulbs, see page 89.* *Spring-flowering bulbs, see page 215.*
	x	*x*	*x*	**CALADIUM** *(Caladium bicolor)* Tender perennial; to 14 inches Foliage plant (seldom flowers)

THE SUPPORTING CAST: FAVORITES FOR FLOWERS, FOLIAGE, FRAGRANCE OR FLAVOR

Sun Conditions
FS   SS   WS   NS

The caladium's gossamer, heart-shaped leaves brighten even dense shade with splashes of white, pink, red and green. Wind protection is necessary. If you have room, dig up and store the corms in autumn for replanting in spring.

x   x

CATNIP or CATMINT *(Nepeta spp.)*
Hardy perennial; to 10 inches, Zone 3
Flowers: pale purple, early summer
These easily grown, gray-green plants are adored both by the gardeners who dry the fragrant leaves for potpourri and the cats who roll on them. *N. cataria* is particularly attractive to cats; *N. faassenii* is better for gardeners and so is *N. mussinii,* although it tends to sprawl. Nip off the spent flowers for repeat bloom. (In many cases nursery labels are confused.)

x   x   x

CELANDINE POPPY *(Stylophorum diphyllum)*
Hardy perennial; to 1½ feet, Zone 4
Flowers: yellow, spring to early summer
I was introduced to this beautiful wildflower by a country friend who gave me a division for my large rooftop tubs. An easily grown plant that prefers rich, moist, well-drained soil, it spreads steadily and also self-sows.

x   x

COCKSCOMB *(Celosia cristata)*
Annual; 12–30 inches
Flowers: yellow, red, orange or purple, all summer to frost
Cockscombs bear velvety crested or plume-feathered flower spikes, often in fantastic shapes. Plant in massed groups to hide the somewhat weedy leaves, and dry the flowers for winter arrangements.

x   x   x   x

COLEUS *(Coleus blumei)*
Tender perennial; over 2 feet
Flowers: Purple; unusually colorful foliage
This easily grown member of the mint family is valued less for its spiky flower than for its richly varied foliage that may be splashed with red, purple, creamy white, yellow or green. New hybrids also have unusual leaf shapes. Pinch the tips to keep the plants bushy.

x   x

CONEFLOWER, PURPLE CONEFLOWER or BLACK-EYED SUSAN
    (Rudbeckia spp. and *Echinacea* spp.*)*
Hardy perennial; to 3 feet, Zone 3
Flowers: yellow, pink or purple, summer
These undemanding, daisylike perennials resemble each other enough to be easily confused. Both flower freely in sunny open exposures and are superb for cutting. Both combine handsomely with Queen Anne's lace *(Daucus carota)* for an easy-care minimeadow. Purple coneflower *(E. purpurea)* has large, slightly drooping,

THE SUPPORTING CAST: FAVORITES FOR FLOWERS, FOLIAGE, FRAGRANCE OR FLAVOR

Sun Conditions

FS   SS   WS   NS

long-lasting purple-pink flowers. Notable cultivars include 'Robert Bloom' and 'Bright Star.' Brilliant yellow flowers are borne on black-eyed Susan *(R. hirta),* which includes gloriosa daisies and the showy coneflower *(R. fulgida).* A notable cultivar is 'Goldsturm.'

x   x

COREOPSIS or TICKSEED *(Coreopsis verticillata)*
Hardy perennial; 1–2 feet, Zone 3
Flowers: yellow, much of the summer
This easily grown plant ignores poor soil, drought and neglect and bears profusions of star-shaped flowers on graceful arching stems. Snip off the spent flowers to encourage repeat bloom. Notable cultivars include the bright yellow 'Golden Shower,' the somewhat shorter, paler 'Moonbeam,' 'Early Sunrise,' which has semidouble flowers, and the dwarf 'Goldfink.'

x   x   x

CORYDALIS *(Corydalis lutea)*
Hardy perennial; to 1 foot, Zone 5
Flowers: yellow, much of the summer
This neat, truly carefree plant with handsome ferny-looking leaves somewhat resembles its cousins, the bleeding hearts. It self-sows easily but is so attractive I don't mind letting it stay.

x   x

COSMOS *(Cosmos bipinnatus)*
Annual; over 3 feet
Flowers: rose, white, crimson, yellow, all summer to frost
Don't be fooled by the feathery foliage. Cosmos is a tough, easily grown, nonstop bloomer that tolerates drying winds, but the tall plants will flop without sufficient sun. Use the lovely, long-lasting flowers in fresh arrangements.

x   x   x

CUSHION SPURGE or MILKWORT *(Euphorbia epithymoides* or *polychroma)*
Hardy perennial; 1½ feet, Zone 3
Flowers: chartreuse yellow, spring
An easily grown member of a large genus of attractive garden plants, the cushion spurge remains demurely in a neat clump. Its stiff, bright green leaves turn bronze-red in autumn. As with most euphorbias, you should avoid touching the milky sap, which may produce an allergic reaction.

x   x   x

DAYLILY *(Hemerocallis* spp.*)*
Hardy perennial; 1–3 feet, Zone 3
Flowers: cream, yellow, pink, purple, orange, red, solids or stripes, summer
The botanical name is Greek and means "beautiful for a day"—the life span of individual blooms. Daylilies do best with rich, well-drained soil and flop over in poor light. With hundreds of new introductions yearly it's hard to keep pace, but handsome hybrids include 'Peach Fairy' (pink-toned blooms), 'Little Grapette' (pur-

THE SUPPORTING CAST: FAVORITES FOR FLOWERS, FOLIAGE, FRAGRANCE OR FLAVOR

Sun Conditions

FS	SS	WS	NS	
				ple) and 'Pardon Me' (red). Good rebloomers include 'Stella de Oro' (golden yellow flowers), 'American Revolution' (wine red), 'Winning Ways' (green-yellow), and 'American Belle' (lavender-pink).
x	*x*	*x*	*x*	**DROUGHT-TOLERANT PLANTS** *Plants that survive with minimal moisture. See page 195.*
	x	*x*	*x*	**EPIMEDIUM or BARRENWORT (*Epimedium* spp.)** **Hardy perennial; 6 inches–1 foot** **Flowers: yellow or pink, spring** These delightful plants have elongated heart-shaped leaves that dance on top of wiry stems. Like many gardeners, I feel compelled to neaten the nearly evergreen foliage late in winter by trimming it back to the soil. This fine underplanting for woodland shrubs is easily divided and easily moved.
x	*x*			**EVENING PRIMROSE or SUNDROPS (*Oenothera fruticosa*)** **Hardy perennial; 2–3 feet, Zone 5** **Flowers: yellow, early summer** Although usually called evening primrose, this bushy perennial freely bears its cheerful flowers most of the day. This steady spreader is easily moved and divided.
x	*x*			**FALSE DRAGONHEAD (*Physostegia virginiana*)** **Hardy perennial; 3 feet, Zone 3** **Flowers: purple-pink, mid to late summer and fall** False dragonhead has stately narrow leaves and spiky flower stalks that are covered with small tubular blooms that make a spectacular and unusual garden effect. A quick grower and spreader that must be controlled, it prefers slightly moist, acid soil.
	x	*x*	*x*	**FERNS** *Ferns do best in rich, moist soil and bright shade with an occasional sunbeam. Most are easily moved, but be sure to water well after planting.* **Christmas Fern (*Polystichum acrostichoides*)** has silvery new leaf buds, or crosiers, which are among the first fiddleheads to uncoil in spring. The 2–3-foot-tall fronds are a leathery dark green and stubbornly endure even when snow beats them down. **Cinnamon Fern (*Osmunda cinnamomea*)** is an easily grown native American with light green, feathery-looking fertile fronds that can reach 5 feet. The name comes from its 2-foot-tall chocolate brown fronds, which resemble a stick of cinnamon. **Japanese Painted Fern (*Athyrium niponicum pictum*)** has exquisite silvery serrated fronds with wine red stems that can reach up to 2 feet. Although it tolerates minimal light, both leaf color and growth are better with some sun.

THE SUPPORTING CAST: FAVORITES FOR FLOWERS, FOLIAGE, FRAGRANCE OR FLAVOR

Sun Conditions

FS   SS   WS   NS

Maidenhair Fern *(Adiantum pedatum)* has brittle, purple-black stems topped with delicate-looking light green leaflets arranged in a fan-shaped pattern. This exquisite slow grower must have evenly moist soil.

Marginal Shield Fern or Evergreen Wood Fern *(Dryopteris marginalis)* has leathery-looking gray evergreen fronds that grow to about 1½ feet. A native American, it prefers evenly moist soil.

Ostrich Fern *(Matteuccia struthiopteris)* has fast-growing, 4-foot-tall, feathery, light green fronds that make a decorative summer screen.

x   x   x

FLOWERING TOBACCO *(Nicotiana alata)*
Tender perennial; 1–3 feet
Flowers: red, pink or white, all summer to frost
Even nonsmokers enjoy this cousin of the plant that yields leaves for cigarettes. Its tall stems bear a profusion of gracefully drooping trumpet-shaped blooms. Moist soil is preferred and the more sun, the better; otherwise the plants flop and flowering decreases. A giant relative, *N. sylvestris,* bears unusually long clusters of white blooms.

x   x   x

FOUR-O'CLOCK *(Mirabilis jalapa)*
Tender perennial; 2–3 feet
Flowers: white, yellow or red, all summer to frost
As its name implies, this plant is a late-afternoon flower with stately funnel-shaped blooms. Although readily grown from seed, it also has tuberous roots that can be lifted in autumn and stored for replanting in spring.

x   x   x

GERANIUM *(Geranium* spp. and *Pelargonium* spp.*)*
Hardy and tender perennial; 1–2 feet
Flowers: vary
This name really adds to a gardener's confusion. The popular window-box specimen is the zonal geranium *(Pelargonium hortorum),* a bushy, tender perennial that flowers freely all summer in white, pink, salmon or red. It thrives in hot, dry, windy exposures but also tolerates as little as 3 hours of sun. The many delightful scented-leaf geraniums flower only briefly but are treasured for fragrant foliage that is suffused with scents like nutmeg, mint, rose or lemon. These long-lasting perfumes make them important ingredients in potpourri. Closely related are numerous hardy perennial geraniums *(Geranium* spp.*).* These grow as low mounds or sprawling, slow-spreading mats that bloom profusely in spring or early summer. Hardy geraniums prefer full sun but often tolerate as little as 4 hours daily. Notable cultivars include 'Johnson's Blue' and the pale pink 'Ingwersen's Variety.'

x   x   x

GLOBE AMARANTH *(Gomphrena globosa)*
Annual; to over 1 foot

THE SUPPORTING CAST: FAVORITES FOR FLOWERS, FOLIAGE, FRAGRANCE OR FLAVOR

Sun Conditions
FS   SS   WS   NS

				Flowers: white, purple, pink or orange, all summer to frost This flower provides long-lasting color both in the garden and later in dried arrangements. It tolerates drought, wind and searing sun.
x	*x*	*x*	*x*	**GROUND COVERS** *Sprawling or low-growing plants to cover the soil. See page 184.*
x	*x*	*x*	*x*	**HOSTA, FUNKIA or PLANTAIN-LILY** *(Hosta* spp.*)* Hardy perennial; 6 inches–2 feet **Flowers: white or lavender, spring or early summer** The many hosta species and hybrids are versatile additions as ground covers, edging or specimen accents in gardens where sun is in short supply. Although the various-sized flower spikes last for weeks, hostas are valued primarily for their foliage. Leaf shapes vary from broadly tall to narrow and small; leaf tones range from rich blue-green to yellow-white and textures are smooth or puckered. Rich, moist soil is preferred, but drought and neglect are tolerated. Notable hybrids include 'Blue Wedgwood' (textured blue-green oval leaves), 'Kabitan' (sword-shaped yellow leaves with green margins), 'Aureo-Marginata' (heart-shaped leaves with irregular yellow-white margins).
x	*x*	*x*	*x*	**HOUSEPLANTS** *Inexpensive tropical houseplants are good fillers in the small summer garden or window box as well as in pots on balconies, rooftops and decks. Fine specimen plants are good accents.*
x	*x*	*x*	*x*	**IMPATIENS or BUSY LIZZIE** *(Impatiens wallerana)* Tender perennial; 1–2 feet **Flowers: pink, purple, salmon, lilac blue, white or striped, all summer to frost** Few other flowers are as reliable as impatiens for shade. Hybrids include the extremely floriferous Super Elfins, which remain under 10 inches. The New Guinea hybrids have narrow, sometimes purple-red foliage but demand sun which to me seems to defeat the purpose of using impatiens.
x	*x*	*x*	*x*	**INVADERS** *Plants that take over where all else has failed. See page 188.*
x	*x*	*x*		**JACOB'S LADDER** *(Polemonium caeruleum)* Hardy perennial; 1–3 feet, Zone 3 **Flowers: blue, late spring or early summer** The filigree of leaflets arranged like rungs in a ladder gives this woodland plant its name. Cool, moist soil and some protection from hot sun are best for a long period of bloom.

THE SUPPORTING CAST: FAVORITES FOR FLOWERS, FOLIAGE, FRAGRANCE OR FLAVOR

Sun Conditions

FS	SS	WS	NS	

FS	SS	WS	NS	
x	x			**JAPANESE ANEMONE** *(Anemone japonica)* Hardy perennial; 1 foot **Flowers: pink, red or white, late summer through autumn** The large flat flowers of this carefree late-summer bloomer rise high above the handsome foliage on graceful stems. Notable cultivars include 'Queen Charlotte,' which has semidouble 2½-inch-high pink flowers, and 'Whirlwind,' which has semidouble 3-foot white blooms.
x	x	x	x	**LADY'S MANTLE** *(Alchemilla mollis)* Hardy perennial; 1–2 feet, Zone 3 **Flowers: chartreuse yellow, late spring or early summer** The frothy flowers contrast well with the handsome, somewhat furry, scalloped foliage. These rounded leaves are fascinating, too, for the magical way they hold shimmering drops of rain. Lady's mantle is easily grown and readily self-sows. If you can spare the space, enjoy the seedings wherever they appear.
x	x	x		**LAMB'S EARS or WOOLLY BETONY** *(Stachys byzantina)* Hardy perennial; to 1 foot, Zone 4 **Flowers: purple-pink, summer** I don't know anyone who can resist stopping to stroke these soft, furry leaves, which look (to this city slicker at least) more like rabbit's ears than lamb's. Its handsome silver tones and habit of sprawling make it a good softener for edging a path or container. This slow spreader needs well-drained soil but rotting may be unavoidable in hot, humid weather. Don't overwater.
x	x	x		**LANTANA** *(Lantana camara)* Tender shrub; 4–10 feet, Zone 8 **Flowers: red, pink, yellow, white or a blend, followed by blue-black berries, all summer to fall** Lantana's cascading limbs and nonstop colorful blooms are versatile enough for covering the edge of a tub on a windy rooftop or as ground cover in a sunny yard. Full sun is best, but dappled shade is tolerated. The rough, pungent leaves sometimes produce an allergic reaction.
x	x			**LAVENDER** *(Lavandula angustifolia)* Hardy perennial; 1–3 feet, Zone 6 **Flowers: lavender (of course), early summer** This delightfully scented, carefree plant with its silver-gray leaves may be used as a single specimen or massed for edge or hedge. Good drainage and full sun is imperative. Harvest and dry the perfumed leaves and flowers for potpourri or sachets. Notable cultivars include the compact 'Hidcote Strain' and 'Munstead Dwarf.'

? container?

THE SUPPORTING CAST: FAVORITES FOR FLOWERS, FOLIAGE, FRAGRANCE OR FLAVOR

Sun Conditions

FS	SS	WS	NS	
x	*x*			**LAVENDER-COTTON** *(Santolina chamaecyparissus)* Tender shrub; 1–2 feet, Zone 6 Flowers: yellow, summer The soft, silvery, fragrant foliage makes this a superb accent or edging plant for herbs. The finely cut leaves do best in full sun, and light sandy soil is preferred. Prune severely after flowering for compact growth.
x	*x*	*x*		**LEMON BALM** *(Melissa officinalis)* Hardy perennial; 2 feet, Zone 5 Flowers: white, summer This lemon-scented member of the mint family is an easily grown addition to potpourri as well as teas, punch and baked goods. It spreads and self-sows readily.
x	*x*	*x*	*x*	**LILYTURF** *(Liriope* spp.*)* and **MONDO GRASS** *(Ophiopogon* spp.*)* Hardy perennial; 1–2 feet Flowers: lilac or white followed by small dark berries in summer There's so little difference in appearance between these two grassy plants that only the botanists know for sure. Lilyturf *(Liriope muscari)* is hardy to Zone 5. I prefer the variegated cultivars with their stripes of creamy white or yellow with green. Mondo grass *(Ophiopogon japonicus)* is hardy to Zone 7 and has handsome dark green leaves. My own favorite is the spectacular purple-black *O. planiscapus* 'Ebony King.' Mondo grass is evergreen. Lilyturf is semievergreen, and its fading leaves should be trimmed in spring to allow the new growth to emerge neatly.
	x	*x*	*x*	**LUNGWORT** *(Pulmonaria officinalis)* Hardy perennial; to 10 inches, Zone 3 Flowers: changing tones of pink, blue and purple, early spring The broad, white-spotted foliage remains perky all summer even in dense shade. It takes a while before crowding occurs but division is easy in spring. A moist soil is best to prevent what the plant explorer, Reginald Farrer, called "morbid-looking heaps of leprous leafage." Notable cultivars include 'Mrs. Moon' and 'Margery Fish.'
x	*x*	*x*	*x*	MOISTURE-TOLERANT PLANTS *Plants that tolerate continually moist soil. See page 194.*
x	*x*	*x*		ORNAMENTAL GRASSES *Usually included in this category are true grasses and bamboos as well as sedges and rushes. Well-drained soil is best.* **Fountain Grass *(Pennisetum alopecuroides)*** has narrow, bright green leaves that grow in mounds up to 3½ feet. Silver-brown flower plumes appear in late summer and remain handsome through winter. Also marvelous are the burgundy-leaved *P. setaceum* 'Rubrium' and *P. arundinacea picta* with its green and white leaves. Good for sun or light shade.

THE SUPPORTING CAST: FAVORITES FOR FLOWERS, FOLIAGE, FRAGRANCE OR FLAVOR

Sun Conditions

FS	SS	WS	NS	
				Black Bamboo *(Phyllostachys nigra)* has dark green stems (called culms) that are covered with purple-black spots when mature. The graceful, narrow leaves have blue-green undersides. It spreads steadily and quickly to over 15 feet. It tolerates both sun and part shade. **Blue Fescue** *(Festuca ovina glauca)* is a low, tufted clump-forming grass that is bright silver-blue. The wiry, fountainlike leaves remain well through winter. It does best in full sun. **Japanese Blood Grass** *(Imperata cylindrica* 'Red Baron'*)* has narrow, scarlet leaves to about 1 foot. Full sun is best but light shade is tolerated. **Purple Moor Grass** *(Molinia caerulea variegata)* has stiffly arching tufts of striped light green and creamy white foliage, 1–2 feet high. It is easily grown in sun or light shade. **Ribbon Grass** *(Phalaris arundinacea picta)* is a quick spreader, easily grown in sun or part shade. The striped green and white narrow leaves grow to about 2 feet and are particularly handsome near birches.
x	*x*	*x*		PETUNIA *(Petunia hybrida)* Annual; 6 inches–3 feet Flowers: white, yellow, pink, purple, red or striped, summer to frost What with ruffles and stripes and double flowers I'd guess there's a petunia for every taste, pot, basket, window box or flower bed. Rejuvenate straggly plants in midseason by cutting the older stems back.
x	*x*	*x*	*x*	QUICK FILLERS *Plants for quick height and bulk. See page 180.*
	x	*x*	*x*	SOLOMON'S SEAL *(Polygonatum biflorum)* Hardy perennial; to 2½ feet, Zone 3 Flowers: small yellow-white, late spring This strong grower has graceful arching stems that are lined in spring with rows of bell-shaped blooms. It does best in rich, moist woodland soil but is quite amenable to less ideal conditions. I use it to line one side of a path. As an echo, opposite I use a variegated form whose leaves have cream white edges and tips.
	x	*x*	*x*	SNAKEROOT or BUGBANE *(Cimicifuga* spp.*)* Hardy perennial; to 3 feet, Zone 3 Flowers: tall white spikes, mid or late summer This handsome, ferny-leaved woodland plant is prized for its stately bottlebrush-shaped flowers. Growth is most vigorous in moist, acid soil. Notable cultivars include *C. racemosa* 'Atropurpurea,' which has purple stems and leaves, and 'White Pearl,' which flowers through early autumn.

THE SUPPORTING CAST: FAVORITES FOR FLOWERS, FOLIAGE, FRAGRANCE OR FLAVOR

Sun Conditions

FS	SS	WS	NS	
x	x	x		**SUMMER-FLOWERING BULBS**

Summer-flowering bulbs should be planted early in spring. Treat those that are not reliably perennial as annuals and toss them out after they bloom (unless you have space to allow the foliage to ripen and time to dig them up and store them for re-planting next year).

Chincherinchee *(Ornithogalum thyrsoides)* has long-lasting spiky white flowers on foot-high stems.

Lilies *(Lilium* spp.*)* now number in the thousands, and with clever selection, you can have hardy bulbs blooming from spring through fall. Flowers vary from upright bowls to pendulous trumpets in nearly every color, stripe and spot. Use short species on exposed rooftops.

Montbretia *(Tritonia crocosmaeflora)* has graceful, arching, 18-inch-high wiry stems topped with sprays of lilylike flowers in yellow, orange, scarlet or red.

Summer Hyacinth *(Galtonia candicans)* has tiny white, bell-shaped blossoms borne along 3–4-foot-tall stems.

Tigerflower or Mexican Shell Flower *(Tigridia pavonia)* has large irislike spotted flowers on 12–15-inch-high stems in yellow, orange or purple.

	x	x	x

SWEET WOODRUFF *(Galium odoratum)*
Hardy perennial; to 8 inches, Zone 4
Flowers: white, spring
The fragrant, whorled leaves and dainty white spring flowers are arranged in neat layers along the stems. This plant makes a fine decorative ground cover under woodland shrubs and is a longtime favorite of herbalists for wines and liqueurs. I also use the shiny leaves as edging for pastries and puddings.

x	x		

THYME *(Thymus* spp.*)*
Hardy perennial; 2–12 inches; zone varies with species
Flowers: white, pink or purple, spring or summer
The thymes include several hundred fragrant creepers, a number of which are semi-evergreen. Common thyme *(T. vulgaris)* has been a culinary favorite since Colonial days, and the decorative hybrids have variegated or lemon-scented leaves. Mother-of-thyme *(T. serpyllum)* is a true groundhugger, and few can resist the charm of the gray, furry-leaved *T. s. lanuginosis,* aptly called woolly mother-of-thyme. Full sun is a must. Poor, alkaline, well-drained soil is preferred.

x	x		

TOMATO *(Lycopersicon esculentum)*
Annual; 1–10 feet
Flowers: yellow, followed by delicious red fruit through summer
There's good reason why homegrown tomatoes have reigned for years as the most popular vegetable (the flip side of the Puritans' view that tomatoes were poisonous as well as evil because of their sensuous color, shape and texture). *Indeterminate*

THE SUPPORTING CAST: FAVORITES FOR FLOWERS, FOLIAGE, FRAGRANCE OR FLAVOR

Sun Conditions

FS	SS	WS	NS

varieties blossom all season on continually growing stems and need a support. *Determinate* varieties are less rangy but bear for a shorter period. Fruit sizes vary from delectable cherry tomatoes to huge beefsteaks. Transplant seedlings so that the new soil line is slightly higher than the old. A sampling of the countless tasty hybrids includes 'Big Girl,' 'Rutgers,' 'Sweet-100,' 'Better Boy,' 'Supersonic' and 'Ramapo.'

x   *x*   *x*

THORNY PLANTS
Plants with unfriendly thorns. See page 187.

x   *x*

VERBENA *(Verbena hortensis)*
Annual; 8–18 inches
Flowers: pink, purple, red, yellow or white, all summer
This brightly colored, free-blooming plant is a graceful addition to hanging baskets, borders and window boxes and also as a ground cover. Drying winds and neglect are tolerated.

    x   *x*   *x*

WILD GINGER *(Asarum spp.)*
Hardy perennial; 6–8 inches
Flowers: brown, spring
If I had to pick a single plant for shade, it would probably be wild ginger, specifically the evergreen European wild ginger *(A. europaeum)*. Its round, brightly polished, dark green leaves slowly spread a handsome blanket over the most dreary or shady areas. The leaves of the deciduous Canadian wild ginger *(A. canadense)* are a dull, matte, light green.

? shady side? container?

x   *x*`

YARROW *(Achillea spp.)*
Hardy perennial; 6 inches to several feet
Flowers: white, yellow or pink, summer
This large genus of easily grown species was named for Achilles, whose wounds it healed (or so they say). Fernleaf yarrow *(A. filipendulina)* grows to 4 feet and has silver-gray, aromatic foliage and stately, freely borne clusters of yellow flowers. *A. millefolium* 'Cerise Queen' bears large cherry red clusters. No coddling this plant; it is happy with poor soil, drought and neglect.

CREATIVE COVERS: CLIMBERS FOR WALLS AND FENCES

Sun Conditions

FS	SS	WS	NS

| x | x | x | x | **BOSTON IVY or JAPANESE CREEPER (*Parthenocissus tricuspidata*)** |

Hardy perennial; Zone 5
Adhesive discs; rapid grower
Autumn: crimson foliage
This plant, which one friend insists on calling "Ivy League ivy" is a native of the Orient and not a Bostonian at all. A wonderfully quick grower, it's superb for covering ugly walls. Mine took a mere 6 years to reach the top of my four-story brownstone. The lustrous, three-part leaves are truly glorious in fall, and the purple-blue fruits are adored by birds. Its cousin, the Virginia creeper (*P. quinquefolia*), has five-part leaves that also turn scarlet in autumn. But it climbs through the use of tendrils and is better for chain-link fencing.

| x | x | | | **CLEMATIS (*Clematis* spp.)** |

Hardy perennial; zone varies with species
Tendrils; moderately rapid grower
Summer: white, pink, purple or striped flowers developing into fluffy-looking seedpods that last through autumn
I admit the reason I began growing clematis on my nineteenth-floor terrace was because I was told the plant wouldn't grow in the city. Alkaline soil is imperative for most species, so at planting time be generous with horticultural limestone and bonemeal. Take your pick from a mind-boggling assortment: *C. montana* 'Elizabeth,' which has pale pink, fragrant spring flowers, *C. jackmani,* which has purple, early summer flowers that continue sporadically through autumn, popular hybrids like 'Comptesse de Bouchaud' and 'Mrs. Cholmondeley,' or the sweet autumn clematis with its profusion of white, late-summer flowers (this plant is usually listed as *C. paniculata,* although its name keeps changing).

?
container w/ support

| x | x | x | | **CLIMBING HYDRANGEA (*Hydrangea anomala petiolaris*)** |

Hardy perennial; Zone 5
Aerial rootlets; moderately slow grower
Summer: white flowers
Maybe the reason this unusually attractive climber is not more widely planted is because it's a slow starter whose lacy, white, flat-topped blooms refuse to appear until the plant is mature. But the attractive leaves more than compensate for the wait for flowers. If need be, you can help young plants gain a quicker foothold by securing them with a bit of adhesive tape.

| x | x | | | **CLIMBING ROSES (*Rosa* spp.)** |

Hardy perennial
Summer: pink, white, yellow or crimson flowers
Winter: prominent seedpods (called hips)

CREATIVE COVERS: CLIMBERS FOR WALLS AND FENCES

Sun Conditions
FS   SS   WS   NS

Roses don't climb, they lean, and one day someone will correct this misnomer. The long shoots or canes of the "climbing" hybrids are good for training along trellis-work or fences. The length of blooming period and flower numbers are proportional to the amount of sunlight, but good repeaters include climbing 'Don Juan' (red), cl. 'Peace' (blend), cl. 'Improved Blaze' (medium red) and cl. 'Golden Showers' (yellow). For prolific blooms, tie the canes so they grow horizontally.

x   *x*   *x*   *x*   **ENGLISH IVY** *(Hedera helix)*
Hardy perennial; Zone 6
Aerial rootlets; moderately fast grower
Winter: dark evergreen leaves
English ivy is believed to have been brought to America by the colonists, but it's certainly much at home here now and seems to flourish everywhere. Young plants have three to five lobes; older plants may look completely different, with nearly oval leaves, small flowers and black fruit. Two particularly hardy forms are 'Baltica' and '238th Street,' and variegated forms are also to be found.

x   *x*   *x*   *x*   **ESPALIER**
Plants that are trained flat against a wall or trellis. See page 231.

x   *x*   **GRAPE** *(Vitis labrusca)*
Hardy perennial; Zone 5
Tendrils; moderately fast grower
Summer: edible fruit
My first grape harvest was on a friend's mid-Manhattan penthouse, where the plants were growing happily in their favorite conditions: full sun, rich soil, a light breeze for good air circulation and a sturdy support to wrap around. 'Concord' and 'Niagara' are two venerable and reliable hybrids that are easily grown and tolerant of a wide range of conditions. But some object to their tough skins. Newer hybrids include 'Steuben' and 'Alden,' both large and juicy blue grapes, 'Seneca,' which is green or white, and 'Suffolk Red' and 'Canadice,' which are red. 'Golden Muscat' is a somewhat less vigorous vine than the others. For the best hybrids for your area contact your state Agricultural Experiment Station.

x   *x*   *x*   **HONEYSUCKLE** *(Lonicera* spp.*)*
Hardy perennial; zone varies with species
Twiner; rapid grower
Spring through summer: yellow, white, pink or red flowers
Winter: semievergreen (some species)
The many sweet-scented honeysuckle vines with their tubular flowers are quick covers for chain-link fences and poles. But watch them carefully and keep them off your trees. Hall's honeysuckle (*L. japonica* 'Halliana') is a vigorous twiner with

CREATIVE COVERS: CLIMBERS FOR WALLS AND FENCES

Sun Conditions

FS   SS   WS   NS

white flowers that fade to yellow. The trumpet honeysuckle *(L. sempervirens)* has long scarlet or golden flowers and oval blue-green leaves.

x   *x*   *x*

MORNING GLORY *(Ipomoea purpurea)*
Annual
Twiner; rapid grower
Summer: purple, pink, white or blue flowers
Strictly an early riser, the morning glory's trumpet-shaped flowers open with the sun and remain open until early afternoon, except on overcast or very hot days. Morning glory is easily grown from seed. Chip the hard outer coating and soak the seed in water overnight to hasten germination. To round out the flowering day, also plant its cousin, moonflower *(I. alba)*. This tender perennial bears fragrant white blooms in the late afternoon or, as one friend insists, "just in time for cocktails."

x   *x*   *x*

SILVER LACE VINE or FLEECE VINE *(Polygonum aubertii)*
Hardy perennial; Zone 5
Twiner; extremely rapid grower
Late summer: green-white flowers
Autumn: lacy-looking seedpods
It's true that this handsome, vigorous grower can cover 20 feet of ugly fence in a single season (lest you doubt, as I did, those mail-order ads that say "plant it and jump back"). Also welcome are the clouds of fluffy white blooms in late summer, when few other woody plants are in flower.

x   *x*

TRUMPET CREEPER *(Campsis radicans)*
Hardy perennial; Zone 5
Aerial rootlets; moderately rapid grower
Summer: yellow, orange-scarlet or red flowers
Autumn: cigar-shaped fruit capsules
A sturdy support is needed for this tropical-looking, rampant woody vine whose many leaflets are borne in a featherlike arrangement along each stem. It is easily grown in any soil and eventually reaches more than 30 feet, at which point it may be quite heavy and need some help. Notable cultivars include 'Flava' and 'Crimson Trumpet.'

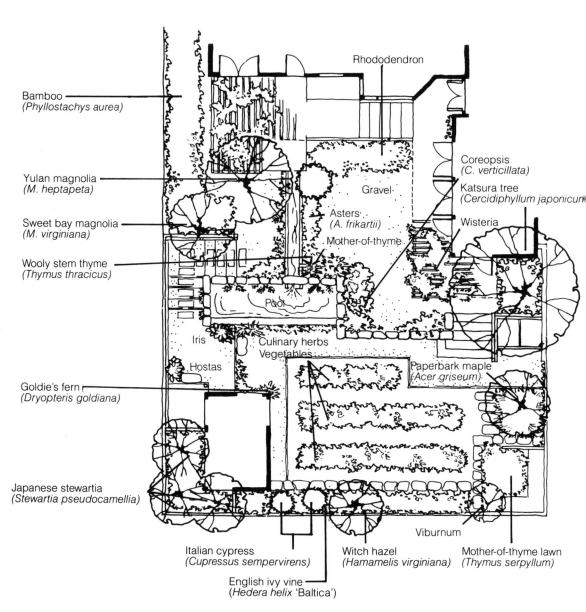

Bamboo
(Phyllostachys aurea)

Rhododendron

Coreopsis
(C. verticillata)

Katsura tree
(Cercidiphyllum japonicum)

Yulan magnolia
(M. heptapeta)

Gravel

Wisteria

Sweet bay magnolia
(M. virginiana)

Asters
(A. frikartii)

Mother-of-thyme

Wooly stem thyme
(Thymus thracicus)

Pool

Iris

Culinary herbs
Vegetables

Hostas

Paperbark maple
(Acer griseum)

Goldie's fern
(Dryopteris goldiana)

Japanese stewartia
(Stewartia pseudocamellia)

Viburnum

Italian cypress
(Cupressus sempervirens)

Witch hazel
(Hamamelis virginiana)

Mother-of-thyme lawn
(Thymus serpyllum)

English ivy vine
(Hedera helix 'Baltica')

NORTH

The terraced levels of a sloping Portland, Oregon, garden are divided by steps, stone retaining walls and a gushing rivulet that empties into a small rectangular pool. Plantings on the 63- by 50-foot site vary from the perennials of the gravelled open area at the top, nearest the house, to the traditional vegetable patch and plastic-topped greenhouse at the bottom, furthest away.

Richard W. Painter and Laurence Ferar, Landscape Architects

Plan for this garden is shown on opposite page.

A mood of classic
order is achieved on a
large gravel rooftop
with symmetrical plant-
ings and a simple
wood plank walk.

A narrow, stucco-
covered planter fitted
against a stair contains
enough soil to support
holly and a cascade
of cotoneaster and
petunias.
A. Billie Cohen, Ltd.

A two-story brick stair
curves back upon itself
to link two floors of
the same house.
Nadine C. Zamichow, Inc.

Curved bluestone steps
are lined with circular
planters filled with weeping hemlocks, azaleas,
English ivy and tulips.
Halsted Welles Associates

Wood deck floors in
portable-size sections
permit easy installation
and removal.

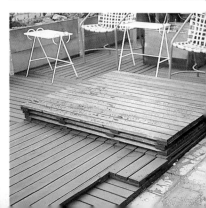

A modular plastic flooring system with removable sections facilitates clearing drains.
Corlett Horticultural Design

Open spaces in between brick paving stones are planted with maiden pinks *(Dianthus deltoides).*

In a London backyard, squares of brick and concrete trace an elegant pattern accentuated by clumps of yellow flowering cushion spurge *(Euphorbia epithymoides).*

A small viewing garden contains a clump of ornamental grass surrounded by bands of black and white stones.
J. Mendoza Gardens

In a San Francisco backyard, a concrete walk with a brick center patio is planted with formally clipped Japanese boxwood, calla lilies and a ring of sycamore trees. An airy, 8-foot-high lattice marks the boundary of the 25- by 125-foot space.

A circular glazed brick patio floor is flanked by symmetrical plantings of bamboo, yew, azaleas and potted Boston ferns.

Robert Lester Associates

Brick paving traces a serpentine path through a Philadelphia backyard that measures 32 by 110 feet. Included are a blue columnar juniper *(Juniperus columnaris* 'Wilsoni glauca'), peppermint geranium, variegated dwarf white pine *(Pinus strobus variegata* 'Nana'), creeping thyme, fennel, purple sage, curry plant *(Helichrysum serotinum)* and variegated myrtle.

*Ann McPhail,
Garden Design*

In a 20- by 30-foot Santa Monica garden, a narrow walk of decomposed granite disappears beneath a frothy floral tide of purple flowering heliotrope, Perez sealavender *(Limonium perezii)*, purple-leaved *Euphorbia* and *Aeoneum arboreum* 'Atropurpureum,' silvery snow-in-summer and sparkling white Montrosa English daisies *(Bellis perennis* 'Montrosa'*)*.
Philip Chandler,
Garden Design

A border of white sweet alyssum edges a grassy path in a New York community garden. Red-leaved perillas *(Perilla frutescens)* contrast with lively masses of cosmos, gazania, lythrum, calendula, nicotiana, lavender and golden marguerites.

A lattice frame artfully
incorporates a free-
standing chimney into
a rooftop garden. Japa-
nese black pines tem-
per the wind and
screen the sitting area.
*Daniel D. Stewart, Stewart
Associates*

The front door sentry
is a boxwood triangle
set within a wrought
iron alcove sculpted in
an appropriately horti-
cultural theme.

A terrace door leads to a wintry setting where clipped privets, moss Sawara cypress *(Chamaecyparis pisifera* 'Squarrosa'*)* and Sargent's weeping hemlock are dusted with snow.

Sliding doors frame a snowy vista of evergreen and deciduous plants and memories of summer dining.

An arbor of steel
I-beams and columns
is a modern support
for purple flowering
wisteria on a rooftop
garden.
Paul Rudolph, Architect;
William T. Wheeler Co., Inc.

A wood and wire trel-
lis planned for clema-
tis frames the city
skyline. Plants include
yucca, a hawthorn tree
underplanted with lav-
ender-flowering asters
(A. frikartii) and bright
golden accents from
flowering black-eyed
Susan *(Rudbeckia
hirta)*, coreopsis and
lantana. The front bor-
der is the grass *Penni-
setum setaceum.*
Oehme, van Sweden and
Associates, Inc.

A hedgerow of 'Sky-rocket' juniper, arbor-vitae and false cypress buffers the wind and adds a year-round evergreen foil. Silvery-leaved dusty miller, pink impatiens and variegated leaf geraniums add summer color.

Corlett Horticultural Design

Snow covered white birches, Japanese white pines and cascading junipers line a "woodland" walk on a narrow terrace.

John Burgee, Architect; Gwen Burgee, Garden Plant Specialists, Inc.

A green blanket of
Boston ivy softens the
brick walls of an entire
block of Chicago
homes.

Peach trees, figs, toma-
toes, grapes and high-
bush blueberries
planted among false
cypress, maple and
roses, provide a dense,
fruitful screen.

Panes of frosted glass temper the wind and add privacy and a bright enclosure to a rooftop space. Plantings include Japanese black pine, junipers, variegated evergreen euonymus *(E. japonica* 'Aureo-marginata'*)* and a crabapple that is preparing to burst into bloom.

Daniel D. Stewart,
Stewart Associates

A 28-year-old climbing hydrangea *(H. anomala petiolaris)* in full flower cloaks the wall of a 20- by 42-foot Chicago backyard. The garden steps are colored with pots of purple and pink flowering dianthus, lobelia, Dalmation bellflower *(Campanula portenschlagiana)* and red-leaved begonias.

Broad-leaved and needle evergreens and deciduous trees, grown in closely spaced containers sunk below a raised deck floor, provide a dense, textured wind screen. Included are early-flowering PJM azaleas, rhododendron, arborvitae, false cypress, holly and crabapple. An English ivy border obscures the floor joint.

William T. Wheeler Co., Inc.

A barrier hedge of yews underplanted with aromatic silvery gray southernwood *(Artemisia abrotanum)* is the periphery of a rooftop terrace. The centerpiece, a three-quartersize whiskey barrel, contains a silveryleaved Russian olive *(Elaeagnus angustifolius)* underplanted with lilac-colored bellflowers.

*John Burgee, Architect;
Gwen Burgee, Garden
Plant Specialists, Inc.*

In a Cambridge back-
yard, a Japanese-style
dry stream of black
pebbles is created by
artfully placed rocks
and small boulders
surrounded by ferns,
hemlock, andromeda
and a ground cover of
European ginger.
Messervy Associates

Bamboo is the polite
fluttering screen be-
tween neighbors in
Portland, Oregon.
*Laurence Ferar,
Landscape Architect*

Not far from downtown Toronto, a path of creeping mother-of-thyme and mosses contrasts with specimen rock and alpine plants in a 55- by 112-foot backyard. Included are pink flowering rock soapwort *(Saponaria ocymoides),* the hardy geranium 'Ballerina,' dianthus, 'Skylands Golden' spruce, golden Hinoki false cypress *(Chamaecyparis obtusa* 'Aurea') and weeping Norway spruce.

Alpines Unlimited

Low boxes planted with 'Bar Harbor' creeping junipers add year-round mounds of green on this 50- by 90-foot terrace. Crabapples and birches are vertical accents; azaleas and yews are bushy winter screens. African daisies *(Arctotis stoechadifolia)* and geraniums add color in summer.
John Mayer,
Landscape Gardener

The formal grassy swath of Rockefeller Center's rooftop terrace in New York can only be seen from surrounding skyscrapers and the neo-Gothic spires of St. Patrick's Cathedral. A clipped 'Newport Blue' boxwood hedge encloses daylilies, golden false Hinoki cypress *(Chamaecyparis obtusa* 'Crippsii') and winged euonymus *(E. alata).*
David Murbach,
Landscape Design

A 60-foot-long, 15-foot-wide, penthouse terrace contains a series of formal and informal outdoor "rooms." These are delineated by architectural elements that include arbors, trelliswork and diverse floor textures of marble tiles, gravel, ceramic tiles and wood decking. The spaces are further defined by containers with vertical plantings (trees and shrubs) that are positioned to contrast with horizontal ones (perennials and annuals).

John Burgee, Architect;
Gwen Burgee, Garden
Plant Specialists Inc.

Plan for this garden is shown on opposite page.

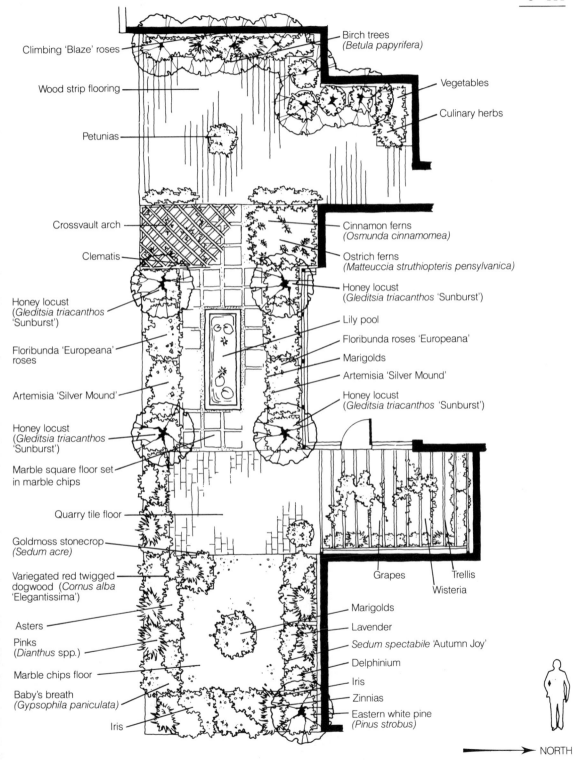

Climbing 'Blaze' roses

Wood strip flooring

Petunias

Crossvault arch

Clematis

Honey locust
(*Gleditsia triacanthos*
'Sunburst')

Floribunda 'Europeana'
roses

Artemisia 'Silver Mound'

Honey locust
(*Gleditsia triacanthos*
'Sunburst')

Marble square floor set
in marble chips

Quarry tile floor

Goldmoss stonecrop
(*Sedum acre*)

Variegated red twigged
dogwood (*Cornus alba*
'Elegantissima')

Asters

Pinks
(*Dianthus* spp.)

Marble chips floor

Baby's breath
(*Gypsophila paniculata*)

Iris

Birch trees
(*Betula papyrifera*)

Vegetables

Culinary herbs

Cinnamon ferns
(*Osmunda cinnamomea*)

Ostrich ferns
(*Matteuccia struthiopteris pensylvanica*)

Honey locust
(*Gleditsia triacanthos* 'Sunburst')

Lily pool

Floribunda roses 'Europeana'

Marigolds

Artemisia 'Silver Mound'

Honey locust
(*Gleditsia triacanthos* 'Sunburst')

Grapes

Trellis

Wisteria

Marigolds

Lavender

Sedum spectabile 'Autumn Joy'

Delphinium

Iris

Zinnias

Eastern white pine
(*Pinus strobus*)

NORTH

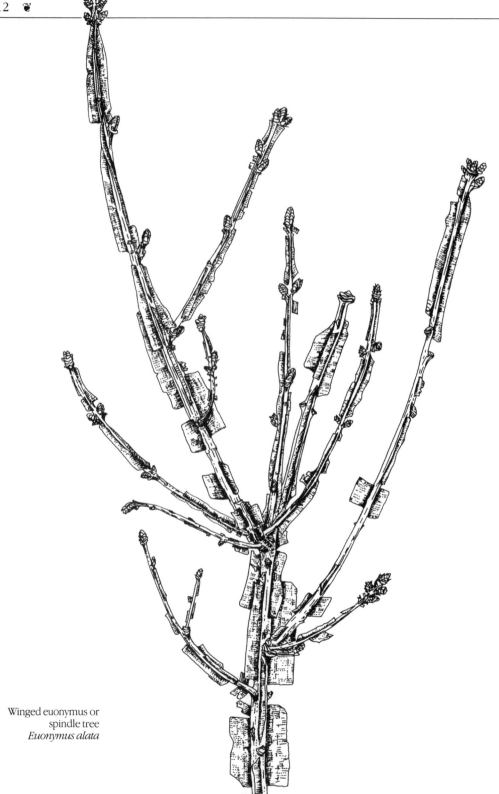

Winged euonymus or
spindle tree
Euonymus alata

Granted that the space is limited, yet it is not only space that
counts today but what you do with that given space.
—Minga Pope Duryea, *Gardens In and About Town,* 1923

5. Finding and Buying Your Plants

I am a nursery addict and obsessive catalogue peruser. I've also had more than one affair with impulsively purchased sirens, plants I'd never seen before, in the flesh, so to speak. Thanks to these romances I've come to disagree with manuals that exhort gardeners to "carefully plan ahead." Some of the most interesting gardens and best garden adventures are to be had by those who don't.

on temptation Advice about limiting plant candidates in advance seems most illogical for the new city gardener not yet able to distinguish between a petunia and a potato. And given the plethora of new hybrids that appear each year, even experienced gardeners must expect the unexpected.

So as far as I'm concerned, yielding to horticultural temptation —i.e., buying and trying unfamiliar species or those not planned for—is a perfectly acceptable way for the city gardener to grow.

where hardy plants The winter-hardy species, you may now agree, are your most important
come from plants. But they are also the most expensive. So how can you find those most likely to succeed?

You can plow through scientific journals or keep notes on everything you read, but an easier method—one that gets you going immediately—is to choose from among plants that have been judged tolerant of your conditions by someone whose business is at stake if they are not.

And that means finding a *local, reputable* nursery.

"Local," for this purpose, means within about a 50-mile radius of where you live. "Reputable" means an established company that has existed for several years, where quality stock is maintained in good health.

But how, you may ask, can I recognize "quality stock in good health"?

You can start by taking a good hard look. A pitiful assembly of wilted, yellowed specimens is not a healthy collection. It's possible, of course, for an experienced gardener to rescue and resuscitate sickly or "bargain" plants. But the novice—and certainly the gardener with difficult conditions in town—is asking for trouble when buying anything less than an established, healthy plant.

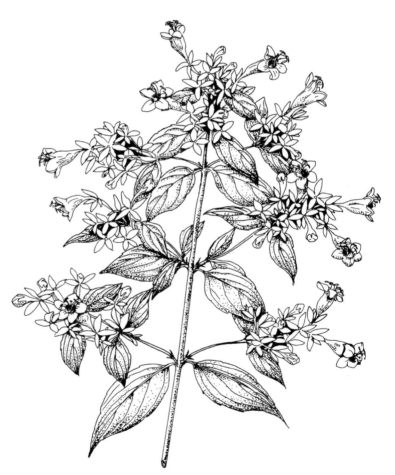

Glossy Abelia
Abelia grandiflora

nursery or florist   For starters, the word "nursery" must not be confused with "florist." Your neighborhood florist may be terribly talented when it comes to fine floral arrangements, wondrous window boxes, or bewitching hanging baskets. Rarely though, are florists knowledgeable about *hardy* outdoor plants, even if they sell them.

finding a nursery   You may have to do some sleuthing to find a good supplier of plants. If you have no neighbors who are also gardeners, the next best source of information is the telephone directory's yellow pages. Check listings like "Landscapers," "Nurserymen," "Garden Centers" or anything similar you think of. With some luck you'll find one a bus or taxi ride away.
Look too for a botanical garden, horticultural society, garden club or block association and ask for a recommendation. And by all means don't forget to check Sunday newspapers; a good amount of local nursery advertising usually appears in spring and fall. You may have to travel a way out of town to reach a well-stocked supplier, but I can assure you I've always been glad when I did—even when it meant splurging on a car rented for a day.

why this trip is necessary   The advantages of visiting a well-stocked garden center or nursery with a copy of your garden sketch in tow become evident the minute you arrive. For let's face it, it's not possible to study the plants in any garden book—this one included—and get an accurate image of what each is like or imagine just how it will fit your space.
All plants have a set pattern of growth that enables gardeners to predict their general form. But no photograph or list of adjectives can hope to depict the infinite modifications of profile, texture or tone. And the plant kingdom is rife with enticing idiosyncrasies.

roaming through nurseries   Although it drives my family to the limits of their patience, I love roaming through nurseries. Even when I've arrived knowing "exactly" the plant I want (which is what I always say), I never fail to change my mind dozens of times before buying. There's so much to be learned simply by walking around.
Many centers now include plant labels with both common and botanical names along with notes on light tolerance, duration of bloom, ultimate size and hardiness or drought resistance—enormously helpful details all.

the importance of roots   The most important portion of your purchase is a healthy set of roots, particularly if you're planting in a container or yard where conditions are less than ideal. Adjusting to urban life is a tough change for woody plants after a perfect nursery home. But the shock of arrival is minimized by an ample supply of established feeder roots that are doing their job.

container plants At the nursery you will find many plants in small containers of one sort or another—metal, plastic, cardboard, peat and occasionally wood. Some shrubs, vines, small trees and perennials are "container grown," which means that the nurseryman has propagated them directly in the container you see before you. Other plants may have only recently been transplanted there. This can spell trouble if the soil mass falls apart when you move it into your garden.

Take a minute to determine if the plant has had sufficient time to establish a root system in this container by poking around in the top layer of soil and around the edges. If you find a mass of roots, transplanting should pose no problem. (Some gardeners muster the nerve to pull the plant out of the container to look, but it's risky to go that far.)

B & B plants Trees and shrubs are also available in the form known as "B & B." This means that the plant has been dug from the ground where it was growing, and its ball of roots and surrounding soil (the first "B") is wrapped in natural or synthetic burlap (the second "B"). It is then tied with cord. Most responsible nurserymen have done a bit of root pruning a season or two before to encourage new feeder roots to form within the area to be balled.

rooftop roots On windy rooftops in particular, a generously proportioned root ball serves as a natural anchor and also ensures the presence of a system of fine feeder roots. So anxious am I for that root ball on the plants I bring home, I willingly bear any extra cost required. So it came as a shock, when I dug up the corpses of some privets that died soon after planting and discovered that the B & B plants I thought I had bought had no roots at all.

I happened to discuss this particular turn of events with a gardening friend who informed me I was yet another victim of "puddled plants," a term I'd never heard before.

puddling When digging a shrub or small tree in the field, rather than making a true B & B plant, some nurserymen remove all the surrounding soil and trim off the "messy feeder roots" (as my friend wryly called them). The root portion is then encased in a heavy, claylike mud, a process called "puddling."

Burlap is then pulled neatly around this mass and the plant is passed

Tomato
Lycopersicum esculentum

along to the retail shop, where buyers assume it's a B & B plant with its feeder roots intact. In fact, there are no roots to penetrate the tough clay shroud and the plant eventually dies. And that is precisely what happened to mine.

Why do nurserymen puddle plants? For convenience, apparently, since the strange clay wrapper works well under certain nursery conditions. How can you recognize when a plant has been puddled? Puddled plants tend to be unusually heavy, with suspiciously symmetrical root balls and a solid, clayey-looking brown soil beneath the burlap.

Unfortunately, the only way you can insure a puddled plant's survival is to wash off the clay (not, by all accounts, so easy) and treat the plant as a bare-root specimen (see page 139).

seedlings Aisles in nurseries and garden shops are also filled with colorful annual flowers, herbs, vegetables and perennials. These are typically in small four- or six-part compartmentalized trays where they've been grown individually from seed. An entire lot of these trays—typically nine, twelve or fifteen—is called a flat, and these are most plentiful in the earliest days of spring. In the "ideal" conditions of the commercial greenhouse, growing periods can be condensed, so flowering annuals are ready to bloom and veggies ready to bear, seemingly at a moment's notice.

beware of But when buying in early spring, remember that your purchases have just
chilly nights come from their cozy greenhouse womb. Cool-weather species like pansies, geraniums, lavender and lettuce tolerate spring's chilly nights. They may be transplanted outdoors immediately. It's prudent to wait until night temperatures stabilize at around 65° F before setting out more tender types like basil or tomatoes.

later may be bigger Unsold seedlings quicky fill their tiny tray homes with roots, so nurserymen continue to move them on to larger quarters. This means that as spring progresses, more mature specimens are available in larger containers. Naturally they are also more expensive. But the cost is offset by a more impressive appearance—and an instant effect is something no city gardener can disparage.

supermarket A surprising assortment of flowers, vegetables and herbs are also avail-
surprises able in supermarkets as well as dime stores and florists and even from the truck vendors who appear as if by magic in spring. Provided you check your purchase carefully for signs of poor health and insects, these small plants can be bought wherever you find them.

mail-order I know only too well that repeated visits to nurseries are not always possi-
catalogues ble. Fortunately there is an alternative—and you don't even have to leave your chair. This is to explore the treasures buried in mail-order plant catalogues (a sampling begins on page 289). Much may be learned from these brochures, which range from unassuming to spectacular. Most include a verbal description of flowers, fruit or leaf color, along with light tolerance and hardiness range. Never mind that much of what's written is an exercise in hyperbole or that the pictures show only impeccable blooms, flawless fruit and nary a hint of munching insects or diseases.

watch those wishes There are indeed real advantages to buying from mail order suppliers. But city gardener, beware.

Sales catalogues they are . . . and sell they will. Browsing on a wintry night with snow swirling about, spring planting seems far away. How easy to believe your conditions are ideal and you've space and time enough for *every* perfect specimen you see.

Take time to read these "wish" books carefully to determine whether what they offer is really right for you. And whether what you see is what you'll get. Restudy the notes on your cardboard plan and keep them firmly in mind.

sowing seeds indoors Particularly tempting, partly because of price, are catalogue offers of seeds. But to successfully grow seedlings indoors you must have a full day of sun. You can increase what you have by adding a reflective surface (a wall of cardboard covered with aluminum foil) or a bevy of grow lights. If this condition can be met and your indoor space is ample, by all means experiment—at least once—with seed sowing indoors. And seed-starter kits—especially those with separate compartments—make growing easier.

Seeds do best when kept evenly moist and warm and when their container is turned regularly to produce even growth all around. It's a good idea, too, to start them a week or two later than the package suggests. This will save you added time-consuming indoor transplantings before it's warm enough to safely move the seedlings outdoors.

Since most packets provide more seeds than any city gardener has room for, plan on sharing with friends or donating leftovers to a community garden or a horticultural society for distribution elsewhere. Don't even think of saving leftover seeds for next year; few have a shelf life of more than one season.

seed problems Unfortunately, maintaining seedlings in a small apartment or townhouse is something few choose to do routinely. It isn't that seed growing is difficult. On the contrary, some—like radishes, morning glory and sunflowers—are ridiculously easy to start. The obstacles are insufficient time (the gardener's, that is), inadequate light, improper temperature and unsuitable space. Also, a good deal more work and mess are involved in starting indoor seedlings than the catalogues imply. Juggling soil and leaking trays of seedlings in a tiny kitchen, then dripping water and/or soil over a living room rug is not the nicest way to welcome spring. And after the seedlings have been "thinned" (that means killing some off to alleviate crowding) and the survivors transplanted to larger pots—yet again—you may start wondering if there's a better way to spend your gardening days. Undoubtedly it's easier in a spacious suburban home.

Bergenia
Bergenia cordifolia

is it worth it? So does it pay for you to grow any—or even some—of your plants from seed?

If there are young children around to whom you wish to demonstrate the miracle of life—which this surely is—the answer is yes.

The answer is yes again if there are hard-to-find species you cannot live without.

seeds outside　　At this point, you may ask, why not sow the seeds directly outdoors? This is indeed the route to take if you're a cost-conscious gardener, vegetable aficionado working a community plot or passionate fan of unusual wildflowers, peculiar herbs or rare annuals or perennials. (Or if, like some city gardeners I know, you regularly toss seeds into street tree pits and abandoned lots to set them abloom.)

The problem is that seeds sown outside often take longer than most city gardeners have space, time or patience for. Seeds won't start to sprout until the moisture and temperature conditions of both soil and air are suitable for germination. This means that if the spring is exceptionally cool, wet or dry, you may not see your flowers or taste your vegetables or herbs until a sizable chunk of the summer is gone.

Buying nursery trays of flowers, vegetables or herbs for a country estate is no small expense. But their cost for a small city yard, balcony or rooftop is manageable—and (for this gardener at least) a blessed alternative.

dormant bare-root　　Seeds are not the only live goods available by mail. Mail-order dealers
plants　　also ship plants. Some sell *dormant bare-root stock*. This means the plants have no leaves (dormant), no soil around their roots (bare root) and they're extremely young. (Who but the young could make such a trip?)

bare-root　　There are several advantages in buying dormant bare-root herbaceous pe-
pros and cons　　rennials by mail. Prices often are cheaper, and with a countrywide choice of nurseries, the selection is greater than any to be found locally. If well packaged (in moist straw, moss or newsprint), perennials can take this trip in their stride. Unfortunately, there are some disadvantages to bare-root ordering of slow growers and woody species in particular. One year at least may be needed by the pathetic specimen gasping for water in its wrapper to recover from the shock of uprooting and the journey through the mail before it begins to resemble the plant you saw in the catalogue.

Then too, you cannot ignore a new bare-root arrival. It must be removed *immediately* from its carton and dropped into a weak fertilizer-and-water solution for a 12–24-hour root soak. It must then be planted without delay—frequently at a time that is less than convenient.

When conditions are ideal (i.e., quick delivery, exemplary garden light, perfect soil moisture, no wind and a good dollop of gardening experience on the part of the receiver) there is nothing wrong with purchasing bare-root stock. It is a favorite with country gardeners since aside from seed planting, it's the cheapest way of building a landscape; no one can argue with bargain 1-foot-tall magnolias for two dollars, and even the mighty oak was once a spindly, leafless "whip." But if you sense I'm not too keen on bare-root stock, you're right. I feel the only times to consider it are when the plant you pine for is so hard to find it cannot be procured any other way, or if the price is so ridiculously low that the risk of loss and tedious wait for maturity is justified.

plants by mail By contrast, it is extremely rewarding to buy plants in containers by mail. This way the plant arrives with viable roots (and often leaves), so there's no need to panic if you haven't time to plant it immediately. Your new guest will remain happy in its plastic pot for days, provided only that you open the shipping carton to light and air and give the plant some water.

determining what When perusing a mail-order catalogue, you must read the fine print care-
will be shipped fully so that you know what it is you will get—seeds, bare-root stock or potted plants. If it's impossible to determine, call the company and ask. Plant dimensions can also be confusing. These may be given either in plant years (which is important for certain fruiting shrubs like blueberries, which must be old enough to bear) or pot size (which may indicate the maturity of the roots).
Remember that there are logistical limits to mailing dimensions and weight. Fancy photos of fruit and flowers notwithstanding, don't expect an instant garden when you order plants by mail.

bulbs by mail On the other hand, there are no such surprises with mail-order bulbs. Mail is often the only way to find truly unusual species for seasons other than spring. Unfortunately, I find that spring bulb catalogues always arrive much too early—I can't stand thinking of next year's tulips while this year's are still going strong.

catalogues as Mail-order catalogues are also superbly inspirational reference tools. And
reference as many a housebound city gardener has discovered, they are useful for what might be called the local nursery telephone order. This procedure is fairly simple, but to do it well takes a little advance planning.
Let's return for a moment to that garden center you found just outside town. During your visit, check to see if, for a minimum fee or reasonably sized order, they will deliver. If so, take the time to introduce yourself and memorize the name of a good-natured salesperson who will remember you and that you're coping with a special city space.

the telephone order After studying your mail-order catalogues and selecting plants that work for your plan, telephone your nursery friend and order from him. If he carries the plant you saw in the catalogue, you can be sure that at least it's hardy for your locale; if he doesn't, he may be able to suggest a suitable substitute.

At the time of your telephone order you can also discuss such critical characteristics as plant shape, color and present total height (including root ball) to ensure that your purchase will fit, and perhaps add to your cache of fertilizers, tools or other supplies. If the plant you've ordered is large, you might ask the nursery to do the planting for you—or at least get them to agree to drop it into the hole or container you've prepared (and that alone can be well worth any additional fee).

While most nursery salespeople try to be patient and helpful, they don't

Summer lilac
Buddleia davidii

always succeed during hectic Sundays in early spring. You may find that like many suburban gardeners, some nurserymen are skeptical about city plants (especially those grown on a rooftop or balcony), but you can overwhelm them with your enthusiasm while you request their indulgence and help.

the wild things Sometimes restraint in matters of horticulture is an ethical imperative— as when the city gardener, out in the country, finds a wild plant that looks "just right" for home. Aside from the fact that taking a plant is called theft when permission has not been granted by the landowner, depending on the plant, it may also be a violation of a state conservation law. To this you must also add the question of whether your prize can even survive the uprooting, transporting and then transplanting to a site that in no way resembles its home.

figuring out Let's say you fall in love with a wild plant (which happens often). And you
what you found don't know what it is (which also happens just as often). Carefully cut off a portion of one twig with just enough leaves, flowers or fruit so that proper identification can be made. Preserve the cutting by flattening it out between several thicknesses of paper (a telephone book is best, if somewhat hard to find in the woods).

Then either take this sample to your nurseryman—who may or may not recognize it—or ship it (reinforced so it isn't damaged) to the nearest expert for help: a botanical garden, horticultural society or your state college's Cooperative Extension Office.

clues for Be prepared, too, to provide as much of the following information as
identification possible:

- the growing habit of the entire plant (is it a tree, shrub, creeper, twiner?)
- the state and habitat where it was found (a vacant Ohio lot, a Maine roadside, dense Catskill forest understory?)
- the light conditions where it was growing
- the season or month it was taken
- the original color of leaves, flower or fruit (some parts fade when dried or pressed)

And don't forget to include your name and address. A self-addressed, stamped envelope for reply is also sure to be appreciated.

scour shops and catalogues

Once the specimen has been identified, scour shops and catalogues for a duplicate of your prize. So long as you regard the venture as an experiment, you won't be upset if it doesn't work. At least you'll know that you've left the *original* plant intact for others to enjoy.

the rose by any Latin name

Whether or not you're intent on tracking down some wild thing, being able to communicate clearly with your nursery friends eventually entails slipping into another language. Even for those who've tossed its polysyllables around for years, botanical Latin can be intimidating. But when it comes to finding and buying plants, it's the only language that does the job.

Take maples, for example—an enormous group full of surprises, with small plants and tall, red-leaved ones and green, and those that yield syrup for pancakes. If it's something special you're after, the only way to be sure of getting the plant you want is to use its botanical name.

Linnaeus and his system

Plant names may seem confusing now, but things were even worse before the Swedish botanist Carolus Linnaeus tidied things up. The system he devised is called binomial nomenclature, and since the eighteenth century it has been the basis of all horticultural naming. Latin was the universal language of scholars (used by botanists since first-century Rome), so it was logical to continue using Latinized words, with a bit of plundered Greek thrown in. Linnaeus dreamed up a two-part identification in which every plant is organized first by the genus to which it belongs (in the case of maples, *Acer*), and then by a species within that genus (the sugar maple is *Acer saccharum,* the Japanese maple *Acer palmatum,* and so on).

there's other meanings in them words

Some botanical names commemorate a person, usually a patron or the plant collector who introduced the species (like *farreri* in honor of Reginald Farrer, or *davidii* for Père Jean Pierre David). Others are descriptive of a flower or leaf outline (*palmatum* for resemblance to an outspread hand, *pendula* for hanging down), leaf or plant size (*nanus* or *pumilus* for small or dwarf), texture (*pubescens* for downy) or color (*purpureum* for purple, *argenteus* for silvery or metallic gray). For example, a popular Japanese maple for city gardens is *Acer palmatum* 'Atropurpureum.' This plant has red-colored hand-shaped leaves.

varieties, hybrids, cultivars

Species are further subdivided into varieties, hybrids and cultivars. Although gardeners frequently use the terms cultivar and variety interchangeably, cultivars are plants produced through human hybridization.

(The word cultivar comes from "cultivated variety" and has been used since 1959 when it was approved by the International Code of Nomenclature for Cultivated Plants.) Cultivar names are either preceded by the abbreviation "cv.," or enclosed in single quotation marks. They are also in a modern language, not Latin, as, for example the popular hosta cultivar *Hosta sieboldiana* 'Frances Williams.'

learning your Latin

No amateur can hope to understand every botanical description or recognize every name. But it sure makes for easier and better gardening if you memorize the ones important to you. I write down new names in large letters—one or two species at a time—and tack up the paper where I see it daily. Eventually even the most complex ones sink in.

facing a move

If there's one constant in city life, it's that sooner or later everyone moves. Leases expire, apartments become too small or too large, and whole buildings are sold. Fortunately, just like furniture, some garden plants can be moved with you. What you take will depend on the degree of devotion the plant deserves, whether it will tolerate the new conditions it will be moved to and the difficulty of finding an appropriate replacement. "Devotion," in this case, also includes the amount of time, money and physical exertion you have for this cause.

you can take it with you

The smaller the plant, the easier to transport. And some furniture movers can be talked (or bribed) into toting plants in manageable-sized containers. While you may be able to dig up and wrap a treasured plant yourself, moving days are often so traumatic it might be better to pay a nurseryman to do the moving and transplanting for you.

gardening safely

A note here on gardening safely. City folk are rarely known for callused hands, so no one will call you a sissy for wearing gloves when toiling with soil or prickly plants.

gloves

Deerskin gloves are great, but heavy cotton, which is cheaper, serves nearly as well and can be discarded in a season or two. Buy the ones with rubbery dots or strips on the palm for a secure grip.
With or without gloves, even a minute cut can develop into a serious infection, so be sure to scrub well with soapy water after working in your garden.

tetanus and aching backs

A tetanus injection is also a wise precaution—once every ten years with booster shots in between. General practitioners rarely keep the serum on hand, but pediatricians do.

And finally, don't let the enthusiasm that comes with early spring allow you to forget that you may have spent a sedentary winter or that you may be in something less than your physical prime. Take it easy that first garden day, and remember that the safest way to lift and carry heavy bags or plants with the least strain is to use the muscles in your legs and thighs, not those in your back.

Dirty fingernails are considered a horticultural badge of distinction; infections and an aching back are not.

Japanese Dogwood
Cornus kousa

The soil is not, as many suppose, a dead, inert substance. It is very much alive and dynamic. It teems with bacteria, actinomycetes, fungi, molds, yeasts, protozoa, algae and other minute organisms.
—J. I. Rodale, *Pay Dirt,* 1945

6. The Secret Is in the Soil

soil is not dirt   If you want to put your friends to sleep, start a discussion on soil. Soil is not "dirt." Dirt (like dust) is found on windowsills and kids' walls; *soil* is what plants must sink their roots into. And there's an important difference. The long-term health of your garden depends on your soil.

new gardeners, old gardens   If you're the new owner of an old or neglected yard, or if you've just acquired an established rooftop terrace garden, soil improvement is needed before you do your planting. (If you're a new container gardener, you must first acquire your soil or there can be no planting—so go on to the next chapter and return here later.)

when to work   Soil improvement can be done in nearly any season, but gardeners seem most inspired in spring. Therefore, once the gray days of winter relent and the soil is no longer soggy, it's time to venture outdoors and begin.

basic tools for soil   First come the tools, and the plethora of handsome implements is overwhelming. For yards and large containers a long-handled fork is best; for windowboxes and small containers, a hand tool. Unless you're wild for gadgets and have lots of space for storage, you only need these five to begin:

- ❧ hand trowel
- ❧ narrow hand trowel
- ❧ hand fork
- ❧ narrow-bladed garden shovel (properly called a spade)
- ❧ garden fork
  (for yard gardeners, a rake is also helpful)

A quality tool is best. And while an expensive one won't make you a better gardener, a comfortable one can. I prefer a spade and fork with a D-shaped handle; you may prefer a handle shaped like a "T," or no handle at all.
Like a toothbrush, the choice of tool is strictly personal.

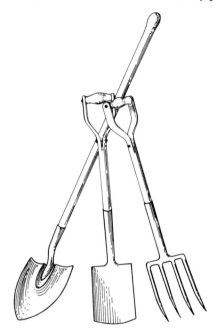

Working a yard that has not previously been restored can be truly backbreaking labor. If the effort is overwhelming, get a rotary hoe or rototiller to help you pulverize the soil—but rent or borrow if possible. Once you begin a maintainance program a power tool should not be needed again.

from sand to clay Soils in their natural state vary from coarse-textured sand at one extreme to fine-textured clay. Sandy soils have individual particles that allow water to drain too quickly; clay soils form hard lumps when dry, are sticky when wet, and hardly drain at all. The ideal soil for most garden plants is something in between called *loam*. Loamy soil is easy to dig, feels fluffy and crumblike, and is slightly gritty when moist. Loamy soils permit water to penetrate easily but also take several minutes to drain.

confronting compaction
It's a simple fact of life that even the best of soils—either in a container or in the ground—loses its porosity and fertility with time. Such soils often become so compacted they resemble concrete, as I discovered when I broke a shovel the first time I dug in my new backyard. So the first order of business is to alleviate compaction, and this is done by turning under a soil amendment known as a lightener. Your choice of lighteners includes three inert rock derivatives: builders' sand, vermiculite and perlite.

sand
Builders' sand is relatively inexpensive, so it's the lightener of choice for many yard gardeners. Builders' sand (not sea sand, which contains salt and is toxic to plants) can be bought in 50-pound bags at garden centers and hardware shops. But sand is so heavy it's not easy to work with. It also makes large containers nearly impossible to move. And because of its weight, sand must be avoided *absolutely* on rooftops and balconies.

vermiculite
Vermiculite is a lightweight, silvery-looking mica-type rock that has been expanded by intense heat. Although sterile, it does contain some elements useful to plants. However, its service as a long-term lightener in yards and large containers is limited by its tendency to compact, so it's best restricted to small pots and windowboxes.
Vermiculite is sold in garden shops in cubic-foot bales. Although not always listed on the label, it is also included in most packaged mixes.
In recent years there have been warnings about occasional asbestos contamination of vermiculite (a result of the way it's mined). You don't have to avoid vermiculite altogether, but do wear gloves when handling it and keep it moist so it doesn't fly into your face.

perlite
Perlite, an expanded, sterile volcanic rock derivative, vaguely resembles tiny white cotton balls, and for both containers and yards it's the most practical lightener of the three. It's easy to use, does not deteriorate or decay with time, and its porous particles trap air and water. If you're working on a windy day, moisten it slightly to keep it under control.
Perlite is sold in garden shops in cubic-foot bales and is also included in packaged potting blends.

how much lightener The amount of lightener needed to loosen the soil varies with its compaction and texture. Heavy clayey soils need more; light, gritty ones less. I can't suggest any specific amount for all conditions, but in the typical soils I've seen, one shovelful of lightener for each 2-foot-by-2-foot square of space is often sufficient.

Madagascar Periwinkle
Catharanthus roseus

where soil space Where soil space is tight—as in a container that's already planted or in a
is limited street tree pit or narrow ribbon of yard—you can make room for the lightener and other amendments by removing handfuls of old soil at random intervals and from around the perimeter. Don't be concerned if

you must cut some roots to do this. Mature species in restricted growing areas eventually become potbound, and this bit of root pruning is helpful.

restoring soil fertility
Once soil compaction is alleviated, you can turn your attention to restoring soil fertility. Truly fertile soil—no matter whether in upstairs containers or downstairs yards—is rich with live microscopic organisms. It is their activity that reduces organic matter to the soluble form that plants can absorb. To encourage the development of these helpful beings, you must create (or recreate) a hospitable environment—and that's a job for the amendment known as a soil conditioner.

the soil conditioner
A soil conditioner is any partially decomposed, organic vegetable matter that makes the soil more workable and adds richness while it continues to decay.

peat moss
The most widely used soil conditioner is peat moss, which comes neatly packed in cubic-foot bags. This is partially decayed sphagnum moss that has been harvested from ancient bogs in Michigan and Canada and has been dried and pressed for easy shipping. Dry peat moss takes awhile to absorb moisture, so wet it a bit before blending it into your soil.

inspiring humus
Another kind of soil conditioner is one that might be called "humus-inspiring." That word "humus," so favored by gardeners, is a peculiar one that's sometimes confusing since it refers both to decayed *and* decaying matter. Classic sources of humus include leaf mold or compost, which you may eventually make yourself (see page 206).

cow manure
Manure is also an important source of the microorganisms that build a fertile, humusy loam. You can find cow manure in plastic bags at garden shops. Some suppliers boast that theirs has been "deodorized," but I stopped believing that the hot day I spent in a car with a bag on the seat beside me.
Eventually you may find its bouquet not at all disagreeable—it does make for romantic notions about checking your livestock—and you know you're a bona fide gardener when you actually begin to *like* it.

how much conditioner
In yard areas or large containers where there are no plants, turn under at least a shovelful of peat moss and cow manure for each 2-foot-by-2-foot space.

in yards In yard areas where plants exist, turn under a half a shovelful for each 2-foot-square of space and work in a ring around herbaceous perennials and small shrubs and trees. Fork the amendments into the soil beneath their "drip line" (the area just below the outer portion of their limbs). If you have one or more truly large trees, use your fork to jab the earth lightly under the drip line just enough to loosen it. Then blend the peat and manure into this top portion of soil (this is called "top dressing").

in containers In containers with shrubs and trees, add a heaping trowelful of peat moss and cow manure for each foot of each plant height and use a hand fork to turn them under the soil around the container's periphery.

earthworms You'll know you're on your way to good garden loam when you find your first earthworm—that headless, toothless, squirmy creature that's a gardener's true friend. Earthworms thrive in moist, rich, organic matter. As they tunnel through earth ingesting dead leaves and other vegetable matter, they improve drainage, open subsurface areas to air, and leave behind "castings" rich in plant growth promoters (called auxins and cytokinins). Earthworms are welcome additions in yards and large planters. But you may find their turmoil too much in a window box.

providing plant food As garden plants begin to make use of the nutrients they find in the soil, those nutrients must be restored or rebalanced. This is true not only for plants in the largest rooftop container (which is still only a pot, after all) but for those in the most spacious yard. Fertilizer does not reappear by magic. So in addition to fostering a humusy, well-drained soil, sooner or later you must also provide your plants with some "food."*

NPK—the Big 3 All members of the plant kingdom—including insect eaters and other strange jungle residents—rely on three major nutrients for good health: nitrogen, phosophorus and potash. Each affects a plant's well-being in many ways, but summarized briefly, these are as follows:

Nitrogen (N) helps give a healthy green glow to leaves and encourages lush growth

Phosphorus (P) encourages strong root formation, good flowering and fruit set and healthy growth

Potash (K) promotes hardiness, disease resistance and root formation and protects from excessive water loss

---

* When speaking of plants, the word "food" is convenient but misleading; humans don't feed plants—plants feed humans. What humans do is supply the nutrients that enable plants to manufacture their own food.

Yucca or Spanish bayonet
Yucca filamentosa

understanding
the label

Garden shop shelves are jammed with a seemingly infinite variety of fertilizers, so the only way to know what you're buying is to read the label carefully. The most important detail you'll find there is the set of three hyphenated numbers, something like 2-1-2 or 5-50-17. These indicate the product's percentage of NPK, and they are listed in order: nitrogen—phosphorus—potash.

target what
you need

Before selecting a fertilizer, target what it is you think you need. If, for example, you must encourage a crabapple tree to flower, boost production of tomatoes, or increase your window box blooms, then the fertilizer you want is one with a higher percentage of phosphorus. Since phosphorus is the middle number in the NPK ratio, look for a proportion on the order of 15-30-15. If your goal, instead, is a general restoration of all soil nutrients, the NPK ratio to look for is on the order of 5-5-5.

Fertilizer percentages in natural products tend to be lower than those of their chemical counterparts, and depending on the organic source, they can also vary for seemingly identical products.

fertilizer sources   There are natural—or "organic"— sources of these Big 3. There are also chemical—or "synthetic"—sources. Synthetic fertilizers tend to be available to plants more quickly than organics because they have been manufactured in readily available form. On the other hand, organic sources improve the tilth and structure of the soil and inspire the development of microorganisms.

In the small city garden organic and synthetic fertilizers need not be mutually exclusive. Both may be useful to plants in much the same way that both balanced, nutritious meals ("organic") and vitamin supplements ("synthetic") are useful to people.

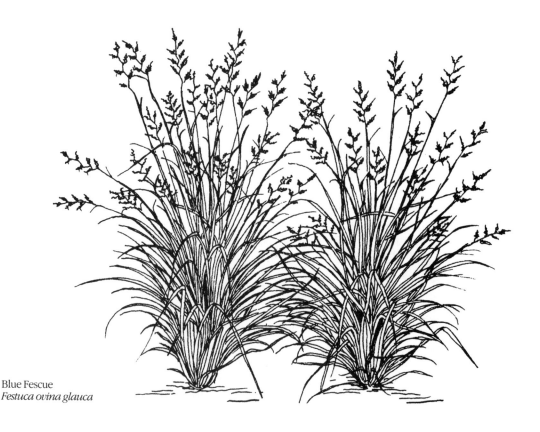

Blue Fescue
Festuca ovina glauca

synthetic sources Chemical fertilizers, or synthetics, typically are marketed under brand names like Miracle-Gro, Rapid-Gro, Hyponex and Peter's. These come in a variety of formulations, and none is necessarily better than another. This detail, of course, doesn't stop gardeners from developing strong preferences, which, I have come to suspect, depend on the gardening method they prefer.

formulations Some synthetic fertilizers are powders that must be dissolved in water before being poured on the soil or sprayed on the leaves (a procedure called "foliar feeding"). Some fertilizers come in a granular form and are to be spread on the soil directly out of the package. Still others are "controlled-release" capsules or sticks. These are to be placed either on top of the soil or in the soil, where they disintegrate over a period of time.
Read the label directions to see which application to use.

organic sources Organic fertilizers are typically marketed under the name of their source, and some sources are pretty exotic. As a city slicker astonished at finding I could *buy* cow manure, I couldn't believe my eyes when I later also found bat guano, poultry manure, sewage sludge, and elephant manure (sold under the name—no kidding—"zoodoo"!). Because they come from natural sources, the actual percentage of NPK in organic fertilizers varies.
The chart will give you an idea of an approximate nutrient content of some organic fertilizers:

NUTRIENT PERCENTAGE OF SOME ORGANIC FERTILIZERS

FERTILIZER	NITROGEN	PHOSPHORUS	POTASH	pH RANGE
Blood meal	13	2	1	acidic
Bone meal (steamed)	2.5	25	—	alkaline
Cottonseed meal	7	3	2	acidic
Fish meal	9.5	7	—	—
Phosphate rock	—	30–40	—	alkaline
Seaweed (kelp)	2.5	1.5	15	—
Soybean meal	7	1.5	2.5	alkaline
Sulphate of potash	—	—	48	—
Superphosphate	—	14–20	—	neutral
Superphosphate (double)	—	40–45	—	acidic
Urea	46	—	—	acidic
Wood ash	—	2	5	alkaline

how much to use The question of "how much" of each of the Big 3 to add to your soil cannot be answered precisely unless you've a resident scientist running tests and continually dispensing advice. The quantity is a function both of the amount already present and the amount the particular plants normally need (e.g., flowers and vegetables have a greater need for phosphorus, grasses and other foliage species need nitrogen). For better or worse, gardening is not so much a science as an art. So while a soil test is certainly useful, most fertilizer packages suggest application amounts that are appropriate for a majority of plants.

translating label quantities While an overdose of organic fertilizer is rarely harmful, an overdose of chemical fertilizer can kill. This is a case where a little may be good, but a lot is fatal.

So never *never* exceed the manufacturer's recommended dose.

And if in doubt, be stingy.

Some manufacturers suggest fertilizer application in terms of hundreds of square feet or acres—which in my city garden is not too helpful. I wasn't the first to be unnerved by this, though, and in a USDA pamphlet by the soil scientist Dr. Charles E. Kellogg entitled "How Much Fertilizer Shall I Use?" these figures were recomputed to be useful for a smaller space. I have further adapted his chart for use in containers.

computing your space But first you must determine your area.

To find the area of a square or rectangular space (either yard or container) multiply its length by its width.

Purple-leaf smoke tree
Cotinus coggygria
'Purpurea'

For round containers, take the radius, square it, and multiply that by 3.14 (Or if you prefer, approximate this by multiplying half the container diameter by itself, and then multiply that amount by 3.) Container areas are not as complex as you might think because height is not a factor—plants, after all, supposedly grow in the ground.

You should now be able to convert label recommendations and determine your needs as follows:

CHART OF REDUCED FERTILIZER QUANTITIES

Where the amount for an acre is:	1,000 pounds	300 pounds	100 pounds
Use for a yard space or tub size:			
2 feet by 1½ feet (2½ square feet)	2 tablespoons	1½ tablespoons	½ tablespoon
2 feet by 2½ feet (5 square feet)	4 tablespoons	1 tablespoon	1¼ tablespoons
2½ feet by 10 feet (25 square feet)	1¼ cups	6 tablespoons	2 tablespoons
5 feet by 20 feet (100 square feet)	2¼ pounds	11 ounces	3½ ounces

the bushel   One other measurement frequently used in garden manuals and by nurserymen that is best committed to memory is the bushel, which is not as arcane as it sounds. A bushel is the equivalent of a container sized 13 by 13 by 13 inches, or 1¼ cubic feet.

trace elements   In addition to the Big 3, scientists have found some twenty other nutrients that plants need in such minute quantities the group is collectively known as "trace elements." Included are such delicacies as iron (most important, especially for evergreens), calcium, manganese, copper, zinc, sulfur, boron and molybdenum. Although their absence can lead to serious problems, the actual quantity required by different species is still unclear. Without a soil test or keen eye for spotting the subtle signs of deficiencies, it's hard to know what you need.

Fortunately, trace elements are present to some degree in organic substances like compost, seaweed, leaf mold and natural ground rock. You may also find several included in synthetic fertilizers. They are typically listed on the label as "secondary plant foods" (a dubious phrase, at best).

professional feeding When it comes to truly large trees, there may be a limit to the "food" you are able to provide. My five-story-high street tree required a truck-mounted pump producing 150 pounds of pressure to force fertilizer through six soil probes to a depth of 2 feet. Street trees like this and mature yard plants may require professional fertilizing, and an arborist is the professional to call.

the mystery of acidity and alkalinity The subject of soil acidity or alkalinity can be intimidating at first, but it's not really the mystery it seems. All soils vary in their chemical composition. These chemicals alter the alkalinity or acidity of the soil (technically called the "hydrogen ion concentration"). This, in turn, affects the nutrients present by making them more *or* less available for different species of plants.

the pH scale Chemists have devised a scale of numbers from 1 to 14—much like a thermometer—to indicate the degree of acidity or alkalinity. This acid-alkaline relationship has as its universal symbol two letters—pH—and they're written just like that.
The higher the number on the pH scale, the more alkaline the substance (a typically alkaline substance is baking soda or limestone).
The lower the number, the more acid (typical is vinegar or grapefruit). Arid desert soils tend to be alkaline, and some have a pH as high as 10. At the other extreme is a peat bog, where the pH may be as low as 3. Smack in the middle is neutral, or 7.

plant preferences The intervals on the pH scale between 1 and 14 are split into logarithmic subdivisions. This means that a soil with a pH of 5 is actually 10 times as acid as one with a pH of 6 (or 100 times more acid than a soil with a pH of 7). But this is of little importance to gardeners. What is important to gardeners is the pH needed by the specific plants they grow. A majority of popular garden plants do best in a pH range that is *slightly* acid, or around 6 to 6.5. Although most are remarkably tolerant, there are a few that are positively neurotic about their soil. These are the ones you must help.

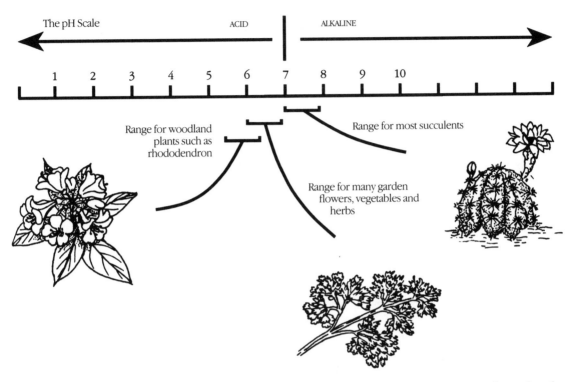

The pH Scale

ACID   ALKALINE

1   2   3   4   5   6   7   8   9   10

Range for woodland
plants such as
rhododendron

Range for most succulents

Range for many garden
flowers, vegetables and
herbs

plants for acid soil   The majority of woodland plants, for example, need a distinctly acid soil,
or a pH close to 5.5. These acid lovers include azaleas, bleeding heart,
blueberry, foxglove, holly, leucothoe, lily-of-the-valley, mountain laurel,
rhododendron, snakeroot and trillium.

lowering the pH   Soil can slowly be made more acid (or the pH lowered) by turning
under peat moss, tea leaves or coffee grounds, oak leaves or cottonseed
meal. Powdered sulfur produces a quicker reaction, and iron sulfate is
quicker still. The fastest by far is aluminum sulfate, which should not be
used around edibles since this may result in aluminum toxicity. Whatever product you choose, follow package directions for dilution and
application.

some like it alkaline   At the other extreme are plants that do better with a distinctly alkaline soil
(which the British call "chalky"). Sun-loving plants in particular seem to
prefer a soil pH that is mildly alkaline or close to a neutral 7. This category includes most culinary herbs, lawn grass, many species of clematis,
desert plants and succulents, and vegetables like asparagus, cantaloupe,
cucumber, tomato and squash.

increasing pH Soil can slowly be made more alkaline (or the pH raised) by turning under wood ashes, pulverized eggshells, clamshells or oystershells, bonemeal or most animal manures. For a faster reaction, use ground limestone or dolomitic limestone (see chart below). Faster still is hydrated lime, which may also burn roots. In any case it's not a good idea to try to raise the soil pH around existing plants by more than one unit per season.

The limestone required to raise the pH varies with the soil structure; more is needed for clayey soils, less for sand. Assuming your soil is a medium texture loam, the following should help you plan:

LIMESTONE NEEDED TO INCREASE SOIL pH BY .5

For a yard space or container of	Use a limestone quantity of
2½ feet by 40 feet (100 square feet)	4½ pounds
2½ feet by 10 feet (25 square feet)	2½ cups
2 feet by 2½ feet (5 square feet)	½ cup
2 feet by ½ foot (typical window box)	¼ cup

analyzing soil If you wish to learn more about the pH or NPK of your soil, you can do so yourself with one of the many inexpensive soil-testing kits available. Most of these kits come with a color chart and jars of liquid chemicals. A small amount of soil is mixed with a small amount of liquid and the resulting color is compared with that on the chart (this should be done three times for accuracy). Even easier, but somewhat more expensive, are the meters that need only be plunged into barely moist soil. The needle on the dial registers the pH number or indicates the amount of nutrient amount of present.

A home test will give you a fair indication of the chemical composition of your soil. It's not absolutely scientifically accurate—but it sure is fun.

professional testing For a more accurate appraisal, mail soil samples either to the extension division of your state agricultural college or a soil testing company (see page 292). Gather your samples from an area about 2–3 inches below the surface of the soil, using a clean spoon or trowel (not fingers). Take your samples from more than one area if the space is large, or wherever there's a variation in light, change of grade or exposure.

After treating your soil, wait about 3 weeks for a chemical reaction to occur before testing to see if further changes are needed.

Compact, barren soil eventually leads to plant decline. The early signs of trouble may be a decrease in the size and number of new leaves, a paling of the general color tone, and a decrease or total lack of flowers or fruit. Too many times when this happens the gardener assumes "that plant can't take the city."

But in fact, the secret of city plant success is in the soil.

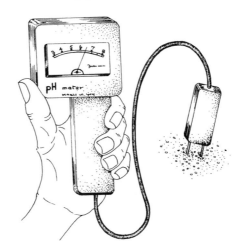

pH soil testing meter

Crabapple
Malus sp.

One plant in a tin can may be a more helpful and inspiring garden to some mind than a whole acre of lawn and flowers may be to another.
—Liberty Hyde Bailey, *Garden Making: Suggestions for the Utilizing of Home Grounds,* 1898

7. Containers for Summer and Winter

Fans of Louis XIV may argue that Versailles was the first container garden of note. But his 3,000 tubbed trees are a mere ho-hum compared to the plants we now jam into pots on a windowsill, rooftop, balcony, terrace, doorstep or porch. Where there's no ground to sink roots into, containers are the only way to grow.

the window box No summer scene is complete without containers of colorful flowers, and window boxes are basic. They may not rank among the world's great landscapes—and snobs may sneer at a "garden" 6 inches deep and 2 feet long—but there's no denying the color they bring to barren streets, the spirit to lifeless buildings, or the pleasure to those who tend them. Whatever the season, it's never too late to begin.

In a crowded urban setting, a window box must be intelligently positioned. This means it must not teeter over heavily traveled sidewalks or obstruct an exit or fire escape.

security for all A responsible window-box gardener must also be sure the container is securely attached. Window-box security is affected by gravity, rain, snow and unexpected gusts of wind. So hang it *inside* the balcony railing, tied with wire to brackets, or perch it on the *interior* surface of a parapet coping or wall, anchored with screws. Stainless steel or coated metal brackets need no further attention; wrought iron must be painted to preserve it from rust.

Remember that an empty window box is deceptively light. So if you're not handy enough to install it safely yourself, hire someone who is. It's a cheap enough way to prevent a lawsuit.

Calendula or pot
marigold
Calendula officinalis

a rule of thumb   The standard for installation and location was best described to me by a New York City Buildings Department inspector, who explained that his personal rule was that "a window box must appear to be no more potentially hazardous than a carefully installed window air conditioner." And that's the sanest rule of thumb I know.

drainage holes   Your window box should have several bottom holes for drainage, at least a half inch in diameter and 7–8 inches apart. Boxes on sills or ledges should also have spacers beneath to raise them enough so that cleaning collected debris is easy. This also ensures that air reaches the soil's bottom and prevents rotting of either the box or the surface it's resting on.

and dripping   Dripping can drive your downstair neighbor wild. So if you like to overwater, add a catch basin or tray. One inventive window box gardener simultaneously prevented dripping and created a self-watering system by snaking a cotton wick from the catch basin up through the drainage hole. Capillary action carried the moisture into the soil.

the quest for planters   When it comes to improvised containers for summer flowers, anything goes. Possibilities include discarded sinks, tubs, teapots, cast iron kettles, wheelbarrows and expired automobile tires. All you really need is a receptacle that is weatherproof, nontoxic to plants, and has a bottom opening for drainage. (If you can't face forging a hole in your prize antique urn, you might try managing without one by watering *very* carefully, keeping the container out of the rain, and adding a generous layer of Styrofoam chips to the bottom before planting.)

There are also ready-made containers. With a little searching of garden shops or mail-order catalogues (see page 290) you can find some handsome original designs or intriguing historic reproductions.

terra-cotta   Materials you will find include terra-cotta or earthenware clay pots, glazed or unglazed. Unglazed pots may become coated with algae or crusted with salts, but you can control this with vigorous scrubbing. Unglazed pots are porous, which keeps roots cool and allows water to evaporate quickly. Unfortunately, it's hard to know in advance which pots have been fired at high enough temperatures to prevent cracking and splintering in subzero cold.

cement or stone   There are also cast cement and sculpted stone. These are durable and are superb natural insulators that buffer extremes of temperature. But large sizes may be much too heavy for gardens upstairs.

plastic   Where weight is a concern, plastic or fiberglass is best. Although once disdained as the ugly ducklings of the container world, plastic and fiberglass have had marvelous face-lifts thanks to new manufacturing techniques. You can now find them in graceful shapes and designs, as well as unusual textures and tones.

metal   Unless your plans are strictly short term, stay away from metal. Metal boxes invariably rust in a season or two. They will also get searing hot in the summer sun and burn your plant roots (and your fingers).

wood   And of course there are fine containers of wood. Usually simple cubes, circles or rectangles, they are typically made in cedar, redwood, fir, oak, maple or pine. Many are held together by steel angles or metal bands. If these are not of stainless steel, treat them with a rust-inhibiting paint to prevent decay.

from the brewery   I'm partial to old wood barrels, both the clean and shiny ones and those that have not yet been "finished." One large barrel I bought fresh from the distillery reeked of brandy for an entire summer. The tree I planted in it was fine—but I did wonder what the neighbors thought when the wind blew their way.

unusual designs

But in fact, if you keep an open mind, you may be surprised at what you find. I once came across a delicate-looking tub of eucalyptus wood bound by bands of bamboo. Unfortunately, I was so afraid it wouldn't last I bought only one—a decision I came to regret when I finally realized the nurseryman had not exaggerated its durability.

homemade containers

If you are of the do-it-yourself school, here's where you certainly can. Homemade planters of redwood, cedar and marine-grade plywood are durable and need no preservative. They are also the most expensive. Use cheaper lumber and extend its life with a coating of tar, shellac, varnish, urethane, epoxy or the preservatives favored by nurseries, such as Cuprinol No. 10 or Barworth. Pressure-treated wood is also an alternative, but avoid wood that has been treated with creosote, inorganic arsenicals or pentachlorophenol and tetrachlorophenol, which are highly toxic to humans.

basics for building with wood

Containers for trees and shrubs should be of planks that are at least ¾-inch thick, especially if the planter will be more than 2 feet long. Avoid wood with knots or other weaknesses, and to save time and sweat, ask the lumberyard to precut the pieces for you. Rustproof screws of brass or steel are imperative, and corner angle irons or brackets are worthwhile. (The minimum size for winter-hardy plants is discussed later.)

a plant coffin

When my husband and I built our first planter many years ago, we used the cheapest pine plywood. Upon completion, the tub was a large, clumsy-looking affair that resembled a coffin, but also fit perfectly across the 5½-foot-deep corner of our balcony. To assure our handiwork's longevity, we stained all pieces several times (thereby giving pine the elegance of "walnut"), coated the inside with tar and drilled a half dozen holes in the bottom for drainage. Our planter was deemed complete after four short wooden strips for "legs" were added to raise it from the floor so the bottom would not rot.

A decade later, although we had long since moved from that balcony, I visited the building and was gratified to see that both the planter and the original plants were still faring well.

Clearly, with a bit of care an inexpensive homemade planter can be built to last.

use containers to create the space

While essential design elements of any individual planting box are style, size, color and shape, even more important is how you place it. On balconies and rooftop terraces in particular, this is the secret to creating an interesting spatial effect.

Use groups of planters to form a sequence of wide areas followed by narrow ones. Or use them to establish a particular style: symmetrically-placed square containers, for example, evoke a mood that's formal, while asymmetrical groups of round ones are more informal in tone. Rows of large, closely spaced tubs can delineate a border, create an enclosure or define boundaries between portions with different uses—dining, childrens' play, sunbathing, storage or repotting.

You can shove the containers around until you've made up your mind, but it's easier to begin with small cut-to-scale pieces and move them on your cardboard plan or buy chalk and make full-size drawings right on the floor.

container gardens for winter

After navigating the huge trees and shrubs on my nineteenth-floor terrace, guests sometimes asked if I took my plants in "for the winter." I knew the question was not in jest, but it did sound strange to even consider bringing into my apartment two blueberry shrubs, a sourwood, birch and crabapples. I finally figured out that what they were really asking was how it was possible for plants to remain outside, *in containers,* all winter long—and *live.*

the hardy ones

As noted in Chapter 3, there are physiological differences between the leading players (hardy trees, shrubs and perennials) and the supporting cast (summer flowers, vegetables and herbs). Any *hardy* plant that can survive a winter in your vicinity *in* the ground, can also be grown *on top* of the ground in a container—although it takes a bit more work.

soil as protector

Hardy species succumb to winter cold when alternate freezing and thawing tear and injure their roots or heave them from the ground. Despite their dormant state, hardy plants continue to need some food and water all winter long.

Soil is a natural insulator. The more soil between the roots and the cold, the greater the chance of plant survival. The more soil available, the greater the area for the storage of nutrients and moisture.

salvation is in the container

The goal, then, with hardy plants is to provide a container that's large enough to duplicate the root-level conditions that sustain them through winter when they grow in the ground. So you might say the "ideal" solution would be to build the largest tub there's room for—from one end of your space to the other. This would yield the maximum soil area and, if made of concrete'or brick, would also be most durable.

the container "ideal" If this ideal is possible—which means you can afford it in terms of both money and room—it is certainly the thing to do. *But it is ideal only if your city garden is downstairs: a patio or sidewalk area on the ground.* If your city garden is *upstairs*—a rooftop, penthouse terrace or balcony —a wall-to-wall masonry planter is not for you.

wall-to-wall Assuming you can even find a qualified landscape mason (not so easy in
disadvantages town), it may not be feasible to commit yourself to the expense entailed, especially if a short rental lease is involved. Furthermore, building codes (not to mention building management corporations and co-op boards) view with appropriate disfavor permanent and heavy new construction on top of completed buildings.

never forget the leak More important (for the gardener, that is), there's the possibility—*never, never to be forgotten*—of leaks to the space below . . . a major headache to repair when there's something permanent and immovable blocking access. But, you say, a well-constructed building should survive for years without a hint of a leak. In theory, that's true; in fact, the leakproof roof is the exception.

Upstairs, then, the only sensible planting solution is *individual* containers.

the practical solution Having established that a generously proportioned container is imperative for winter-hardy species, the question, next, is what is the safe *minimum* size for the plant that is also practical for the gardener? The container, after all, must share its balcony or terrace home with humans. It must also be small enough to handle. This means being small enough to transport up a stairway or in an elevator and then be hauled out through a window or door.

a safe minimum In New York City where I garden (on the cusp of Zones 6 and 7), I have found that a practical *minimum* dimension for containers for hardy plants is 14 inches—width, height and length. In colder zones this minimum must be increased; in warmer climates, it can be reduced.

how little is small Now, I can hear some cheeky gardener out there muttering that this 14-inch dimension is a rather conservative figure—and actually, I agree. For years I grew hardy sedums in a hollow piece of driftwood with barely a thimbleful of soil. I also watched a neighbor tend 3-foot-high yews in a window box that was maybe 8 inches deep. For in truth, there's no magic number for every hardy species or microclimatic condition.

bigger is better

But *maintenance* chores are inversely proportional to container size. Grow your hardy shrubs, trees and perennials in small containers, and you can be sure that your watering, fertilizing and root pruning chores will be monumental. This is something no sane gardener can ignore. Therefore, where space and finances permit, the *bigger the container, the better.*

where there's wind

A generously proportioned tub is also better where terrace winds are severe. Hedges or "windbreaker" trees and shrubs especially need the largest planters that fit. Their roots need every bit of anchoring space, and their moisture needs are considerable.

containers built for root pruning

The long-term health of container trees and shrubs depends on their ability to grow new roots, so root pruning is essential. Although this can be done from above (see page 235), it's easier to prune from the side. If you're building your own containers, you might create your own version of Andre Le Nôtre's seventeenth-century design, which had removable side panels expressly for this purpose. In the basic version of the Versailles Caisse, as Le Nôtre's container is called, each side is constructed separately. They are then linked together with removable bolts or with tie rods hooked together at top and bottom. If the wood is thick enough, the rods can also be concealed in tunnels bored through the sides.

container or plant first

Deciding which to get first—the container or the plant—is sort of like asking about the chicken and the egg. In the case of a homemade container, it makes sense to have your planter finished before your plants arrive.

There's greater flexibility with ready-mades. With the sketch of your garden in hand—to confirm that you have the space—buy the planter that appeals and find a suitable plant later. Or buy on impulse a plant you can't live without (assuming it fits your conditions) and find a suitable planter later. Most nurseries will hold purchases that are paid for a reasonable time.

watch your weight

When experienced rooftop gardeners talk about weight, it's not a beer belly they're concerned with but building department regulations. Rooftop construction must conform to local building department codes for "live loads"—which means anything that lands on top of the structure after it's completed. This includes rain, snow and your garden.

The acceptable live loads for existing buildings vary not only with locale, but with the code in force at the time of construction. In New York City, for example, several years ago, code allowances for live load were reduced from 40 to 30 pounds per square foot. On the other hand, some buildings are planned specifically to bear extra-heavy rooftop construction (for pools, for example) as well as gardens. Such rooftops are designed for weights much higher than the amount normally called for by code.

basic safety first　Records in your town's building department should show the allowable design load for your rooftop, terrace or balcony. If your garden plans call for only a few containers, there's probably no need for concern. In any case it's prudent to adhere to basic weight controls like using lightweight containers and lightweight soil, keeping large planters close to the building's edge or above supporting walls and posts, or adding a deck to distribute the weight of planters over a larger area.

Then too, most structures are designed with an extra margin of safety. If, however, extensive landscaping is planned, you should adhere to the actual code your building was designed for. In this case you will need to consult an architect and/or landscape architect.

preparing for planting　When I was a rooftop terrace gardener, spring always started with a particularly heroic undertaking: dragging heavy bags of pungent cow manure past disdainful doormen and impeccably coiffed neighbors onto the elevator and out through the apartment window (the builder having succeeded in cutting costs on one of my terraces by omitting the door). I was simply preparing my soil for planting.

Cucumbers, peppers, peas and beans

happiness is a good
container mix

The health of a container garden (and thus the happiness of its gardener) begins in the soil. The advantage of gardening in containers is that soil can be "customized" however you wish and every plant can be treated to exactly what it needs: rhododendrons or blueberries can wallow primarily in peat, clematis and herbs in lime (see Chapter 6). But while a degree in both chemistry and botany would be helpful, it's also possible to blend an "all-purpose" mix that satisfies most of your plants. This basic blend, which can be used as a starting point for all containers, is not complex, and the recipe is as follows:

- ❧ 1 part topsoil
- ❧ 1 part soil lightener (perlite or vermiculite)
- ❧ 1 part soil conditioner (peat moss)
  Mix above ingredients together well.
  Then add:
- ❧ A handful of a granular 5-10-5 fertilizer for each 6 inches of planter height
- ❧ A trowelful of dehydrated cow manure for each 6 inches of planter height (adds flavor and zest)
  Stir well
  Serve (in large containers)

no stolen topsoil

You can see that roughly one third of the total mix is topsoil. Good topsoil, which is also called loam, is rich in nutrients and crumbly in texture. Good topsoil is very important, and it is *not* acquired by digging up the nearest park or street tree pit. Aside from the fact that city parks and trees are too valuable to be subject to garden larceny, the soil you find there is unlikely to be what you need. The soil you need is likely to be found, instead, in the nearest garden center, typically packed in 50-pound bags. (Around the middle of spring I reach a point where I am capable of toting home such a load . . . but if you're not yet up to such exertion, arrange for delivery directly to your site.)
All other ingredients are explained in Chapter 6.

the mixing

Mixing soil for a large planter will be familiar to anyone who has worked with houseplants or mixed a cake: just measure, then stir. But watch out. Stirring huge batches of soil, then dumping it into containers, is extremely demanding, even downright overwhelming. If you aren't used to physical labor, start with one tub at a time. (This may be just what you need for getting in shape.)

where to mix   Blend your soil mix either directly in the tub to be planted or, if there's room, on a large plastic sheet on the floor. It can be a challenge to find a place in which to do this mixing. And having solved that, to find a place in which to store (or hide) whatever's left over for future use. If possible, set aside a large plastic garbage bag, pail or box for both mixing and storing. Otherwise prepare only what you need immediately.

working ahead   You can prepare your planting mix any time that the bags of topsoil are neither muddy, wet or frozen. Some gardeners find it useful to work a season ahead of the actual planting—sort of like making a stew and letting it sit so the flavors blend. This is a particularly efficient strategy, especially if you expect to do most of your planting at once. With tubs filled in advance, your planting day is reduced to merely dropping the plants in—and that can be more than enough effort for one session anyway.

the moisture test   If you've never worked with soil before, take time to test a batch of your first mix with a gallon or two of water. This is a potentially messy experiment, but well worth the trouble. If the water goes through too fast, more conditioner and some topsoil should be added. If the water takes longer than 5–10 minutes, increase the lightener. In any case, allow your mix to dry a bit before making corrections.

prepackaged planting mixes   Prepackaged planting mixes vary in content depending on the manufacturer. Most popular soilless blends are based on a formula developed by Cornell University and include peat moss, perlite and vermiculite, along with dolomitic limestone, superphosphate, calcium nitrate and trace elements. It is the absence of humus or soil that results in the blend's light weight as well as its sterile property. There are no weeds, no bugs, no diseases—and also no living microorganisms.
I admit to a certain antipathy to these sterile packaged blends, but I work at keeping an open mind since I know that many find them useful.

pros   On the pro side, packaged blends are convenient and do indeed save a good deal of time: slit open the package and you're ready to plant. Then too, their minimal weight makes them good for window boxes, hanging baskets and small potted houseplants. Their sterile quality makes them good for starting new plants and seeds.

and cons   So why do I insist on mixing my own when I can tote home a "fast-food" package of soil?

To begin with, "sterility" is expensive. If you have more than one large terrace tub to fill, it's cheaper to blend the mix yourself. A sterile soil (one that's free of pests) is useful for potted plants *indoors. Outdoors* it won't be sterile for long.

But in any case, it's this sterile aspect that rankles.

For as Charles E. Kellogg, former head of the National Soil Survey, USDA said, "an essential feature of soil is *living* microorganisms. No life, no soil." With soilless blends, chemical fertilizers must be used continually to add the nutrients that ensure soil fertility. Furthermore, because of their weightless quality, soilless mixes provide little or no root hold or support. (And I believe in growing large trees.)

reducing soil weight But, you say, isn't lightness precisely what's needed by upstairs gardeners plagued by worries with weight? It is indeed, but there are other ways to cope.

One method—described to me by a clever rooftop gardener who needed to save time, if not money—is to blend into the soilless mix up to one fourth volume of humus and cow manure. This assures the development of natural microorganisms.

Another method is simply to alter that basic soil recipe. The heaviest part of that mix (which is also the part that's missing from sterile blends) is the topsoil. There's no need to eliminate topsoil completely. It's enough simply to reduce its proportion. All that's needed is a *minimum* of 10% humus or soil to encourage the life that's the "essential feature" Dr. Kellogg refers to.

In which case the basic soil recipe would be:

❧ 1 part topsoil
❧ 5 parts lightener
❧ 5 parts conditioner

there's more than soil Having prepared your soil, it's time to prepare your container for
down there planting.

First cover the drainage holes with rounded pieces of broken cups or flower pots (called crock) with their curved side up.

drainage Then comes the drainage layer. For this, you can choose such classic materials as pebbles, marble chips, crock, or any other rough, inert material that permits an easy flow of water. However, these are pretty heavy, and rooftop gardeners have now discovered something better: Styrofoam packing chips. This white, fluffy fill, which is such a headache when you're trying to neatly unpack a crate, makes a feathery-light

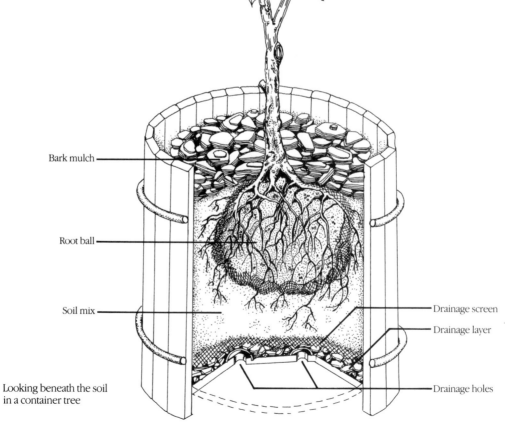

Bark mulch

Root ball

Soil mix

Drainage screen

Drainage layer

Drainage holes

Looking beneath the soil
in a container tree

drainage layer for containers. It is also virtually indestructible.
The depth of the drainage layer varies with the depth of the container.
Allow about an inch of drainage for each foot of planter height, or a half
inch of drainage layer for window boxes and planters that are under a
foot tall and up to 3 inches for tubs that are 3 feet tall.

a barrier screen   Once the drainage layer is in place, add a barrier to keep the soil mix
from sneaking through. Eventually the roots of the plants prevent this
erosion within the container just as they do on hillsides. But it
takes time for the roots to develop and until they do you'll have a muddy
mess on the floor every time you water. You can prevent this with a
fiberglass screen placed on the drainage layer or a thin sheet of rough
sphagnum moss (not *peat* moss). Or if you prefer, equally useful—and
very cheap—is a thin layer of shredded newspaper or barely decayed
leaves.

preparing the "hole"   Once the drainage layer and screen are in place, add the soil mix if it's already prepared (or carefully mix your ingredients in the tub). Fill the con-
tainer only three quarters full, leaving a "hole" for the root ball. Set aside
enough to fill in around it later.

watch those workers   If you hire a nursery to do the preparation and planting for you, remind
the workers that the final soil mix must be friable and drain well. I
learned this the hard way when I lost a beautiful (not to mention expensive) dwarf Japanese maple because its roots could not survive the ex-
ceedingly heavy blend in which it was planted. It was too late when I
realized that I should have watched the workers more closely. However
well meaning, many do not understand the importance of a good
soil mix and tend to be careless. Don't assume they know what they're
doing.

be fearless   A final note on growing compatible species together within a container.
Space is limited, so take advantage of every inch. Underplant your roses
with a silvery artemisia or dusty miller. Or surround a weeping crabapple with sweet alyssum. Encircle tomatoes or eggplant with basil or
tarragon. And add astilbe or ferns as an understory for azaleas or rhododendron.
Don't be afraid to experiment, and ignore what others say about what can
(or can't) be grown in containers.

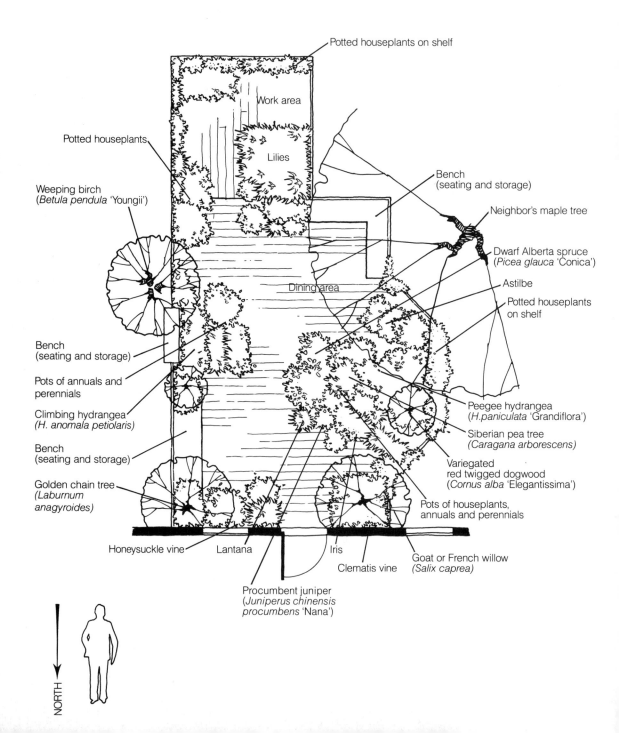

Potted houseplants on shelf

Work area

Lilies

Potted houseplants

Weeping birch
(*Betula pendula* 'Youngii')

Bench
(seating and storage)

Neighbor's maple tree

Dwarf Alberta spruce
(*Picea glauca* 'Conica')

Astilbe

Potted houseplants
on shelf

Dining area

Bench
(seating and storage)

Pots of annuals and
perennials

Climbing hydrangea
(*H. anomala petiolaris*)

Bench
(seating and storage)

Golden chain tree
(*Laburnum
anagyroides*)

Peegee hydrangea
(*H. paniculata* 'Grandiflora')

Siberian pea tree
(*Caragana arborescens*)

Variegated
red twigged dogwood
(*Cornus alba* 'Elegantissima')

Pots of houseplants,
annuals and perennials

Honeysuckle vine   Lantana

Iris

Clematis vine

Goat or French willow
(*Salix caprea*)

Procumbent juniper
(*Juniperus chinensis
procumbens* 'Nana')

NORTH

Closely spaced containers on a 30-foot-long rooftop deck create a meandering path that leads around the dense collection of plants, past a dining space, to a small work area. Rectangular storage units are built along portions of the periphery with upholstered, cushioned tops that double as seating benches.

Plan for this garden is shown on opposite page.

THE PUBLIC FACE

A Charleston front garden faces the street with symmetrical plantings of cycas, azaleas and lilyturf.

Wisteria in full flower hides its sturdy wire support and embellishes an entire townhouse facade.

An English ivy carpet and twin junipers clipped to neat cork-screws add to the formal air of a front door.

A Portland, Oregon front lawn is replaced by an ever-changing mix of perennials, annuals and shrubs. Included are golden yellow yarrow and 'Early Sunrise' coreopsis, white candytuft and pearly everlasting *(Anaphalis margaritacea),* along with massed plantings of lavender, coral bells, daylilies, Japanese anemone, lilies, phlox, primula, goldenrod and delphinium.

A curved apartment building entry is a brilliant burst of spring tulips and azaleas.

An Alexandria garden gate is flanked by cherry laurels *(Prunus laurocerasus)* under-planted with lilyturf. Sourwood trees in their crimson autumn garb overhang boxes of white impatiens.

A matched set of graceful weeping birches adds to the symmetry of a front entrance.

A Brooklyn extravaganza of Queen Anne's lace and sunflowers is grown from seed. The brilliant pink petunias are descendants of hybrids that reverted to the natural species after being allowed to self-sow.

Chrysanthemum cascades in a front garden and a curbside strip improve a public sidewalk.

A hedge of Australian tea tree *(Leptospermum laevigatum)* in a San Francisco front garden effectively obliterates the street.

A Portland, Oregon gardener's whimsical sense of front-yard humor is a bare-bottomed juniper and neat globes.

Hanging gardens, London-style.

The overhanging ever-greens of a Kyoto, Japan home hint at the private garden within. Hidden behind wooden doors, stepping stones wend through a 16- by 64-foot moss-covered space, past a Japanese red pine whose bent trunk is artfully supported by two cedar poles. Plantings include ferns, Japanese holly, quince *(Chaeno-meles lagenaria)*, rhododendron, andromeda, *Cryptomeria japonica*, Japanese aucuba *(Aucuba japonica)* and cape-jasmine gardenia.
Nakane and Associates

A white flowering shrub althea *(Hibiscus syriacus)* overhangs a walled street facade. Inside, a curved path with raised bluestone beds accommodate shade-tolerant plants that include white fringed bleeding heart *(Dicentra eximia 'Alba')*, snakeroot *(Cimicifuga racemosa),* variegated lily-turf, plumbago, hosta and a *Kirengeshoma palmata,* with its oak-shaped leaves.

Nicolas H. Ekstrom, Garden Design

**CONTAINERS FOR
EVERY SEASON**

Not bathtub gin.

Plant pots come in
assorted shapes and
sizes.

Container planting begins with bottom holes, then a drainage layer (covered with a screen) and topsoil, perlite, peat moss and cow manure mixed well before planting.

Late in autumn a heavy planter is moved with the multiple roller method.

A container tree shares
its soil with spring
flowering bulbs.

Spring color along New York's elegant Park Avenue is from closely spaced tulips in broad planting beds that contain a scant two feet of soil.
Peter Van de Wetering, Inc.

Eggplant seedlings turned upside down are removed from their nursery tray for transplanting to their new home.

Ripening tomatoes are supported on a simple wood frame.

Marigolds share space with Egyptian or tree onions *(Allium cepa)* on a Manhattan rooftop.

On a small balcony, arborvitae and a late blooming rose are accompanied through autumn by window-box dwarf chrysanthemums.

A half-size whiskey barrel is a winter home for hemlock.

A black-tiled swimming pool is tucked into an L-shaped Georgetown garden that is 80 feet long and 42 feet at its widest portion. The excavated soil was used to create the gentle change of level that adds a third dimension and the impression of greater space. A dense, richly textured plant mix screens the pool from neighbors and the lower garden.

Oehme, van Sweden and Associates, Inc.

Plan for this garden is shown on opposite page.

Shrub althea
(*Hibiscus syriacus*)

Metake bamboo
(*Pseudosasa japonica*)

Pennyroyal
(*Mentha pulegium*)

Sweet bay magnolia
(*M. virginiana*)

Lythrum
'Morden's Pink'

Inula helenium

Hostas

Ferns

Black tiled swimming pool

Sedum spectabile
'Autumn Joy'

Rudbeckia
(*R. fulgida* 'Goldsturm')

Rudbeckias

Bluestone
steps

Oriental dogwood
(*Cornus kousa*)

Sourwood tree
(*Oxydendrum arboreum*)

*Calamagrostis
acutiflora* 'Stricta'

Japanese snowball
(*Styrax japonicus*)

Lilyturf (*Liriope
muscari* 'Big Blue')

Leatherleaf mahonia
(*M. bealei*)

*Brunnera
macrophylla*

Chinese witch hazel
(*Hamamelis mollis*)

Yucca
(*Y. filamentosa*)

Fountain grass
(*Pennisetum alopecuroides*)

Holly
(*Ilex fosteri*)

NORTH

Maiden grass
(*Miscanthus sinensis*
'Gracillimus')

Arbor

Plumbago
Ceratostigma plumbaginoides

There is nothing like the first hot days of spring when the gardener stops wondering if it's too soon to plant the dahlias and starts wondering if it's too late.
—Henry Mitchell, *The Essential Earthman,* 1981

8. Planting and Other Earth-Shattering Ideas

"You're lucky—your garden's complete," a neighbor grumbled at me one spring. I was so astonished I couldn't refute this case of misplaced envy. No garden is *ever* "complete." At least, I've yet to meet the gardener who thinks his is. Planting or transplanting (that's rearranging plants you already own) is, quite simply, a labor without end.

an early beginning   With locations for new plantings logged in on a copy of your cardboard plan, start planting hardy species as early in spring as you can face toiling outdoors. Assuming, that is, that your soil is no longer frozen or soggy wet. (If your soil is also no longer *friable*—crumbly and easily worked—don't even think of proceeding until you've read Chapter 6.)

prepare ahead   Upstairs gardeners should prepare their containers in advance by having them partially filled with a soil mix (see page 153).
Downstairs gardeners should prepare a hole that's large enough to accommodate a root ball comfortably.

a third dimension downstairs   Excavating holes in yards sometimes results in an abundance of soil, which you can use creatively to add to your third dimension. My leftover earth was piled in two parallel mounds. Each was about a foot high, 5 feet long and set far enough apart to walk between. The mounds were later planted with a mix of closely spaced annuals and perennials. By midsummer it looked like a colorful cottage garden lining a "sunken" path.

shrubs, small trees, hardy perennials

To prepare yard or container soil for a woody plant or hardy perennial, thoroughly stir into the area one handful of a granular 5-10-5 fertilizer for each foot of plant height. The new soil line around the plant's base must match the old, so this is the time to examine the planting hole's depth to be sure it matches the root ball's height. If you don't trust your eye, measure the hole by marking lengths on your shovel or trowel. Or test with easily moved plants by dropping them briefly into their future home.

B & B plants

Lift your B & B plant by supporting its root mass from *below.* This is especially important when raising it up to the rim of a tall container. Don't grab the trunk and let the root ball hang, or you'll tear all the roots you've paid for.

Lower the ball gently into its hole. Then stand back and see how it looks. This is your chance to rotate or tilt it and start branches heading the way you want them to grow. Once you're satisfied with the plant's appearance, cut and remove the cord encircling the top of the root ball and loosen the upper burlap.

cutting away the burlap

Yard gardeners can tuck the ends of natural burlap back into the hole since this material eventually disintegrates. Synthetic wrappers do not, so remove as much as you can reach without breaking the ball. Container gardeners should save all their tub space for soil and cut away as much wrapper as possible.

plastic or metal nursery pots

Hardy species in nursery pots should be watered just before planting. A good dousing is always beneficial, but it also makes it easier to slide plants out from containers. To slip a small plant from its nursery pot, turn it upside down while holding your open hand flat against the soil to keep it in place. If the plant refuses to move, sharply rap the *top* rim of its container.

You can handle a large plant easily by laying it on its side (preferably on a large sheet of plastic) and rapping its rim all around. When it slips out, use the sheet to support the root mass and lift the plant into its new home.

Plants in metal nursery pots are easier to cope with if the sides are slit. If the nursery didn't do this for you, do it yourself with metal shears—not pruners.

peat pots

Perennials and small woody species are also sold in heavy peat pots. These are supposed to disintegrate to allow the roots to come through. But that may not happen. Unless you *see* the roots infiltrating the sides of the pot, treat the plant like other containerized purchases and slide it out before planting.

pot-bound roots After extricating your plant from its container, look at its roots. Plants that have been in a nursery pot for any length of time will have a tight, dense mass of roots. But plants are not too smart. If you don't loosen their roots before you transplant them, the roots will weave themselves into ever tighter balls and the plant will die. You must help your purchase get started by *vigorously* scoring and scraping its surface roots. If your fingernails don't work, use a pruner, trowel or fork. Then tug the surface roots out all around.

plantable cardboard A few plants are sold in "plantable boxes." Roses from the Jackson & Perkins Company, for example, are typically tucked into these cardboard packs in specially blended soil. In this case, the box is essential for holding both new roots and soil together, so for fail-safe growing, follow the directions for planting the box, cutting away only the topmost portion. Unlike metal, plastic or peat, this pot will disintegrate.

Red chokeberry
Aronia arbutifolia
'Brilliantissima'

spacing for now and then It makes sense to heed the words of experienced nurserymen who warn against crowding plants that need air circulation or room to expand. But if nature abhors a vacuum, city gardeners abhor empty space. There's nothing more disheartening than looking at toothless gaps while your shrubs and trees mature.

You could choose to plant closely now and prepare to transplant in a few seasons (which is what happens anyway, when you change your mind about design). Or you can plant for an immediate effect by using "quick fillers" among the slower growers.

Here are some flowering plants for adding quick height or bulk:

FLOWERING QUICK FILLERS

| Sun Conditions | | | | | Annual or Tender Perennial | Hardy Perennial |
FS	SS	WS	NS			
x	x	x		Ageratum *(Ageratum* spp.*)*	x	
x	x			Aster *(Aster frikartii)*		x
	x	x	x	Astilbe *(Astilbe* spp.*)*		x
x	x	x		Begonia *(Begonia semperflorens)*	x	
	x	x	x	Bleeding heart *(Dicentra eximia)*		x
x	x			Butterfly weed *(Asclepias tuberosa)*		x
x	x	x		Caladium *(Caladium bicolor)*	x	
x	x			Canna *(Canna generalis)*	x	
	x	x	x	Celandine poppy *(Stylophorum diphyllum)*		x
x	x			Cockscomb *(Celosia* spp.*)*	x	
x	x	x	x	Coleus *(Coleus blumei)*	x	
x	x			Coneflower *(Rudbeckia* spp.*)*		x
x	x	x		Four-o'clock *(Mirabilis jalapa)*	x	
	x	x		Foxglove *(Digitalis purpurea)*		x
x	x	x		Geranium *(Pelargonium hortorum)*	x	
x	x	x		Globe thistle *(Echinops exaltatus)*		x
		x	x	Hollyhock *(Althaea rosea)*	x	
	x	x	x	Hosta *(Hosta* spp.*)*		x
	x	x	x	Impatiens *(Impatiens wallerana)*	x	
x	x			Lantana *(Lantana camara)*	x	
x	x	x		Lily *(Lilium* spp.*)*		x
x	x			Love-in-a-mist *(Nigella damascena)*	x	
x	x	x		Nicotiana *(Nicotiana alata)*	x	
x	x	x		Petunia *(Petunia hybrida)*	x	
x	x			Portulaca *(Portulaca* spp.*)*	x	
x	x			Russian sage *(Perovskia atriplicifolia)*		x
x	x	x		Salpiglossis *(Salpiglossis sinuata)*	x	
x	x			Spider flower *(Cleome spinosa)*	x	
x	x			Sunflower *(Helianthus* spp.*)*	x	
	x	x		Torenia *(Torenia fournieri)*	x	
x	x	x	x	Tropical houseplants (may not flower, but are good fillers anyway)	x	

seedlings of flowers, veggies and herbs

Once the danger of frost has passed, you can plant seedlings of cool-weather species outside—vegetables like lettuce, spinach, cabbage, broccoli, radishes and cauliflower, herbs like tarragon, thyme, sage, oregano and parsley, and flowers like pansies, petunias, sweet pea and stock. But wait until nighttime temperatures stabilize around 65F° before planting basil, tomatoes, peppers and eggplant and most other tender annuals. Transplant these seedlings late in the afternoon or on a cloudy, calm day when they're less likely to be burned by the sun and wind they're not used to.

plastic trays and peat Seedlings in plastic trays can be slid out by pushing them up from the bottom, or by turning them upside down and catching them in your outspread hand. Plant peat pots (the thin-shelled kind like "Jiffy-7's") after soaking them well and making a vertical slit down each side so that roots can exit easily. Cut the rim off too so that after planting it is completely covered with soil and moisture is not wicked into the air by capillary action.

setting the soil line Once your plant is in place, backfill the surrounding area. Shrubs, vines and trees should be planted no higher or lower than they were originally grown. You can see where this was by the line of dry, woody bark at the base of their trunk.
Seedlings of flowers, vegetables or herbs, however, are best planted slightly deeper than originally grown to ensure that all roots are buried.

backfilling Eliminate subsurface air in the soil by tamping firmly around your newly planted plant. Yard gardeners can do this by pressing gently with their foot or the broad handle of a shovel. Leave a shallow surrounding moat so that rainwater is directed toward the roots. Container gardeners can use their palm or fist to firm the soil, but make sure it stops at least an inch below the rim of the container. This keeps the soil from sloshing over the top and leaves room for the final planting layer—the mulch.

the importance of mulch A mulch is a protective soil surface cover that reduces the caking and crusting caused by rain, wind and sun. For gardeners—both upstairs and down—mulches help stabilize soil temperatures, keep the soil moist and inhibit the growth of weeds. Like sensible footwear, some mulches are fundamentally practical; others, like party frocks, are strictly decorative. The trick is to combine the best of both.

newsprint Take newsprint, for example. When it comes to cheap and practical, a newsprint mulch ranks high. It also is highly ugly. Newsprint is best used tucked beneath a decorative blanket of bark chips, pebbles or shells. It's best, too, to use layers of two or three sheets shredded to a width of several inches to allow the soil to breathe and the rain to penetrate. Since a newspaper mulch eventually decays, at season's end you can turn it under the soil when you cultivate. (After reading the news it's consoling to know that my *Times* at least helps my plants.)

A CHOICE OF MULCHES

Mulch	Comments
autumn leaves	
bark chips or shreds	usually darkens with age; good for windy rooftops
bird cage droppings	
black pebbles	more decorative than useful
black plastic	smothers weeds like nothing else; perforate so water penetrates
buckwheat hulls	fine texture; blows easily in wind
cat litter	must be unused only
cocoa bean shells	adds the aroma of chocolate for weeks
coffee grounds	for acid-tolerant plants only
compost	partially decomposed is best
Christmas boughs	a good way to recycle
finely chopped eggshells	superb for herbs and vegetables; the white color discourages dog owners from visiting street trees
freshly pruned leaves	chop before using
grass clippings	
licorice root	very handsome and very hard to find
marble chips	not for woodland plants
newsprint	cheap and efficient
peanut shells	good source of nutrients; may attract rodents
salt hay	may contain weed seeds; blows easily in wind
seashells	not for acid-tolerant species
seaweed	hose off sea salt
tea leaves	for acid-tolerant species only
wood fireplace ashes	good for herbs, flowers and vegetables; blows easily in wind
wood shavings or sawdust	add nitrogen if the shavings are fresh

making a choice   With so many choices, it's hard to know which to use. But in the small city space aesthetics come first. Small-scale mulches are for small tubs, window boxes and narrow paths. Dark colors add a quiet backdrop. White brightens shade. Mulches should also be chemically compatible with the plants they surround. Marble chips and seashells leach lime, so keep them away from plants like rhododendrons that need acid soil; tea and coffee grounds are acidic, so keep them away from vegetables and herbs (see page 141). Avoid peat moss mulch altogether; when wet and soggy, it encourages stem rot and when dry, it's an impervious crust.

the outdoor carpet   Grass has been used as an outdoor carpet since ancient times, so if concrete sidewalks get you down, the antidote may be a greensward. The cheapest way to grow a lawn is to start from seed, and botanists have developed hybrids for every soil and light condition. Since a blend of grasses is usually most practical, seed is sold in mixtures. In cool climates, for example, a box of grass seed might include fescue, ryegrass, Kentucky bluegrass and bentgrass, while a warm climate mix may include Bermuda grass, carpetgrass, St. Augustine and zoysia. The assortment you find at your local nursery is very likely the best for your area, so read the package label to find the one that sounds right for you. Look for mixtures of named varieties like 'Victa' Kentucky bluegrass or 'Pennant' perennial rye grass and choose a mix that contains a low proportion of weed seeds and other undesirable ingredients.

the instant lawn   But as with any plant started from seed, if growing conditions are not ideal—if it's too hot, sunny and dry or too cold, shady and wet—grass seed germination can be slow, or not at all. If the idea of an instant lawn appeals, the answer is sod. Sod eliminates the wait and possibility of failure. Sod also eliminates the battles with rampaging children, pets, seed-eating pigeons, rats and other city marauders. Sod comes in precut strips, typically 1½ feet by 5 feet. There are also different sods for different conditions.

upstairs or down   To prepare a downstairs garden for sod (or grass seed), loosen the soil to a depth of 4–6 inches and scratch into the surface several shovelfuls of lime and a 5-10-5 fertilizer. Using a spade or heavy pruning shears, cut the sod sheets to size. Fit them in, press them firmly in place and water well.
Sod can also be grown on a rooftop garden (assuming no drainage hole is covered and no management's complaints are filed). To prepare an upstairs garden for sod, cover the portion to be planted with a protec-

tive polyethylene sheet. Edge it with 2-by-4-inch wood strips or a flexible plastic garden border. Add a 4–6-inch layer of container soil mix (see page 153) blended with several trowels of lime. Cut and fit the sheets, and water well (as noted above). And presto: instant lawn.

lawn alternatives   But think before you grow. And beware of grass addiction. A lawn can take over your life.

Grass demands continual attention to watering, fertilizing, refurbishing—and mowing. Having watched in disbelief as my husband "mowed" our 5-square-foot "lawn" with a pair of scissors on his hands and knees (is it indigenous to the genus *Husbandius* to *naturally* begin to mow?), I decided it was time for a ground cover.

ground covers   Ground covers, as you will quickly discover, are handsome, hassle-free alternatives to grass. They are also practical planting solutions for steep slopes and a decorative planting solution for open spaces between paving stones.

Here's a sampling of ground covers to try:

PLANTS TO USE AS GROUND COVERS

Sun Conditions					Deciduous	Evergreen	Flowers
FS	SS	WS	NS				
	x	x	x	**Astilbe** *(Astilbe chinensis* 'Pumila'*)*	x		x
x	x	x	x	**Boston ivy** *(Parthenocissus tricuspidata)*	x		
x	x	x	x	**Bugleweed** *(Ajuga reptans)*		(semi)	x
	x	x	x	**Bunchberry** *(Cornus canadensis)*		x	x
	x	x	x	**Canadian ginger** *(Asarum canadense)*	x		
x	x	x		**Cotoneaster** *(Cotoneaster horizontalis)*		x	x
	x	x	x	**Dead nettle** *(Lamium maculatum)*		(semi)	x
x	x	x	x	**English ivy** *(Hedera helix* 'Baltica'*)*		x	
	x	x	x	*Epimedium* spp.		(semi)	x
x	x			*Euonymus fortunei minimus*		x	

PLANTS TO USE AS GROUND COVERS

FS	SS	WS	NS		Deciduous	Evergreen	Flowers
Sun Conditions							
	x	x	x	European ginger *(Asarum europaeum)*		x	
	x	x	x	Foamflower *(Tiarella cordifolia)*	x		x
	x	x	x	Gill-over-the-ground *(Glecoma hederacea)*	x		
x	x	x		Hen-and-chickens *(Sempervivum tectorum)*		x	
	x	x		Lily-of-the-valley *(Convallaria majalis)*	x		x
x	x	x		Lilyturf *(Liriope* spp.*)*		(semi)	x
	x	x	x	Lungwort *(Pulmonaria officinalis)*	x		x
x	x			Maiden pink *(Dianthus deltoides)*	x		x
	x	x		Moneywort *(Lysimachia nummularia)*	x		x
	x	x	x	Moss		x	
x	x	x	x	Mint *(Mentha* spp.*)*	x		x
x	x	x	x	Pachysandra *(Pachysandra terminalis)*		x	x
x	x	x		Periwinkle *(Vinca minor)*		x	x
x	x	x		*Phlox divaricata* and *P. stolonifera*	x		x
x	x			Pussytoes *(Antennaria dioica)*		(semi)	x
x	x			Snow-in-summer *(Cerastium tomentosum)*	x		x
x	x	x		Stonecrop *(Sedum* spp.*)*		x	x
x	x	x		Sweet woodruff *(Asperula odorata)*	x		x
x	x			Thyme *(Thymus serpyllum)*	x		x
	x	x		Violet *(Viola* spp.*)*	x		x
		x	x	Wintergreen *(Gaultheria procumbens)*		x	

East meets West in town

Not since the nineteenth century, when the Victorians "discovered" Japan, has Oriental garden design held such appeal, especially in town, where space is a luxury. A true understanding of Japanese garden design can take a lifetime, but some useful techniques can be briefly summarized for use in a small urban site.

some useful techniques

Particularly effective are such architectural elements as white stucco walls to add brightness, weathered stones or irregular and rough-surfaced paths for texture, and diagonal paths, which give an illusion of space.

When it comes to planting, asymmetry is the rule, and plants are grouped in odd numbers—three, five or seven to a cluster. To add an illusion of depth, the eye may be forced through a kind of false perspective. One method is through a duplication of plant form or shape. In the foreground, for example, there might be a large-leaved, rounded plant like rhododendron or a perennial like hosta 'Big Daddy.' A similarly shaped but smaller-leaved species—an azalea or *Hosta lancifolia*—is then placed toward the rear. Or a Japanese black pine, which has relatively coarse, long needles, might be echoed by a Japanese white pine, which has finer-textured needles that are half as long.

Since the Japanese think of their garden as a year-round spatial arrangement, evergreens are important. Color is used with restraint and plants define, rather than decorate, the space.

the front-door garden

Open to the street but not public, within the property line but not private, a front-door planting is a most peculiar garden. On narrow sidewalks this foyerlike transition to the house or apartment may actually start with a street tree or a single tub at the curb. Front-door plantings are exceptionally vulnerable. Daffodils may disappear before fading in spring. Branches may be ripped and defoliated in summer. And chrysanthemums may evaporate even before Halloween.

It was no joke when my neighbor's rare rhododendron was stolen, but front-garden vandalism does occasionally have its ludicrous moments. There was the time when the huge golden heads of a row of 5-foot-tall sunflowers disappeared, one each night, for a week.

Weeping crabapple
Malus 'Red Jade'

advantages of the cheap or well anchored

Dedicated frontyard gardeners manage to shrug off these depressing aspects (I try to convince myself that plant vandalism is ignorance born of horticultural enthusiasm). But on heavily traveled streets it's prudent to resist the temptation of trying to impress your neighbors with exotic or expensive species or containers, and concentrate on those most likely to remain.

You may wish, for example, to discreetly bolt portable containers to the sidewalk or wall. One nurseryman I know secures the root balls of expensive shrubs and small trees by encircling them with heavy wires or chains prior to planting and then anchors these to weights hidden beneath the soil.

Another ploy is to use only commonly found, inexpensive plants whose loss or destruction will be less painful for you to bear. Or use plants with natural barbs whose removal is too painful for the vandal to bear.

natural barbs

This approach to "offensive gardening" was honed to a fine point by one desperate gardener who twined barbed wire unobtrusively through her ground cover and around her roses. The following list of hardy thorny plants—which may succeed as a deterrent—was compiled by a friend and fellow frontyard gardener, Patti Hagan:

PLANTS WITH OFFENSIVE THORNS

Sun Conditions					Deciduous	Evergreen
FS	SS	WS	NS			
x	x	x		American holly *(Ilex opaca)*		x
x	x	x	x	Barberry *(Berberis* spp.*)*		*(semi)*
x	x			Blackberry *(Rubus* spp.*)*	x	
x	x			Carline thistle *(Carlina acaulis)*	x	
x	x	x		Firethorn *(Pyracantha coccinea)*		*(semi)*
x	x	x		Globe thistle *(Echinops ritro)*	x	
x	x			Hardy orange *(Poncirus trifoliata)*	x	
x	x			Prickly pear cactus *(Opuntia compressa)*		x
x	x			Roses:	x	
				Father Hugo's rose *(Rosa hugonis)*		
				Sweetbriar rose *(R. eglanteria)*		
				Scotch rose *(R. spinosissima)*		
				R. rugosa		
x	x			Scotch thistle *(Onopordum acanthium)*	x	
x				Sea holly *(Eryngium maritimum)*	x	
x	x			Stinging nettle *(Urtica dioica)*	x	
x	x			Teasel *(Dipsacus sylvestris)*	x	

useful invaders There's a time and place for every plant, and that includes the group derisively called "invasive." A rapid spreader or a plant that sprawls without shame may be just what's needed in a spot so troublesome nothing else grows. This could be a problem corner of your backyard or rooftop—or a vulnerable front door. Here's a sampling to try:

USEFUL INVADERS

Sun Conditions					Deciduous	Evergreen
FS	SS	WS	NS			
x	*x*	*x*	*x*	Ajuga *(Ajuga reptans)*		*(semi)*
x	*x*			Bamboo *(Phyllostachys* spp.*)*	*x*	*(some)*
x	*x*	*x*		Beebalm *(Monarda didyma)*	*x*	
x	*x*	*x*	*x*	Boston ivy *(Parthenocissus tricuspidata)*	*x*	
x	*x*	*x*		Cinquefoil or Creeping potentilla *(Potentilla canadensis)*	*x*	
	x	*x*	*x*	Dead nettle *(Lamium maculatum)*	*x*	
x	*x*	*x*	*x*	English ivy *(Hedera helix)*		*x*
x	*x*			Evening primrose *(Oenothera fruticosa)*	*x*	
x	*x*			Goldenrod *(Solidago* spp.*)*	*x*	
	x	*x*	*x*	Goutweed *(Aegopodium podagraria)*	*x*	
x	*x*			Lamb's ears *(Stachys byzantina)*		*(semi)*
	x	*x*		Lily-of-the-valley *(Convallaria majalis)*	*x*	
x	*x*			Loosestrife *(Lysimachia clethroides)*	*x*	
x	*x*			Maiden grass *(Miscanthus sinensis* 'Gracillimus'*)*	*x*	
x	*x*	*x*		Mint *(Mentha* spp.*)*	*x*	
x	*x*			Mugwort *(Artemisia vulgaris)*	*x*	
	x	*x*	*x*	Pachysandra *(Pachysandra terminalis)*		*x*
x	*x*			Plume poppy *(Macleaya cordata)*	*x*	
x	*x*			Purple loosestrife *(Lythrum salicaria)*	*x*	
	x	*x*	*x*	Snakeroot *(Cimicifuga racemosa)*	*x*	
x	*x*	*x*		Spiderwort *(Tradescantia virginiana)*	*x*	
x	*x*	*x*		Stonecrop *(Sedum acre)*		*x*
	x	*x*	*x*	Violet *(Viola* spp.*)*	*x*	

floor cleanups The planting day ends with the cleanup.

Large garbage bags are handy for the many items to be disposed of. Also handy where there's more sidewalk than soil are a broom and dustpan. I have a plastic set exclusively for outdoor use—and that's just where I keep them. But then I admit to a certain determination about keeping my garden path clean. I also believe in cleaning rooftop terrace tiles sailor style, swabbing away with an outdoor mop. Folks who are less fussy should find a broom will suffice.

water at last After the planting debris is removed and the walks are swept, *water* all your newly planted additions thoroughly. Then, at last, you can sit back—chilled drink in hand—and take the time to admire your handiwork. Having made it this far, there's nothing wrong with some discreet self-satisfaction.

Columbine
Aquilegia sp.

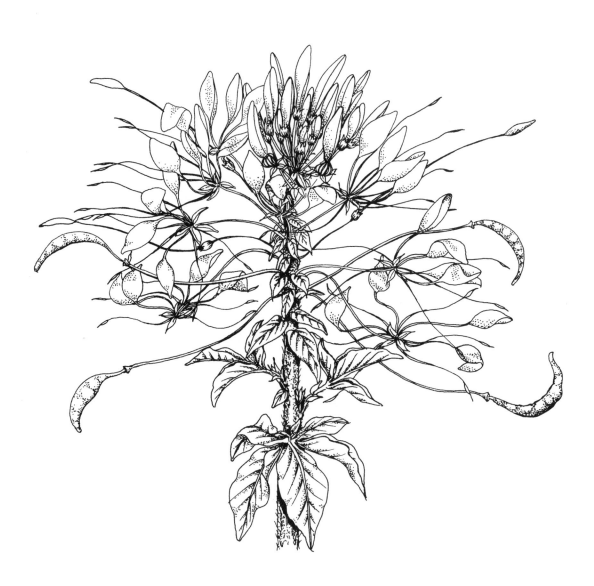

Cleome or Spiderflower
Cleome spinosa

It will soon be clear that until it has been tamed, a hose is an extraordinarily evasive and dangerous beast, for it contorts itself . . . jumps . . . wriggles . . . makes puddles of water, and dives with delight into the mess it has made.
—Karel Čapek, *The Gardener's Year,* 1931

9. Water Comes Not from Heaven Alone

In the hanging Gardens of Babylon water was hauled in leather buckets to a topside storage area for later distribution to planting levels below. Those ancient gardeners knew better than to rely on gods for moisture—and neither should you.

the finger test   The question, then, is, how do you know when your plants need water? No one who heard him will forget the spirited reply of the late Louis Politi, horticulturist at the New York Botanical Garden. When queried by his students, he would answer with passion, "Don't be afraid to ruin your manicure—stick your fingers into the soil and find out how wet it is!" And I can't beat that for accuracy and succinctness.

when to water   I always try to water my garden first thing in the morning. The air is sweet and fresh, and there's no more glorious beginning to a day than peaceful moments among fragrant flowers and herbs. More important, an early-morning watering gives plants the maximum daylight hours in which to make use of the moisture in their soil. When the morning is inconvenient, my plants get a mid- or early-afternoon shower. Long ago I chose to ignore the old saw that insists "plants must never be watered in full sun." As with all such tales, this myth includes a little bit of fact and a lot of fiction.

There is only one truth in watering, and that is its goal: a *thorough* wetting of the entire root zone.

a myth explored　Let's say that each day the gardener appears promptly at noon and lightly sprinkles the parched soil. In their search for moisture, roots grow *up* toward this miserly offering. If superficial watering like this occurs repeatedly, the roots eventually surface and the sun is sure to burn them. Of course, the plant then weakens and dies, lending credence to the warnings on midday watering. On the other hand, if the water quantity is sufficient to permeate the entire root mass, the roots have no reason to move upward. Safely below ground, where they belong, no fiery sun can harm them.

wet foliage　Often bandied about, too, is a belief that wet foliage is "burned" by sunshine. For years I hosed my plants in midday sun—with nary a dire consequence—ignoring yet another tale I suspected was fallacious. My observations were confirmed by the late T. H. Everett, the eminent horticulturist, who wrote in his definitive *Encyclopedia of Horticulture,* "In high summer, when light is most intense, bright sunshine frequently follows showers, commonly with advantage to growing plants."

never in darkness　Unfortunately, garden lore gives insufficient space to the dangers of evening watering. Moisture and darkness is the environment of choice for many impudent pests, among them slugs and mosquitoes, as well as a range of nasty diseases like downy mildew and black spot. To habitually water at night is to needlessly open your garden to trouble.

roots in the ground　When it comes to coping with watering, gardeners with plants growing *in* the ground definitely have an easier time of it than those with plants on top of the ground in containers. Roots of plants in the ground are free to find water in areas other than immediately at their base. (Although in utility-riddled, rocky subsurfaces like New York this quest isn't always easy.) It's not unusual to find roots of mature trees, shrubs or vines dozens or even hundreds of feet away from their trunk. Moisture from rain may remain for days to quench plants' thirst in ground-level gardens.

roots in containers　Plants in containers have less soil to begin with. And confined roots have nowhere else to search. Moisture disappears quickly from containers, leaching out the bottom, and evaporating from its sides. Life is even harder for plants like rhododendrons and ligularias, whose dense canopy of large leaves acts as an umbrella and sends the rain over the container's side. There may be times when nothing at all reaches the soil.

So while a light summer shower may possibly benefit plants in the ground, it is positively harmful for those in containers; the gardener is fooled.

save that hole   Maybe you're tempted at this point to solve the problem by using containers with no drainage holes at all. And I admit it sounds great in theory. But in fact a pond of stagnant water will collect at the container's bottom and the plants will die from rot or lack of oxygen around their roots. Bog plants and aquatics are the only plants that can grow in a tub with no drainage.

overwatering   Which brings up the question of overwatering container plants outside.
containers   I've already stressed the importance of a good soil mix, an adequate drainage layer and drainage holes. Assuming these are in order, it is rare that a container plant on a rooftop, balcony or terrace dies from overwatering. Trees and shrubs in containers outdoors usually die from *underwatering*. (Their situation should not be confused with houseplants *indoors,* where environmental conditions are so different.)

to each its own   Most trees, shrubs, vines and flowers—whether grown in containers or in the ground—do best with a regular, deeply penetrating watering that's generous enough to soak the entire root ball. (Or, as I used to say when nagging the workmen who tended the street trees in front of my apartment building, "Put enough water into the soil to reach the top of the tree.")

A majority of plants, then, prefer to achieve a *nearly* dry state before the watering is repeated.

When you buy a plant, find out if it falls into this category or if its water preference is at one of the extremes—which range from bog to desert.

some like it wet   Although summer vegetables like cucumbers, melons, squash and tomatoes need good moisture to develop, plants whose natural habitat is close to streams or forests do best if they're always somewhat damp. Unless you're prepared to spend your garden hours watering, put plants like these in a spot that suits them. Maybe you have an artificial bog or subsurface stream that was long ago buried by civilization's steady march. If you do, here are some plants you can grow:

PLANTS THAT TOLERATE MOIST SOILS

FS	SS	WS	NS	Sun Conditions	Flowers
x	x	x		Bamboo (*Phyllostachys* spp.)	
	x	x	x	Bleeding heart (*Dicentra eximia*)	x
	x	x		Bog rosemary (*Andromeda glaucophylla*)	x
	x	x		Cardinal flower (*Lobelia cardinalis*)	x
x	x	x		Corkscrew willow (*Salix matsudana* 'Tortuosa')	
x	x	x		Feather reed grass (*Calamagrostis acutiflora stricta*)	(*plumes*)
	x	x	x	Horsetail (*Equisetum hyemale*)	
x	x	x		Japanese sedge grass (*Carex morrowii* 'Aurea Variegata')	
	x	x	x	Ligularia (*Ligularia* spp.)	x
x	x			Marsh marigold (*Caltha palustris*)	x
	x	x	x	Maidenhair fern (*Adiantum pedatum*)	
x	x	x		Mint (*Mentha* spp.)	x
		x	x	Mosses	
	x	x	x	Ostrich fern (*Mattencia struthiopteris*)	
x	x	x		Pussy willow (*Salix discolor*)	
x	x	x		Red osier dogwood (*Cornus sericea*)	x
	x	x	x	Royal fern (*Osmunda regalis*)	
	x	x		Summersweet (*Clethra alnifolia*)	x
	x	x		Sweet flag (*Acorus calamus*)	x
		x	x	Trillium (*Trillium* spp.)	x
	x	x	x	Turtlehead (*Chelone* spp.)	x
	x	x	x	Violet (*Viola* spp.)	x

the dry ones At the other extreme are plants that prefer arid conditions—that are not happy with "wet feet" (as gardeners anthropomorphically put it). These are the plants to use where winds are hot and dry, as on a windy, exposed rooftop. You can recognize many of these by their thick, fleshy stems or leaves or silvery color.

xeriscaping Water can no longer be regarded as the cheap, unlimited resource it was once thought to be, and in some regions restrictions are now a daily fact of life. Drought-tolerant plants have become increasingly important as water conservation is mandated by more and more communities. Water-sensible gardening or xeriscaping (from the Greek *xeros* for dry) means selecting plants that can survive with reduced rations. The xeriscaping movement began in Denver, Colorado, where landscapers worked with the water department to develop a conservation approach for gardeners. If your region has regular water shortages, look for local xeriscape organizations and programs to learn more about the most suitable plants. Here's a sampling to start with:

Fountain Grass
Pennisetum alopecuroides

PLANTS WITH MINIMAL WATER NEEDS

FS	SS	WS	NS	Sun Conditions	Flowers
x	x			Bar Harbor juniper *(Juniperus horizontalis* 'Bar Harbor'*)*	
x	x			Black-eyed Susan *(Rudbeckia hirta)*	x
x	x			Blue fescue *(Festuca ovina* 'Glauca'*)*	
x	x			Chicory *(Cichorium intybus)*	x
x	x			Coreopsis *(Coreopsis verticillata)*	x
x	x	x		Cotoneaster *(Cotoneaster* spp.*)*	x
x	x			Cleome *(Cleome hasslerana)*	x
x	x			Dusty miller *(Artemisia stellariana)*	
x	x			Goldenrain tree *(Koelreuteria paniculata)*	x
x	x			Goldenrod *(Solidago virgaurea)*	x
x	x	x	x	Hall's honeysuckle *(Lonicera japonica)*	x
x	x	x		Honey locust *(Gleditsia triacanthos)*	
x	x	x		Japanese barberry *(Berberis thunbergii)*	x
x	x	x		Lamb's ears *(Stachys lanata)*	x
x	x			Lavender *(Lavandula angustifolia)*	x
x	x			Lavender cotton *(Santolina chamaecyparissus)*	x
x	x	x		Lilyturf *(Liriope mucari)*	x
x	x			Mullein *(Verbascum phoenicum)*	x
x	x			Portulaca *(Portulaca grandiflorum)*	x
x	x			Quaking grass *(Briza maxima)*	*(plumes)*
x	x			Queen Anne's lace *(Daucus carota)*	x
x	x	x		Russian olive *(Elaeagnus angustifolia)*	
x	x			Russian sage *(Perovskia atriplicifolia)*	x
x	x	x		Sedum *(Sedum* spp.*)*	x
x	x			Shasta daisy *(Chrysanthemum superbum)*	x
x	x	x		Smoketree *(Cotinus coggygria)*	x
x	x	x		Spiderwort *(Tradescantia* spp.*)*	x
x	x			Sunflower *(Helianthus* spp.*)*	x
x	x			Tamarix *(Tamarix* spp.*)*	x
x	x			Thyme *(Thymus* spp.*)*	x
x	x			Yarrow *(Achillea* spp.*)*	x
x	x	x	x	Yew *(Taxus* spp.*)*	
x	x			Yucca *(Yucca filamentosa)*	x

confronting your retention

Your plants' water needs may also be affected by your microclimates—wind, sun, walls or other environmental aspects. Because of these small climatic conditions, a plant at one end of your yard or rooftop terrace may demand much more water—or much less—than the same plant at the other end. You don't have to transplant them, but you do have to change your watering procedure accordingly.

upstairs dehydration

Upstairs gardeners in particular may find certain corners unusually hot and dry in summer and cold and dry in winter. Environmentally caused dehydration may differ in origin from that caused by the plant's food-making process or photosynthesis, but the need for water can be even greater.

Black Bamboo
Phyllostachys nigra

controlling soil moisture

And then there's the water-retaining property of the soil itself. If your planting area is a manageable size, you just might effect one of the following changes:

To *decrease* the soil's moisture-holding capacity and improve drainage, mix in more sand or perlite.

To *increase* the soil's moisture-holding property and help retard drainage, mix in more organic matter like humus, compost and peat moss.

soil polymers The latter method, of course, is the old-fashioned way to increase a soil's moisture-retaining ability. But now, thanks to the magic of modern science, there is an even fancier way, which is by adding synthetic polymers (or polyacrylamide). Synthetic polymers are substances that act like little sponges and absorb up to several hundred times their weight in moisture. By holding onto moisture that normally drains away, plants that normally need watering every few days may now be left for a week or more. First tested by the USDA in the 1970s, soil polymers were originally available only to commercial growers. They are now marketed to home gardeners under trade names like Water Grabber and Broadleaf P4, and (according to the manufacturers) their water-holding ability is good for up to 5 years.

Blend soil polymers into the soil in quantities listed on the label (typically 1 ounce per 60 pounds of soil). Although it's possible to add them around plants already in place, it's more efficient if you stir them into the soil before planting.

container compatibility Containers permit enormous design flexibility. But where two or more plants are growing together, they should have compatible soil and water needs—ferns with azaleas, say, or portulaca with yucca. Use separate tubs if you want woodland and desert plants to be amenable neighbors.

the mystery of the missing faucet As an economy measure for construction companies, high-rise apartment terraces are sometimes built without outdoor spigots. So the caring gardener is forced through the living room with pitchers of water for thirsty plants. If you find that you must face this chore (as I did), you'd better decide quickly how you intend to cope. For in an understandable effort to save yourself work, you will certainly water less than you should.

the watering can One solution is the lightweight plastic watering pail, and I found that a 2-gallon can was ideal. Less than 2 gallons means too many trips back to the faucet; more than 2 gallons is too heavy to carry and is impossible to fill at a kitchen or bathroom source.

indoor hookups But however tiny your space, if there's more than one shrub to care for, a hose is a must. And don't despair if there's no outdoor spigot. Thanks to a gadget called a snap coupler, you can hook a hose to the nearest kitchen or bathroom faucet, snake it out through a window or door and thus

reduce your watering job to merely running back and forth to modulate water pressure and temperature—which still beats using a pail.

Snap couplers are sold at hardware or plumbing suppliers. Before you run out and buy, check the position and measure the threads on the faucet you choose to hook up to.

the hose

Lightweight 25-, 50- or 100-foot hoses with a ½- or ⅝-inch diameter are sold at garden shops as well as hardware or dime stores. Prices vary considerably, but this is no time to scrimp. A cheap hose kinks so easily you'll curse every time you use it.

for chores

This hose, after all, will also come in handy for other chores, like cleaning off your sidewalk, terrace or balcony floor, not to mention washing your awning, windows, outdoor furniture—*and* plants. The city is a sooty place, and if you think your windowsills are grimy, your plants' leaves are too.

keep those plants clean

While a good friend will not notice your dirty foliage, this is a problem beyond mere aesthetics.

Plants are living things. A coat of soot reduces their ability to take advantage of sunlight and manufacture their food. In so doing they "breathe" by absorbing carbon dioxide and other pollutants through the stomata or microscopic openings on their leaves. Oxygen is then released into the atmosphere. If they can't do this, they eventually falter and die.

If you need a cosmic excuse to keep your plants clean, remember that *each* leaf is a filtering mechanism that creates fresh air. Or, as someone once said, plants are the "oldest, cheapest and most efficient air purifiers on earth."

when you're away from your containers

If you're a container gardener who must be away during the growing season, you must also face the problem of who will water your plants. If your trip is only for a day or two, you can leave them in nature's care. But for a longer stay it's better to find a responsible friend willing to accept the privilege of enjoying your garden in return for caring for plants.

Remember that the tendency for the uninitiated will be to *underwater*. So provide your caretaker with graphic instructions about which species need what (like: "drown that rhododendron—but ignore the sedums"). If your friend enjoys gardening, directives can be minimal. But if the friend is just being friendly . . . well, you can console yourself with the thought that most healthy plants have remarkable powers of regeneration.

houseplants outdoors There's nothing like treating houseplants to a summer vacation outside. But tiny pots can be unbelievably demanding. To reduce watering chores, group small pots together in a large container and surround them with soil, newspaper or sphagnum moss.

Lamb's Ears
Stachys lanata

dreams of water automation At some point it's natural to dream of easing the burden of watering, and sprinklers were once *the* method of choice. Unfortunately, sprinklers are not only inefficient but grossly wasteful of water. They are also useless, of course, for the container garden upstairs.

a basic watering system Years ago, on the large rooftop garden I owned at the time, I added one of the earliest irrigation systems then available to home gardeners. It was a simple setup that consisted of a main water line of ¾-inch-diameter self-sealing polyvinyl tubing. Plugged into this main at intervals as needed to distribute water to each plant, was a series of "spaghetti" feeders (so called, I presume, because that's what they look like). Their numbers were increased or decreased, according to each plant's water needs. For a while I controlled—manually—both the length of time of each watering and the number of times each week it was done. And since I am somewhat old-fashioned, it took several seasons before I felt it appropriate to relinquish this job to an automated clock.

more systems   Since that time, many manufacturers have aspired to satisfy demands of increasingly sophisticated gardeners, and many new devices have appeared. Collectively known as "drip irrigation," they are marketed under such picturesque names as Drip Mist, Sunshower, Rain Bird, Hydro-Grow, Rainjet, Gardena and the Leaky Pipe (really!). When you finally opt for one of these systems, remember that a change from manual labor to automation is easier said than done. And a homemade installation can be quite a challenge.

The basic idea remains simple. One or more primary lines bring the water to the yard or rooftop terrace. Secondary lines—now a choice of soakers, drippers or sprays—distribute this water to the plants.

and gadgets   Optional gadgets include an automated timer (operated by electricity or battery) or soil moisture sensor (which controls the flow depending on what is already in the soil). There are also water pressure regulators (to ensure an even supply), backflow preventers (required by some municipalities to keep water from siphoning back into the system), filters (to prevent clogging), shutoff valves (to control the water flow) and fertilizer injectors. It's a bewildering array of hardware, to be sure, so pick and choose selectively. Except for the choice of timer or moisture sensor, it is entirely likely you will find you need nothing extra at all.

Some gardeners are up to planning and installing a watering system themselves. Others are better off hiring a company that specializes in this work and guarantees continuing support. Whatever you choose, a successful irrigation system is worth every bit of time, effort and money it takes.

gray water   Gray water is the term used for household wastewater used as an alternative source of moisture for plants. Some enthusiasts enjoy dreaming up methods of collecting it and devices for transporting this treasure outside. Others may wonder if this is mostly a quixotic endeavor. It is important in any case to try to reuse whatever water you can, and the safest, most practical place to start is the kitchen.

It's not all that hard to keep a large pot handy to catch rinsewater from fruit and vegetables for recycling outdoors. Also recyclable is water run from the tap before hot water appears, and be sure too, to save water from boiled eggs (a good source of minerals) and that used for vegetables or frozen food packets (but remember to let it cool before tossing it onto your roses). Water with a hint of soap—as from rinsed dishes—is also acceptable for the garden providing there's no trace of grease, fat or oil.

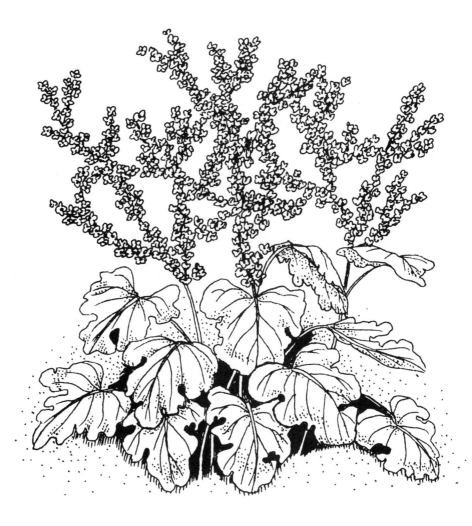

Colewort
Crambe cordifolia

watering containers in autumn

As the days of autumn shorten, plants enter a period of rest. While water requirements slowly decrease, some moisture is needed. If autumn rain is sparse, you must make up for its lack. As in the summer, the factors determining watering frequency include the species' needs, the daytime temperature, the amount of sun and wind the area receives and the soil type (in yards) or container size (on terraces).

You can safely stop watering *nearly* completely after the first killing frost or when all deciduous leaves are gone. Later, when winter slides into spring, the plants begin their period of growth and watering chores resume.

don't forget winter If you have come to realize the uselessness of a light summer shower for container plants, you may now realize the uselessness of light *winter* rain or snow. In winter, hardy trees and shrubs are dormant—not dead.

Again, it's up to you to notice the amount of winter rain or snow that has fallen over a period of months and determine its adequacy for your conditions and plants.

Winter needs of evergreens on a windy rooftop, for example, are greater than those of deciduous plants in a sheltered yard. Your neighbors may think you're nuts, but there may be times when you must water container plants in winter.

watering containers when it's cold The best time for winter watering is early morning during a week when temperatures have been above 40F°. This minimizes the possibility of the water freezing too quickly to be of benefit to the plant. Since hoses are often stored away and your outdoor spigot is likely inoperable, a watering can comes in handy. Fill it indoors, with *cold* water only, and remember that while the frequency of watering has diminished, the principle of a thorough drenching is unchanged.

the balcony ceiling A balcony ceiling completely eliminates the supply of natural water— summer rain and winter snow. In summer, your plants' need for moisture is obvious: the rains come, but the flowers droop from lack of water. In autumn and winter, with no wilting blooms as reminders, you can easily forget that your plants' need for moisture continues. When I was the owner of this kind of sheltered garden, it took two consecutive winters of losing expensive shrubs and trees to teach me the importance of year-round watering.

use your snow It's not for nothing that snow has been called the "poor man's mulch," and a clever city gardener takes advantage of whatever falls. Downstairs gardeners can shovel fresh snow from the sidewalk onto the soil around evergreens and street trees. Upstairs gardeners can scoop the snow from the floor and pile it onto the tubs (I convinced my children this was a great after-school game). Snow is the ideal winter insulator. It helps prevent rapid fluctuations of freezing and thawing and keeps plants dormant. But more important, melting snow is the best source of winter water.

will it rain today? Just as farmers have done for centuries, so the city gardener may glance upward, wondering if there will be rain or snow. Several years ago I splurged on a barometer so that I could have an idea of what to expect. Atmospheric pressure is indicated within a 5-hour period; a rapid rise means fair weather coming, a rapid fall means a storm. While the strength and direction of wind is also a factor (I still need that TV meteorologist), a barometer is a handy, handsome wall fixture that makes dispensing advice about umbrellas easier.

the rain gauge After the thunder and lightning are through, how do you know if enough moisture has fallen? The answer is a rain gauge. This inexpensive item is well worth its weight in gold. A rain gauge is nothing more than a clear plastic tube, maybe 10 inches high, that's marked with calibrated graduations. After a light summer sprinkle—or a major winter storm—the rain gauge tells the number of inches that really landed.

And you can be sure this rarely, if ever, is quite what you thought.

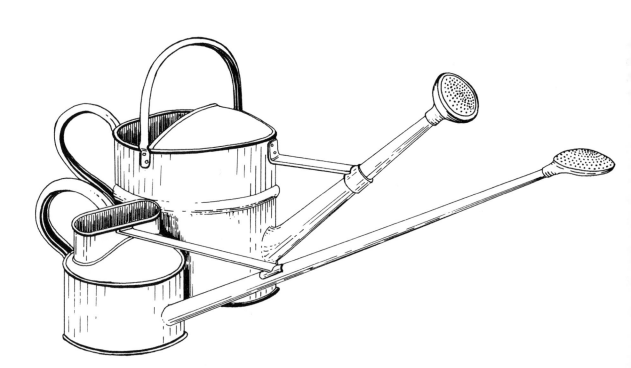

Autumn Crocus
Crocus speciosus

. . . come quick, sharp early frost! Obliterate some of this beauty!
Clear decks for the majesty of Autumn!
—Richardson Wright, *The Gardener's Bed-Book,* 1929

10. Continuing Through Autumn

The magic of the shifting seasons belongs to city folk who garden. It is our kaleidoscope of leaves that heralds winter's gray. But as the warmth of summer merges with the chill of fall a peculiar mood sets in. It's called the end-of-season blues.

end-of-season blues But this is not a mourning of the summer's passing. It is, instead, a longing for the months of dormancy to begin. Slowly but surely it overtakes the most devoted gardener.

I'm ashamed to say it, but every fall I think I've lost all interest in my treasured haven. Each day the garden grows a little less than perfect. Exhausted annuals fade. Weary perennials topple. And another shrub or tree falls prey to some mysterious marauder. Paths vanish under leaves as this once-conscientious gardener looks the other way. The sweeping, staking, pruning, hosing—all the joyous chores of sunny summer mornings —now are burdens more than I can bear.

Fall marks the start of a new school year and renewed civic involvements. Seasonal household chores demand the time that was once so peacefully spent outdoors. The sun seems to race to the horizon, and early darkness thwarts the pleasures of the garden at dusk. The job of taking in houseplants seems monumental. All I say is, "Lord, I hope spring never comes." I know I'm not alone in this yearning for the peace of winter.

It's autumn, after all. And people too must have a time of rest.

But it's still too soon to cover up the chairs and close the garden door for good. Autumn is for reassessing. With rude remembrances of summer's chores as well as pleasures, there's no better season for a truly objective view. There's no better time to deal firmly with experiments that failed, flowers that disappointed, plants whose leaves or outline proved unsettling, and species with immoral appeal for insects or disease.

Plants can *survive* demanding city conditions, but that's no guarantee of a performance to make you proud. For some species it's a case of wrong light. For others it's the wrong space. Or wrong scale, or wind. Or maybe just the wrong garden.

I've found that our feelings for plants are much like those we have for people. Some plants we truly love, others we truly abhor. I once had a fruiting shrub that for years refused to bear and a rose so thorny it threatened all who approached.

I admit to the greatest relief when both were gone.

Each autumn I think anew of that formidable mistress of Sissinghurst, Vita Sackville-West, who wrote, "if it displeases you the first year, get rid of it, for it will succeed in displeasing you every year thereafter."

With or without a "rational" reason, if a plant yields constant distress, don't agonize. Just get rid of it. Autumnal cleanup must include a cleansing of the soul.

Small or inexpensive plants are easily discarded. If the roots won't budge, cut the offender back and sever new shoots in spring. Expensive or unusual species are not so casually tossed in the trash, but you can absolve your guilt by sending your discard to a loving new home.

Canvass friends with gardens where a gift is appropriate, or look for a horticultural group that provides plants to community gardeners. In New York, for instance, an intrepid band called the Green Guerillas actively seeks and catalogues garden discards for redistribution. You could also consider donating the offender to a nonprofit institution. (But since you're the one who will foot the bill for transporting and replanting, save this method for last resort and check on a possible tax deduction for your "donation.")

Whatever method you choose, don't dispatch container plants to sites where they must remain in tubs unless you're sure the recipient is able to care for them. Schools, hospitals, and churches rarely can.

Throw unwanted plants away. Or give them away.

But spend your garden time enjoying every inch of your space.

borrowed autumn ambience

In my first autumn on a balcony, I had too few mature plants to generate what I considered proper seasonal ambience, so I "borrowed" some oak leaves from a country friend and tossed them all over the floor. I look back at this performance with astonishment. Autumn leaves are essential to the healthy city garden; *importing* them is going too far.

a leafy sweep

While country cousins furiously rake their fallen autumn leaves from lawns, we city folk—with more paving than soil—celebrate the season with dustpan and broom. Moist, rotting leaves collect in corners and behind, between and beneath furniture and plant containers. This provides a cozy haven for multilegged creatures and microscopic organisms—the next generation of summer's pests. A trip to the trash seems the simplest way to thwart their plans and ensure that rain and melted snow have a clear route down the drain.

life without a compost heap

But autumn leaves are nature's gift to gardeners. Left to decay, leaves release nutrients and improve soil by promoting a crumbly structure. Some years after my oak-leaf exchange, I moved to a larger terrace, where I finally had more autumn ambience than space. What a pity, I thought. Now I'm forced to discard these useful objects—but why can't I compost, just like country gardeners do?

At that point, the only compost piles I had seen were multicompart-mented contraptions that were also lingering eyesores. I couldn't imagine coping with compost in a small city space until, shortly thereafter, I met a rooftop gardener who did.

coping with compost

His heap was a study in simplicity: a slatted wood box about the size of an orange crate (which maybe it had been), raised an inch or so off the floor and topped with a hinged cover stained a nondescript shade. Into this went autumn leaves as well as summer clippings, chopped kitchen vegetable scraps and the commercial compost activator he felt he needed for the microbes that inspire decay. His compost pile did not smell. Nor was it visually offensive. It also occupied hardly any space at all. As he proudly dug through handfuls of homemade humus, I knew the time had come for me to give this composting business a try.

a whiskey barrel try

The only place I could find for my venture that year was a half-size whiskey barrel prepared for a plant I'd never bought. It measured 20 inches wide and high, had several holes in the bottom, and a shallow drainage layer of pebbles and twigs covered with soil. Into this tub I heaped all the fallen leaves I had. Every few inches I added a thin layer of soil and some packaged cow manure. Through the rest of the autumn I turned the pile whenever I remembered to do so (or could convince my children this churning was "fun") and watered between rains.

Late the following spring the original pile of leaves was reduced in volume. They were now a moist, crumbly, black-brown loam with a sweet aroma that reminded me of the woods. To my astonishment this "fresh" humus was also filled with squirming earthworms, leading me to accept, momentarily, that ancient belief that some creatures arise "spontaneously." (I suspect that eggs are present in the manure.)

For weeks thereafter, no one I encountered could escape any detail of my impressive achievement.

humus without tears   The secret to making compost is simply to mimic nature's example. And if you've ever been in a forest, that model is clear: any loose pile of leaves eventually decays—and this is true even if you stand around and do nothing. An organized approach merely speeds things along and ensures a rich yield that's there when you need it.

To do this in a small space, you need to balance moisture, air and the organic materials that produce high interior temperatures (the ideal is over 140F°). Heat accelerates decay and ensures the destruction of overwintering insect eggs and spores from summer's diseases. In a tiny pile, truly high temperatures may not be possible, but you can get reasonably close if you chop the soft ingredients into small pieces and leave out hard things like twigs.

no fungus, please   Mildew, fungus, or a malodorous stench are signs your pile is in trouble. The new additions may have been heaped too high or the ingredients packed too tightly. Regular turning facilitates the entry of air and distributes the microorganisms that promote decay.

compost additives   You can buy an "accelerator" to increase the presence of these beneficial microbes or increase your cache simply by adding cow manure. Also good is blood meal, cottonseed meal and fish meal.

Other useful ingredients to toss in your compost heap include:

banana skins	peanut shells
coffee grounds	seaweed (hose off the salt)
eggshells	straw or hay
fish scraps (turn under well)	sunflower hulls
fruit peelings	tea leaves
grass clippings	vegetable scraps
newspaper (shredded)	wood ashes

Animal fats from the kitchen should not be used. Neither should pet litter or manure from cats or dogs.

compost "makers" My whisky barrel has since been replaced by a variety of more fancy-looking compost "makers." The worst was a flimsy, round, plastic enclosure that jiggled merrily when the pile was turned. The best—from a mail-order catalogue and still in use—is a rigid, dark brown polyethylene affair that measures a squarish 2 feet wide by 2½ feet high. Narrow side slats allow air to enter, and a sliding bottom panel allows the compost to be easily removed. This composter also blends discreetly into the shadow of a shrub. I've since seen many elaborate compost "recipes," but my own remains unchanged: all the autumn leaves that fit, soil and cow manure layers—and, when I'm lucky, "gifts" from the horse stable of a sympathetic (if amused) country friend.

Polyethylene composter

dormant means Autumn is when hardy plants prepare to enter their winter dormancy.
sleep Dormancy means slowed life processes, not *NO* life processes. "Dormant," after all, means *sleep*.

As with the hibernation of animals, it is a time of diminished activity in response to shortened days, lowered temperatures, and reduced hours and intensity of sun. Yet even through winter, some food and water continue to be needed. By autumn the plants have depleted the nutrients in the soil, which may now also be quite compacted. If next year's garden is to thrive, nutrients must be replenished and a friable soil structure restored.

soil restoration   The best time for autumn soil work is when most of the leaves have dropped from deciduous trees. Begin by pulling out the dead or dying annuals. Removing these summer skeletons helps to loosen the soil and to expose subterranean insects to the elements and birds. Harvest your herbs (freeze them for later use in plastic containers and don't forget to label them), and trim spent perennials too. Leave only the flower stalks of stately late bloomers or the foliage of tall species whose silhouettes will add to your winter scene.

city plowing   Yard gardeners can then begin, with a long-handled fork, to loosen the
downstairs   soil around hardy plants, digging down and gently wobbling the tool. Where the soil is starting to resemble concrete, turn under a shovel of perlite or builders' sand. And to inspire humus-making organisms, also turn under as many fallen leaves as fit. Autumn feeding begins with one heaping shovel of packaged cow manure for each 4 feet of plant height. For every foot of plant height, also turn under a trowel of cottonseed meal or blood meal, a trowel of superphosphate, and half a trowel of potash rock or greensand marl. (If your friends or neighbors ask what you're up to, tell them you're just another city farmer plowing your autumn field.)

and upstairs   Container gardeners can do their autumn "plowing" in tubs of hardy species with a narrow hand fork. Dig as deep as you can in several random spots around the outer portions of the container. Loosen the soil and turn under chopped pieces of leaves. Also add the same fertilizers noted above, but only in half the amounts. To gain space for these fresh additions, remove a half-dozen handfuls of old soil from around each shrub or tree. And don't worry about cutting some roots. Hardy plants have many more roots than they use, and pruning old roots helps inspire the growth of new young feeders (see page 234).

sampling autumn's   While there's no better time than fall to eliminate the plants that have
splendor   failed, there's no better time to study those that make autumn special. Few city gardens warrant inclusion in a glossy color calendar, but take advantage of newly opened sites for species that contribute to autumn. Here are some to consider:

PLANTS FOR AUTUMN

Plants for gardens with more than 5 hours of autumn sun:

	Late Flowers	Foliage Color	Berries or Pods
herbaceous perennials			
Aster *(Aster* spp.*)*	x		
Autumn crocus *(Colchicum autumnale)*	x		
Black-eyed Susan *(Rudbeckia hirta)*	x		
Blue fescue *(Festuca ovina* 'Glauca'*)*		x	
Chrysanthemum *(Chrysanthemum* spp.*)*		x	
Eulalia grass *(Miscanthus sinensis)*		x	
Fountain grass *(Pennisetum alopecuroides)*		x	
Japanese anemone *(Anemone japonica)*	x		
Liatris *(Liatris* spp.*)*	x		
Meadow sage *(Salvia pratensis)*	x		
Michaelmas daisy *(Aster novae-angliae* and *A. novi-belgii)*	x		
Nippon or Montauk daisy *(Chrysanthemum nipponicum)*	x		
Oxeye daisy *(Chrysanthemum leucanthemum)*	x		
Phlox *(Phlox paniculata)*	x		
Plumbago *(Ceratostigma plumaginoides)*	x	x	
Sedum *(Sedum spectabile* 'Autumn Joy' or 'Ruby Glo'*)*	x		
Shasta daisy *(Chrysanthemum superbum)*	x		
White mugwort *(Artemisia lactiflora)*	x		
shrubs and trees			
Abelia *(Abelia grandiflora)*	x	x	
Barberry *(Berberis* spp.*)*		x	x
Beautyberry *(Callicarpa americana)*			x
Birch *(Betula* spp.*)*		x	
Blueberries *(Vaccinum corymbosum)*		x	
Callery pear *(Pyrus calleryana)*		x	
Caryopteris incana	x		
Cotoneaster *(Cotoneaster* spp.*)*		x	x
Firethorn *(Pyracantha coccinea)*			x
Fothergilla *(Fothergilla* spp.*)*		x	
Gingko *(Gingko biloba)*		x	
Hawthorn *(Crataegus* spp.*)*		x	x
Mountain ash *(Sorbus aucuparia)*		x	
Ornamental grasses (many kinds)	*(feathery plumes)*		
Peegee hydrangea *(Hydrangea paniculata* 'Grandiflora'*)*	x		
Smokebush *(Cotinus coggygria)*		x	
Snowball *(Viburnum macrocephalum)*	x	x	

Garden Phlox
Phlox paniculata

PLANTS FOR AUTUMN

Plants for gardens with less than 5 hours of autumn sun:

		Late Flowers	Foliage Color	Berries or Pods
herbaceous perennials	Autumn crocus *(Colchicum autumnale)*	x		
	Bleeding heart *(Dicenta eximia)*	x		
	Boston ivy *(Parthenocissus tricuspidata)*		x	
	Cyclamen *(Cyclamen hederifolium)*	x		
	Japanese anemone *(Anemone japonica)*	x		
	Lilyturf *(Liriope muscari)*	x		
	Mistflower *(Eupatorium coelestinum)*	x		
	Northern sea oats *(Chasmanthium latifolium)*		x	
	Sedum *(Sedum spectabile* 'Autumn Joy' or 'Ruby Glo'*)*	x		
	Snakeroot *(Cimicifuga simplex)*			x
shrubs and trees	Barberry *(Berberis* spp.*)*		x	x
	Birch *(Betula* spp.*)*		x	
	Cotoneaster *(Cotoneaster* spp.*)*		x	x
	Gingko *(Gingko biloba)*		x	
	Hawthorn *(Crataegus* spp.*)*		x	x
	Japanese dogwood *(Cornus kousa)*		x	x
	Oakleaf hydrangea *(Hydrangea quercifolia)*	x		
	Red chokeberry *(Aronia arbutifolia)*		x	
	Sourwood tree *(Oxydendrum arboreum)*		x	x
	Star magnolia *(Magnolia stellata)*		x	x
	Winged euonymus *(Euonymus alata)*		x	
	Witch hazel *(Hamamelis virginiana)*	x	x	

autumn alterations And what about that perennial autumn question—to plant now, or wait until spring? Nurserymen have long encouraged gardeners to extend their planting time through fall. Many take heart from the work of Jim Cross, a wholesale nurseryman in Long Island whose experiments show that most hardy perennials, shrubs and trees may safely be planted as long as soil temperatures remain above 40F° (which, where I live, can be as late as Thanksgiving). He found that in autumn, with foliage growth slowed or completed, there is less competition for the nutrients needed to develop new roots and plants can concentrate energies where they're most needed—under the soil.

This means that as long as temperatures are mild, yard gardeners can continue to buy and plant. After all, autumn meeans comfortable work weather and unfrenzied browsing in garden shops where salespeople have more time for questions.

autumn planting downstairs

Planting in autumn is not so different from planting in spring. But a number of plants bought now have been in the nursery since summer. Since these are apt to be quite potbound, take the time to loosen the surface roots well.

After planting, add a mulch to lock in the warmer soil temperature. This enables the subsoil development to continue and new feeder roots to form. Water well, and remember to water whenever autumn rains are sparse.

autumn upstairs

However, autumn planting is not advisable for all.

If your trees and shrubs are in rooftop or terrace containers, stick to note making and postpone your nursery delivery till spring. Even the hardiest plant is better equipped to cope with winter after a summer of producing new roots. It is also apt to remain more firmly in place.

rearranging planters

Since there's no planting upstairs, use the brisk days for a critical study of your view, and for rearranging the plants you already own. You can move even the largest container with relative ease thanks to the multiple roller method devised by bonsai gardeners.

First, raise one side of the tub you want moved just enough to slide beneath it a broom handle, sturdy wood dowel or metal pipe.

Then slip a second roller under the other side and a third in between. Depending on the container's size, a fourth or fifth roller may be needed. Push the planter along on top of the rollers, and as you go transfer the one left behind to the front. Repeat this procedure until your plant has reached its destination.

tulipomania

Whether you garden upstairs in a container or downstairs in a yard, autumn is planting time for spring-blooming bulbs, the most popular of which is the reliable tulip.

Tulips came to Europe from Turkey in the fifteenth century, and the name is a corruption of the Persian word for turban (which Europeans thought the inverted flower resembled). By the end of the sixteenth-century tulip hybridizing in Holland had become such a passion that wealthy buyers throughout Europe, anxious to acquire unusual strains, were trading species that were still underground. In a bizarre frenzy that came to be called "Tulipomania," homes and estates were mortgaged and fortunes made and lost as the hysteria over the plants spread.

Tulipomania finally ended in 1637 with a financial crash that nearly ruined the country.

a spring plot for bulbs　I do look forward to the emergence of my own favorite tulip (the purple-black 'Queen-of-the-Night' which is every bit as sublime as the Mozart aria I assume it's named for). But tulips alone should not be expected to carry the spring. Many other spring bloomers add a dazzling diversity of shapes and colors.
And autumn is when you must plant them.

early is better　Spring-blooming bulbs need time to develop roots before frost. One New York gardener I know procrastinates planting until Christmas. Depending on your zone, plan on starting to get them underground shortly after Labor Day.

bulbs in containers　Spring bulbs are not for yards only. A container that's large enough for hardy shrubs, trees, or perennials (see Chapter 7) is large enough for hardy bulbs. You can also add as many bulbs as fit to tubs already planted with trees. And fill empty planters to overflowing. Short species are particularly good on a windy balcony or rooftop terrace or where garden light or growing conditions are poor. The earlier the bloom, the shorter the stem, so plant them where you can see them from indoors.

easy planting　Spring bulbs do not require special soil. They do need good drainage or they may rot. They may also rot if planted in freshly added compost or manure. (If you've just rejuvenated your soil, wait a week or two before adding bulbs.)
For a good display, plant them close together, no more than 1 to 1½ diameters apart, and never in quantities less than five. Bulbs are conveniently shaped for easy handling. The planting procedure is simple:

ᔍ Dig a hole two to three times deeper than the bulb's size
ᔍ Position the bulb *flat* side down
ᔍ Cover with soil
ᔍ Water well

A mulch of leaves or evergreen boughs is useful too, to keep the soil temperature stable and the area moist. A mulch is also nicer to look at in winter than naked soil.

plotting a spring sequence　The key to a brilliant spring spectacle lies in plotting the bulb sequence in fall. Spring-blooming bulbs have a built-in timetable, and mail-order catalogues make it pleasurable to experiment with a lengthy display. Armed with a copy of your garden outline, it's easy to orchestrate a protracted exhibit.
While precise calendar dates for flowering are not guaranteed, there is a

Crown Imperial or
Fritillary
Fritillaria imperialis

general sequence. Here are some favorites in their approximate order
of appearance:

EARLY BLOOMERS	MID-SPRING BLOOMERS
Winter aconite *(Eranthis hyemalis)*	**Triumph tulip**
Snowdrop *(Galanthus nivalis)*	**Darwin tulip**
Crocus *(Crocus* spp.*)*	**Greigii tulip**
Dwarf iris *(Iris reticulata* or *I. danfordiae)*	*Fritillaria persica*
Squill *(Scilla siberica)*	**Hyacinth** *(Hyacinthus orientalis)*
Anemone blanda	*Fritillaria imperialis*
Chionodoxa luciliae	
Dwarf daffodil	**LATE SPRING BLOOMERS**
Dwarf tulip	**Single and double late tulip**
Botanical tulip	**Parrot tulip**
Grape hyacinth *(Muscari botryoides)*	**Lily-flowered tulip**
Daffodil	*Hyacinthoides hispanica*
Single and double early tulip	**Cottage tulip**
Trout lily *(Erythronium revolutum)*	*Camassia cusickii*
	Allium giganteum

The actual flowering dates vary with exposure and soil temperature.
Bulbs in a balcony container in full sun, for example, will bloom before
those in a shady backyard.

the windy city The city's peculiar configurations of solids and voids (structures and
open spaces) mean that some gardens are so windswept in autumn that
few plants can manage and most people would rather not. You can't
stop the wind, but you can soften the gusts with a barrier of tolerant
species.

The best windbreak is a mix of evergreen and deciduous trees or tall shrubs. Plant them in multiple rows if there's room. Here's a sampling of shrubs and trees that tolerate wind:

PLANTS THAT TOLERATE WIND

Sun Conditions				
FS	SS	WS	NS	
x	x			Bayberry *(Myrica pensylvanica)*
x	x			Beach plum *(Prunus maritima)*
x	x	x	x	Birch *(Betula* spp.*)*
x	x			Cinquefoil *(Potentilla* spp.*)*
x	x	x		Cotoneaster *(Cotoneaster* spp.*)*
x	x	x	x	Crabapple *(Malus* spp.*)*
x	x	x		Firethorn *(Pyracantha coccinea)*
x	x	x	x	Forsythia *(Forsythia* spp.*)*
x	x	x		Honey locust *(Gleditsia triacanthos)*
x	x			Japanese barberry *(Berberis thunbergii)*
x	x			Japanese black pine *(Pinus thunbergiana)*
x	x	x		Juniper 'Skyrocket' *(Juniperus virginiana* 'Skyrocket'*)*
x	x	x	x	Privet *(Ligustrum vulgare)*
x	x	x		Pussy willow *(Salix discolor)*
x	x			Red cedar *(Juniperus viginiana)*
x	x			Roses: *Rosa canina, R. rugosa, R. wichuriana*
x	x	x		Russian olive *(Eleagnus angustifolia)*
x	x	x	x	Shadbush *(Amelanchier* spp.*)*
x	x			Summersweet *(Clethra alnifolia)*
x	x			Tamarix *(Tamarix* spp.*)*
x	x			White spruce *(Picea glauca)*
x	x	x	x	Yew *(Taxus baccata)*
x	x			Yucca *(Yucca* spp.*)*

a winter setting

It's tempting to ignore the winter garden. Long forgotten are summer's vibrant blooms, and the russet hues of autumn have faded in the icy wind. To dismiss your vista now is to lose a quarter of the year.

The winter setting is a study in outline and pattern. Architectural features are compelling, but with no summer blossoms for distraction, winter's the time for plants with distinctive textures and tones. Use these dreary days to assess your space and dream up ways to improve next year's scene.

patterns, textures and tones

For a sculptural touch, there are espaliers and topiaries as well as small weeping trees (see lists pages 231 and 229 respectively). There's no planting now, but a nursery visit is good for leisurely scouting. You can buy now and arrange for delivery in spring.

Conifers are always good for a hint of hue, but there's no need to live by winter green alone. At a well-stocked nursery you may find your pot of gold in a yellow-tipped arborvitae (like *Thuja occidentalis* 'Aurea') or a golden-hued false cypress (*Chamaecyparis pisifera* 'Filifera Aurea'). In winter, some azaleas and leucothoes are colored bronze or reddish-brown, as is the spreading juniper (*Juniperus horizontalis*). Keep winter blues in the garden with a 'Blue Princess' holly (*Ilex meserveae,* 'Blue Princess') or a silvery-blue juniper (like *Juniperus squamata* 'Blue Star').

Deciduous plants need not be forgotten. Here's a sampling of those with winter appeal:

Winter heath
Erica carnea

DECIDUOUS PLANTS FOR WINTER

Sun Conditions
(during the growing season)

FS	SS	WS	NS	
x	x	x	x	**Birch** *(Betula papyrifera* or *B. populifolia)* white exfoliating bark
x	x	x	x	**Chinese witch hazel** *(Hamamelis mollis)* star-shaped late winter flowers
x	x			**Corkscrew willow** *(Salix matsudana* 'Tortuosa') twisted, brown-gray twigs
x	x			**Harry Lauder's walking stick** *(Corylus avellana* 'Contorta') spiral, contorted limbs
x	x			**Highbush blueberry** *(Vaccinium corymbosum)* jagged, red-hued stems
x	x			**Magnolia** *(Magnolia* spp.*)* silvery gray bark, prominent furry flower buds
x	x			**Oriental cherry** *(Prunus serrulata)* glossy brown-red bark
x	x	x		**Paperbark maple** *(Acer griseum)* cinnamon-red exfoliating bark
x	x	x		**Red osier dogwood** *(Cornus sericea)* bright red branches
x	x	x		**Shadbush** *(Amelanchier canadensis)* silver gray bark
x	x			**Stewartia** *(Stewartia pseudocamellia)* reddish-brown exfoliating bark, light brown underneath
x	x			**Trifoliate or hardy orange** *(Poncirus trifoliata)* very thorny, light green asymmetric stems
x	x	x		**Winged euonymus or spindle tree** *(Euonymus alatus)* corky, irregular growth on dark stems

Oak-leaf hydrangea
Hydrangea quercifolia

winter protection   Gardening books abound with suggestions on burlap or wood buffers to "protect" shrubs and trees from winter. These are devices I determinedly avoid. I prefer to look at my *plants* in winter—not shrouded sculptures or grotesque forms. A few windburned tips are a small price to pay for viewing a natural scene, and any species that can't survive on its own doesn't deserve to remain.

antidesiccants   An antidesiccant or antitranspirant spray, however, can be helpful. There are rubber- or plastic-derived products that form a colorless film that retards moisture loss from leaves, limbs and twigs. Should you decide to use an antidesiccant spray, read and follow the label directions precisely.

recycling the   Once they're no longer magical with ornaments or lights, Christmas
Christmas tree   greens can be recycled as a decorative winter mulch for yards and containers. Use leftover holiday branches, too, for shielding vines and young shrubs from the drying effect of winter wind and sun. Strategically sited around street trees, holiday greens sometimes succeed in keeping visiting dogs at bay—especially civilized city creatures whose

owners are loath to subject them to prickly needles. Recycle boughs, too, under bird feeders to make foraging harder for pigeons.

But there is an art to denuding a Christmas tree, and heavy gloves and pruning shears are a must. If it's not possible to haul the tree outdoors first, use a plastic sheet to keep the mess of fallen needles and sticky sap from ruining your rug.

safe deicing   A fresh dusting of snow envelops the city in peaceful beauty. But problems lurk in deicing compounds, which can kill or stunt front-area plants and street trees. The safest way to deice the sidewalk around your plants is to use a nontoxic, abrasive material like sand, sawdust or cat litter. Also useful is calcium nitrate or a urea-containing fertilizer. Cinders and fireplace ashes are useful too, but only where they cannot be tracked indoors.

Avoid salt or products containing sodium chloride or calcium chloride.

If your front area plants die as a result of a deicing compound (evergreens may succumb by spring; deciduous species take longer), replant the area only after you counter the soil toxicity with gypsum (the common name of calcium sulfate). It should be turned under at the rate of a minimum of 10 pounds for each 250 square feet (or a 10-foot-wide-by-25-foot-long area).

Bus drivers and commuters may hate it, but city gardeners can delight in the magic of snow. Part of the pleasure comes from knowing that a snowy garden means no planting, no watering, no weeding, and no feeding.

All that's left is viewing.

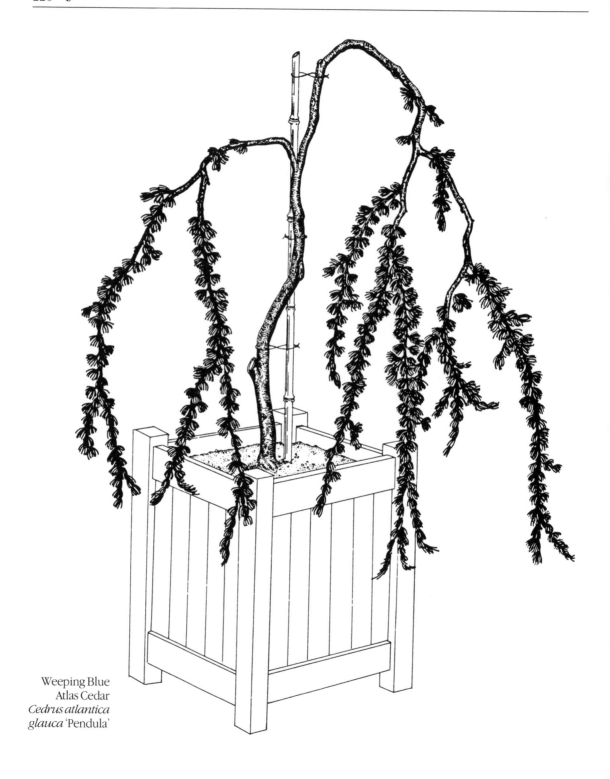

Weeping Blue
Atlas Cedar
*Cedrus atlantica
glauca* 'Pendula'

. . . shrubs overgrow paths. Sometimes you can move the path but if not, then girth control must be imposed.
—Christopher Lloyd, *The Well Chosen Garden,* 1984

11. City Girth Control

nature's rampant growth   The only way to ensure room for both plants and people is to impose girth control, which usually means *pruning,* or cutting away portions of plants. In a small city space it's not feasible to permit the rampant growth nature prefers. And crowded conditions are no better for plants than for people.

Left to their own devices, plants overtake paths, patios and utility lines, and block sidewalks or views. They also strangle, shade or crowd themselves or their neighbors to death.

Skillful pruning improves a garden's appearance just as a skillful haircut improves the gardener's appearance. As with a haircut, there is no "pain" —for either cutter or cuttee—and with rare exceptions what's removed grows back in one form or another.

no negatives   Yet pruning evokes some peculiar reactions, as I discovered in an old English gardening book. The author likened pruning to a *surgical operation* and called it a "necessary evil." This ghastly view of such a creative endeavor is, to say the least, unproductive.

the bonsai influence   I prefer to draw inspiration from the Japanese bonsai gardeners. The word bonsai (pronounced BONE-sigh) means "tray planting," and bonsai gardeners are masters at keeping mature trees and shrubs healthy and handsome in limited confines. Which is just what every city gardener must do.

controlling the woody crowd   Your first goal, then, is to alleviate or prevent crowding. Truly overgrown shrubs and trees may need drastic reduction, and entire branches may have to go. Some plants may also be reshaped through the use of *directional pruning.*

directional pruning   Directional pruning is based on the premise that buds point in the direction of future growth, so a limb's ultimate path is predictable. To alter a stem's route, prune back to just *above* a bud that is pointing in a desirable direction. Use directional pruning to change the course of branches headed back in to crowd the plant's center, to remove those that overlap or rub against other limbs, and to cut away those that block light and air —from that plant, from other plants, or from you.

string and wire   Bonsai gardeners also prevent crowding and change plant shapes by bending limbs and securing them with copper wire. After several seasons the branch is permanently redirected and the wire is removed (This is where that canard—"as the twig is bent so grows the tree"—resonates.) You too can change the path of a misguided limb by tying it with heavy packing cord or laundry line (copper wire is expensive and impractical for large plants) and securing it to something solid—a fence, balcony railing or another strong plant. After several seasons, the cord can be removed.

arborist cables   The limbs of large or mature trees can also be redirected or supported with steel cables installed by an arborist or tree surgeon. An arborist is a professional horticulturist who specializes in tree care. Look for a state-certified arborist in the yellow pages of your telephone directory (check under "Landscapers" or "Tree service") or get a recommendation from a botanical garden or nursery.

staking   On a smaller scale, girth control is also needed for floppy flower stalks or stems of annuals and perennials. Support them with judiciously placed bamboo canes or metal or wood stakes and plastic ties. I also use twigs pruned from shrubby plants like privets. Rammed into the soil next to the plant, these stiff stems, called *pea sticks,* make a fine natural scaffold.

sculptured limbs   Bonsai gardeners use artful pruning, too, to display the structure of shrub limbs and tree trunks or reveal a plant's sculptural form. This is done by snipping off twigs, stems, or leaves that have emerged close to the point of major branching, or, as one bonsai teacher so graphically put it, "just eliminate the underarm hair."

pruning for deadwood   Pruning is also a way to improve plant health, and the first thing to do is remove dead twigs. Dead portions are trimmed all the way back to the first vigorously growing set of leaves or branches.

deadheading Removing dead parts frequently includes *deadheading,* or neatening of annuals, perennials and flowering shrubs by snipping off expired blossoms. And don't dismiss this as trivial—deadheading is more than a cosmetic affair. With its spent flowers gone, rather than set seed, the plant can concentrate on making new buds. Deadheading summer bloomers —roses, butterfly shrubs, cornflowers, daisies and petunias—inspires the formation of new flowers immediately. Deadheading spring bloomers—rhododendrons, lilacs and mountain laurels—inspires the formation of new flower buds for the following spring.

damaged wood The logical extension of removing dead limbs is removing those that are damaged or broken, and it doesn't matter if these were a result of a brutal storm or a brutal trip from a nursery.

diseased wood Prune, too, to control insects and diseases. The pests known as aphids, for example, enjoy clustering on tender new shoots, while diseases like powdery mildew may coat only a single twig. Eliminate these afflicted parts, and you've eliminated much of the problem. You may find times when it's better to eliminate an *entire* plant—and I admit to being an enthusiastic practitioner of this form of "pruning."

improving flowering In old or neglected gardens deciduous and broad-leaved evergreen
or form shrubs like forsythia or rhododendron may grow tall and straggly or lose their ability to bloom. The plant can be rejuvenated with some drastic pruning and a three-year plan. The first year, cut to the soil line up to one third of the oldest branches. The second year, cut another third and the last year, the remaining third. This will inspire vigorous young shoots to rise from the base.

division With age too, many perennials will spread beyond their alloted space or lose their ability to bloom, but this can be corrected with a method called *division.* Dividing perennials means either separating the clumps of roots by hand or using a pruner or spade, cutting in half the masses of hairy-looking (or "fibrous") roots. If the center of a large cluster of perennials is dead, dig up that part (and discard it), add fresh soil, and replant the area with pieces severed from the healthy outer portions.
In cool climate zones, it's easiest and safest to divide most perennials in early spring while the leaves are still small, but you can wait until after the early-spring bloomers like arabis or lungwort are finished flowering.

making your cut Prune deciduous plants and broad-leaved evergreens by cutting just *above* the first set of healthy leaves or stems, or close to a live bud or

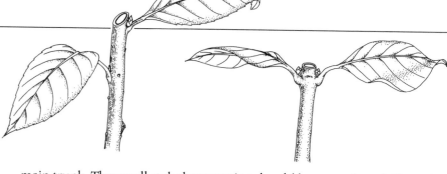

Make pruning cuts smooth and close to the nearest healthy set of leaves

main trunk. The small stub that remains should be smooth and, if possible, sloped downward to hasten healing.

the wound Although horticulturists once believed that pruning wounds on a woody plant needed protection with a coat of shellac or gooey black tree paint, scientists now feel that no cover is needed to help with healing. Aesthetics, however, is another issue. When I asked an arborist hired by a neighbor why he had painted a newly pruned cut, he said he felt compelled to do so because "the *owners* hate the sight of the plants' open wounds."

needle evergreens Deciduous plants and broad-leaved evergreens have extraordinary powers of regeneration. They make fresh limbs quickly, renew themselves from their trunk, and usually recover even from the most severe pruning. Unfortunately, most needle evergreens cannot. Therefore, regular trimming and shaping of evergreens must begin while these plants are young, and yearly trimming is needed to keep them in bounds.
Make pines, spruces and firs bushier by cutting off half of the tip of the newest growth. (This prevents the development of large terminal buds and inspires many smaller ones.) Yews, hemlocks, arborvitae and junipers can be sheared more severely.

think before you cut Artful pruning is crucial in a small city space where *every* tree and shrub is important. Whatever the species under your knife, *think* before you cut and take time to develop your eye by studying plants that are skillfully groomed. You can learn a great deal on a pleasant afternoon simply by walking around a botanical garden and seeing what they've done.

pruning for special effects Artful pruning is useful for a number of special effects. When I was growing up in Brooklyn I was annually tempted into unspeakable Halloween pranks by a cantankerous neighbor's carefully clipped hedge—an inviting green wall. Only now do I appreciate his gardening skill and the advantages of a living barrier that helps define space, camouflages ugly city views and adds a polite screen for neighbors and passersby as well as an elegant backdrop for flowers.

A hedge can also temper the wind and muffle the sound of traffic.

creating a hedge   A good hedge needs good pruning, but it begins with good spacing. That spacing depends on the rate of growth and ultimate size of the species you choose. The further apart, the longer it takes for the hedge shape to form. Use as a guide the plant's mature width. Rooftop plants and those to be formally sheared can be closer; unsheared or informal hedge plants should be given more room. Stagger species that will be used as wind-breaks or place them in multiple rows if there's space.

Container-grown or balled and burlaped plants are best for hedges. They are also more expensive. But they're easier to plant and less likely to die. More important, they're often well branched, so they won't need the severe pruning at planting time that bare-root plants must have.

pruning for hedge mass   Immediately after planting in spring, trim deciduous plants and broad-leaved evergreens to make the hedge mass uniform and force new growth and multiple branching. Give them a light shearing again in summer. The following spring, reduce the shoots of the previous year's growth by about one third. Or, as one experienced nurseryman told me, "to make a *tall* tight hedge, you must first develop a *small* tight hedge—and then let it grow. Don't wait until it reaches the height you want before you start shearing."

Needle evergreens should be sheared only in spring, with the exception of yews, which will need trimming again in summer.

formal or informal   If a hedge with a neat formal line is your goal, don't trust your eye; use temporary stakes at each end and run a taut string as your guide. Keep the top branches from shading those on the bottom by sloping each side slightly to create a somewhat wider base. A rounded top reduces injury from the weight of piled-up snow. Hedges can also be an informal clump like the hedgerows that have divided fields in Britain since the Middle Ages. But these too must be clipped occasionally to keep them from degenerating from carefree to careless.

And be sure to site your hedge one foot, at least, within *your* side of a property line. As the plants mature and spread, a petulant neighbor has the right—legitimately—to chop off the intruders.

plants for hedges   Many trees and shrubs can be used for hedges. You might discourage trespassers with thorny species like roses (see list page 187). Or use flowering shrubs like forsythia for a decorative divider. For a formal design choose plants like Japanese holly that are particularly amenable to repeated clipping. And if you prefer to mix and match, combine species that have a similar rate of growth and that are equally tolerant of shearing. Here's a sampling of plants to choose from:

PLANTS FOR HEDGES

tall or medium-tall hedges	FS	SS	WS	NS		Deciduous	Evergreen
					Sun Conditions		
	x	x			Arborvitae *(Thuja occidentalis)*		x
	x	x	x		Bamboo *(Phyllostachys* spp.*)*	x	*(some)*
	x	x			Corkscrew willow *(Salix matsudana* 'Tortuosa'*)*	x	
	x	x	x	x	English holly *(Ilex aquifolium)*	x	
	x	x			False cypress *(Chamaecyparis pisifera)*		x
	x	x	x		Firethorn *(Pyracantha coccinea)*		*(semi)*
	x	x	x		Forsythia *(Forsythia* spp.*)*	x	
	x	x	x		Hardy orange *(Poncirus trifoliata)*	x	
	x	x	x		Hedge cotoneaster *(Cotoneaster lucidus)*	x	
	x	x	x		Hemlock *(Tsuga canadensis)*		x
	x	x	x	x	Inkberry *(Ilex glabra)*		x
	x	x	x	x	Japanese holly *(Ilex crenata)*		x
	x	x	x		Juniper 'Skyrocket' *(Juniperus virginiana* 'Skyrocket'*)*		x
	x	x			Lilac *(Syringa* spp.*)*	x	
	x	x			Mock orange *(Philadelphus* spp.*)*	x	
	x	x	x		Peegee hydrangea *(Hydrangea paniculata* 'Grandiflora'*)*	x	
	x	x	x	x	Privet *(Ligustrum vulgare)*	x	
	x	x			Quince *(Chaenomeles speciosa)*	x	
		x	x	x	Rhododendron *(Rhododendron* spp.*)*		x
	x	x	x		Rugosa rose *(Rosa rugosa)*	x	
	x	x			Russian olive *(Eleagnus angustifolia)*	x	
	x	x	x		Shrub althea *(Hibiscus syriacus)*	x	
	x	x			Vanhoutte spiraea *(Spiraea vanhouttei)*	x	
	x	x			Washington hawthorn *(Crataegus phaenopyrum)*	x	
	x	x			White pine *(Pinus strobus)*		x
	x	x	x		Winged spindle bush *(Euonymus alatus)*	x	
	x	x	x	x	Yew *(Taxus baccata)*		x

PLANTS FOR HEDGES

low hedges, borders or edging hedges

Sun Conditions FS	SS	WS	NS		Deciduous	Evergreen
x	x	x	x	**Dwarf Japanese holly** *(Ilex crenata convexa)*		x
x	x			**Dwarf white spruce** *(Picea glauca* 'Conica'*)*		x
x	x			**English box** *(Buxus sempervirens* 'Suffruticosa'*)*		x
x	x			**Japanese barberry** *(Berberis thunbergii)*		(semi)
x	x	x		**Japanese box** *(Buxus microphylla)*		x
x	x			**Japanese flowering quince** *(Chaenomeles japonica)*	x	
x	x			**Lavender** *(Lavandula angustifolia)*		x

globes, pyramids and other topiary shapes

In one garden I saw, the new owner had transformed the previous owner's 6-foot-long hedge into a whimsical caterpillar complete with undulating profile. It was a reminder that pruning to create a hedge is not so different from pruning to create a globe, pyramid or bird. If you've the time and energy you can save yourself money by making one of these fanciful topiaries yourself. Choose a small leaf species and select your nursery specimen carefully; it helps to begin with a plant that already resembles the final shape.

multistemmed trees

If you reverse the hedge-making process and cut out all but a few strong trunks, you can create an elegant, multistemmed "tree" from bushy shrubs like star magnolia, peegee hydrangea, privet or lilac.

standards

Or take this pruning to its extreme and create the single-stemmed lollipop known as a *standard.* Use any woody-stemmed perennial like holly, rosemary, scented geranium, myrtle or chrysanthemum. If possible, choose a plant with a strong vertical stem, or use a stake and ties to support a weak one. Prune all branches along the lower portion, leaving only the twigs on top. When the stem reaches the height you want, clip it off and prune to shape the rounded head. Continue clipping through the growing season to encourage multiple branching. And if the plant is in a container, rotate it regularly for even exposure to sun.

You should have a respectable-looking standard within 18 months.

understock shoots

Whether or not it's a topiary standard you're after, there are certain basal shoots that must be removed. These are stems produced by grafted roots.

Sargent weeping hemlock
Tsuga canadensis
'Pendula'

Grafting is a propagation method in which the stem or twig of one plant (called the *scion*), is severed from its own roots. It is then attached (or "grafted") onto the roots of a related, more vigorous or hardier plant (called the *stock* or *understock*). This tough understock may send up its own shoots, which then compete with the stems of the plant above the graft—the plant you thought you bought. If you don't remove the understock suckers, they'll crowd out the scion.

On bushy plants like roses, understock suckers can be hard to spot, but look for stems with leaves that are coarser or differently shaped from those of the scion, or bark that is rougher or thornier.

when you can't grow up Small weeping species, like flowering crabapples or cherries, are among the trees favored for grafting as standards. These, along with naturally pendulous plants, make truly romantic accents in summer and striking sculptures in winter. Weeping trees add distinction to any city space, and since they grow *down,* not up, they're particularly useful on tiered balconies or under awnings.

beautiful weepers   Small pendulous trees must not be confused with the massive, majestic weeping willow—this is a rampant grower that always grabs more than its fair share of space. It's a plant I do *not* recommend!

WEEPING TREES

Sun Conditions					Flowers	Evergreen
FS	SS	WS	NS			
x	x			Weeping Alasakan or Nootka false cypress *(Chamaecyparis nootkatensis* 'Pendula'*)*		x
x	x			Weeping American arborvitae *(Thuja occidentalis* 'pendula'*)*		x
x	x	x		Weeping birch *(Betula pendula* 'Gracilis'*)*	*(catkins)*	
x	x	x		Weeping blue Atlas cedar *(Cedrus atlantica* 'Glauca Pendula'*)*		x
x	x			Weeping blue spruce *(Picea pungens* 'Glauca Pendula'*)*		x
x	x			Weeping Camperdown elm *(Ulmus glabra* 'Camperdownii'*)*	x	
x	x			Weeping cherry *(Prunus subhirtella* 'Pendula'*)*	x	
x	x			Weeping eastern white pine *(Pinus strobus* 'Pendula'*)*		x
x	x	x		Weeping flowering crabapple *(Malus* spp.*)*	x	
x	x	x		Weeping fringed Siberian pea *(Caragana arborescens* 'Walker's Pendula'*)*	x	
x	x	x		Weeping golden chain *(Laburnum alpinum* 'Pendula'*)*	x	
x	x			Weeping Katsura *(Cercidiphyllum magnificum* 'Pendulum'*)*		
x	x			Weeping Pear *(Pyrus salicifolia* Pendula 'Silver Frost'*)*	x	
x	x	x		Weeping Sargent hemlock *(Tsuga canadensis* 'Pendula'*)*		x
x	x			Weeping Serbian spruce *(Picea omorika* 'Pendula'*)*		x
x	x	x		Weeping Siberian pea *(Caragana arborescens* 'Pendula'*)*	x	

The weepers to look for instead are the slower growers or smaller species that are easily controlled with pruning. Although the design effect may be similar, there are in fact several kinds of weeping plants. Plants like the weeping hemlock or weeping beech for example, typically grow on a trunk that is naturally pendulous. Plants like the weeping spruce or weeping crabapple typically are standards: a naturally drooping variety grafted onto the straight stem of an upright form of the same genus. The graft union for the weeping portion may be as low as a foot off the ground, or as high as 6 feet. So weeping plants of the same species may have markedly different appearances.

why do some plants weep? You might wonder, as I did, what makes a species pendulous or drooping in the first place. Peter Del Tredici, a former propagator with the Arnold Arboretum, explained to me that the weeping plant form is a mutation. Most plants have a single growing point that remains dominant so that the whole trunk grows vertical and straight. In weepers, this control mechanism is somehow disrupted. Instead of developing an upright trunk from a vertical growing shoot, weepers develop by superimposing one layer of horizontal growth on top of the previous one. This horizontal growth pattern is called plagiotropism.

pruning weepers Despite this horizontal direction, however, pruning is needed by some weepers for size control as well as appearance. If left unpruned, a Red Jade crabapple, for example, can reach a height of about 18 feet and a width of 30 feet.

When pruning a weeping plant it's important to accentuate the cascading form and avoid creating a mop-like head. This is done by thinning or removing several limbs from the area closest to the trunk. Tall growers or spreading plants are then kept in bounds by removing several outside limbs as well.

espaliers Where space is limited but a divider or wall cover is needed, grow an espalier. Use a lattice or wire form as your guide and bend the limbs of a flexible shrub or tree to conform to this shape. Tie the branches with rubber bands or plastic ties just tight enough to allow them to grow without strangling. Secure new shoots as they emerge and regularly snip and pinch out stragglers to keep the outline clean.

Here's a sampling of shrubs or trees to espalier:

WOODY PLANTS TO ESPALIER

| Sun Conditions | | | | | Flowers | Deciduous | Evergreen |
FS	SS	WS	NS				
x	x	x	x	Crabapple *(Malus* spp.*)*	x	x	
x	x	x		Firethorn *(Pyracantha* spp.*)*	x		*(semi)*
x	x	x		Forsythia *(Forsythia* spp.*)*	x	x	
x	x	x	x	Japanese holly *(Ilex crenata)*	x		x
x	x			Mock orange *(Philadelphus coronarius)*	x	x	
x	x			Pear *(Pyrus communis)*	x	x	
x	x	x		Pfitzer juniper *(Juniperus chinensis* 'Pfitzeriana'*)*			x
x	x			Quince *(Cydonia oblonga)*	x	x	
x	x	x		Red-twigged, variegated dogwood *(Cornus alba* 'Argentea-marginata'*)*	x	x	
x	x	x		Rockspray cotoneaster *(Cotoneaster horizontalis)*	x		x
x	x			Snowball *(Viburnum macrocephalum)*	x	x	
x	x	x	x	Spreading cotoneaster *(Cotoneaster divaricata)*	x	x	
x	x	x		Star magnolia *(Magnolia stellata)*	x	x	
x	x	x		Winged euonymus *(Euonymus alata)*	x	x	
x	x	x	x	Yew *(Taxus* spp.*)*			x

the right tool   Having the right pruning tool is useful. I remember watching a neighbor hacking away at his birches. The reason for his mighty struggle was that he was trying to trim his trees with hedge shears. Since he was really having a time of it, it should have been obvious that it was the wrong tool for the job.

hand shears   If your budget allows only one pruner, it should be a set of hand shears to allow you to sever limbs up to a half inch. There are two kinds available: one works like a scissors, the other has a sharp blade that hits against an anvil. I've used both for years, and confess I find no advantage in one over the other.

loppers   The cost of a long-handled pruner or lopper is justified, too, if you have any number of mature shrubs or trees and need to cut through limbs up to 1½ inches.

saws for thick   If there are really thick branches to cut, you must resist the temptation of
branches   the saw in your toolbox. A carpenter's saw was not designed for live wood: it has the wrong teeth and wrong shape for pruning, and it invariably gums up and sticks. A *tree* saw is the pruner you need. I prefer the bow-shaped one that folds into a safe, storable package, but there's also a large, double-sided kind with coarse teeth for quick work and fine teeth for smoothing the cut.

the pole pruner   The largest weapon most home gardeners can handle is the pole pruner. Its telescoping pole can extend your reach 20 feet and more, if you're also willing to climb a stepstool. Pole pruners come with interchangeable parts: a tree saw and spring-loaded blade that's worked with a rope.

tall plants upstairs   Rooftop gardeners must begin controlling trees and shrubs when they're young. Once out of reach, the limbs are difficult, if not downright danger-

Chinese Juniper
Juniperus chinensis

ous, to prune. Trees in containers, after all, are planted several feet above the floor and their branches can stretch well beyond the parapet or railing. There is a sensible limit to how far even the bravest, most devoted city gardener should climb.

and downstairs Yard gardeners, however, can hire an arborist to prune *in situ*. Arborists are trained to scale tall trees and come equipped with hard hat, climbing boots and an impressive tangle of ropes. For streetside locations they may also come equipped with a hydraulic lift. It's a lot less dramatic, but just as efficient. (Limbs cut from your trees can be saved to use in a fireplace—except for ailanthus, which burns with a terrible smell.)

a late-winter Around about Valentine's Day, the gray city begins to weigh heavily on
tradition gardeners. The lengthening hours of sunlight are a reminder that summer will finally be, and pruning chores are a welcome respite from stuffy rooms. Late winter and early spring are traditional times for pruning. Trimming bare branches means you can see what you've done, and plant wounds heal quickly in spring with the rapid movement of sap.

spring bloomers But beginner, take care. If you prune *spring* bloomers before they flower, you prune off all your spring buds. Shrubs and trees like forsythia, rhododendron, crabapple and blueberry set their spring flowers the previous summer. To avoid cutting them off, prune them immediately *after* they bloom. (Or prune lightly in winter, drop the branches in a water-filled vase, and enjoy your blossoms indoors.)

pruning time In general, any time is the right time to prune dead, damaged or diseased wood. Immediately is best, since the idea is to avoid leaving plants in a vulnerable state for long (although you needn't brave snow and ice to remove winter-damaged limbs). Any time is a good time, too, for fast growers (like privets or Boston ivy) that are completely out of control. Prune summer bloomers, like roses or butterfly shrubs, early in spring after the final frost, and shear evergreens and hedges in early summer. By autumn, pruning of woody plants should stop. Food is stored in the branches and every bit is needed to see them through winter.

coping with roots When houseplants mature and become *potbound* (that means they fill
in containers their pots with roots) they are lifted and moved to larger quarters. Rooftop, terrace and balcony trees and shrubs in containers also become potbound. But lifting and moving them is crazy, and clearly another solution is needed.

Strange as it sounds, that solution is to *cut their roots*. Stranger still is to discover that this too, is an ancient concept.

origins of root pruning

As with so much in garden history, the origins of root pruning and maintaining trees and shrubs in containers are hazy. Although the western world associates the art with Japanese bonsai, the practice originated in China, where the word for pot plants is *pen-tsuai*. Some believe the technique reached Japan as early as the third century A.D.

confronting the act

When I first realized that my terrace trees and shrubs were potbound, I turned for inspiration to the bonsai master gardeners. After all, my plants were similar to those I had seen in bonsai collections. The only difference was size: my trees and shrubs were larger and so were my containers.

I learned that bonsai trees and shrubs are regularly root pruned, usually in spring. Some bonsai masters are most meticulous. They slide the plant from its pot and then disentangle the root ball and cut each root area carefully. Others are less persnickety and merely chop the roots straight across, equidistant from the trunk, all around. (This did seem a bit severe, but was certainly useful information. It was useful, too, to realize that root pruning is not a scientific endeavor.)

purpose of root pruning

After pruning, the bonsai masters add fresh nutrients to the soil and return the plant to its pot.

This procedure has two critical effects:

First, potentially large trees and shrubs are dwarfed. This enables them to live comfortably in the same small container.

Second, new feeder roots develop. This is crucial since old roots are merely passageways; it's the young roots that do the job of absorbing water and nutrients.

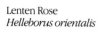

Lenten Rose
Helleborus orientalis

Having come to accept that bonsai trees and shrubs are *regularly* root-pruned to keep them under control, I realized it was time for me to do likewise. The only question at that point was, "HOW?"

Given my rooftop conditions and the size of my plants, I could not follow bonsai procedures literally (although I was advised by an *expert* to "hire a crane and do it right" . . . experts are not always very helpful). Since my containers were not built with removable side panels, the only logical access was to enter the tubs from *above*. And this, as you may come to agree, is disarmingly easy.

root pruning
container trees and
shrubs

In spring dig into your tubs as far as you can reach along the outermost portion of one side of the container, using a narrow shovel or spade (preferably one that's been sharpened). Sever bunches of old roots and remove each mass. Cut away at least half a dozen good-sized clumps from mature shrubs or trees or those that have become potbound, fewer from immature or less crowded plants.

Repeat this procedure on the opposite side of the container but leave the remaining two sides for the following spring.

how often

You can determine how often to root prune by watching how quickly each plant's new roots grow. As a rule of thumb, plan on root pruning deciduous shrubs and trees once every 2–3 years.

Root prune broad-leaved evergreens once every 3–4 years, needle evergreens once every 3–5 years.

The exceptions are exuberant growers like privets, forsythias and most woody vines. Plants like these fill their containers so quickly, it's best to root prune yearly.

On rooftop gardens, manageable-sized containers should also be tilted to remove the roots that have grown through the drainage holes (before they find openings in the floor). Set larger containers on legs that raise them sufficiently so the area beneath them can also be cleared.

compensating for
root loss

Once their root-pruning work is done, bonsai masters trim the upper limbs and twigs. This is to keep the plant dwarfed and looking as it should, based on a tradition of classic styles. But more important, this is also to reduce above-ground parts to compensate for the reduction of roots.

You, too, must prune away some branches and twigs after root pruning. Since you're not restricted to classic forms—and for your purposes "dwarfed" may be reasonably large—you can be more flexible about how and when you do this. (I usually top prune before I root prune simply because a cold or rainy spring may delay working in the soil.)

signs of insufficient compensation   As spring progresses, be sure you watch your newly root-pruned plants carefully. If too little top growth has been taken, the plant will wilt—a sign to ignore at your peril. *Immediately* trim off several more large branches or many small ones and water the plant well.
Once you've struck the right balance, this wilting will stop.

wilting   And while on the subject of wilting, I must add that this can also be a serious problem with *newly planted* trees and shrubs. In the case of B & B species, it occurs when the grower has not sufficiently compensated for the root loss of a recently dug specimen. To correct this, top prune the plant *immediately*—monitor as noted above—and keep it well watered. In the case of container-grown species, it occurs when the outer surface of pot-bound roots have not been loosened sufficiently at planting time. To correct this, open the soil area surrounding your new planting, then scratch and loosen the side surface roots all around as described on page 179. In either case, do not add fertilizer.

Lewisia tweedyi

too big   If you're prepared to do regular—occasonally drastic—pruning, there's no plant that's too big for any city garden or container. But having said that, I must admit to battles lost with truly rapid growers—among them weeping willows, poplars and striped maples. These plants are not only exhausting, they're downright discouraging. They are simply too fast at taking over more than their fair share of space, and I now avoid them.

or not too big   At the other extreme are the dwarf shrubs or alpines, which are genetically programmed to remain tiny for years. Here are some diminutive shrubs to try:

DWARF SHRUBS

Sun Conditions					Deciduous	Evergreen
FS	SS	WS	NS			
x	x	x		Bearberry cotoneaster (*Cotoneaster dammeri*)		x
x	x	x		Blue star juniper (*Juniperus squamata* 'Blue Star')		x
x	x			Bog rosemary (*Andromeda polifolia* 'Nana')		x
x	x			Bronx forsythia (*Forsythia viridissima* 'Bronxensis')	x	
x	x			Compact Korean spice viburnum (*Viburnum carlesii* 'Compactum')	x	
x	x	x		*Daphne cneorum*		x
x	x			Dwarf Alberta spruce (*Picea glauca* 'Conica')		x
x	x	x		Dwarf azalea and rhododendron (*Rhododendron* spp.)		x
x	x			Dwarf Hinoki false cypress (*Chamaecyparis obtusa* 'Nana')		x
x	x	x		Dwarf Japanese maple (*Acer palmatum* 'Dissectum')	x	
x	x			Dwarf littleleaf boxwood (*Buxus microphylla* 'Compacta')		x
x	x			Dwarf mugo pine (*Pinus mugo* 'Compacta')		x
x	x			Hudson's balsam fir (*Abies balsamea* 'Hudsonia')		x
x	x			Japanese alpine spiraea (*Spiraea japonica* 'Alpina')	x	
x	x	x		Japanese holly (*Ilex crenata* 'Compacta')		x
x	x			Prostrate Korean fir (*Abies koreana* 'Prostrata')		x

City gardens may lack the scenic splendor of the Alps, but dwarf species are well suited not only to backyard rockeries and mixed borders, but to window boxes, rooftops, balconies and doorways. They are good, too, for gardeners who prefer to leave their pruning shears in a drawer.

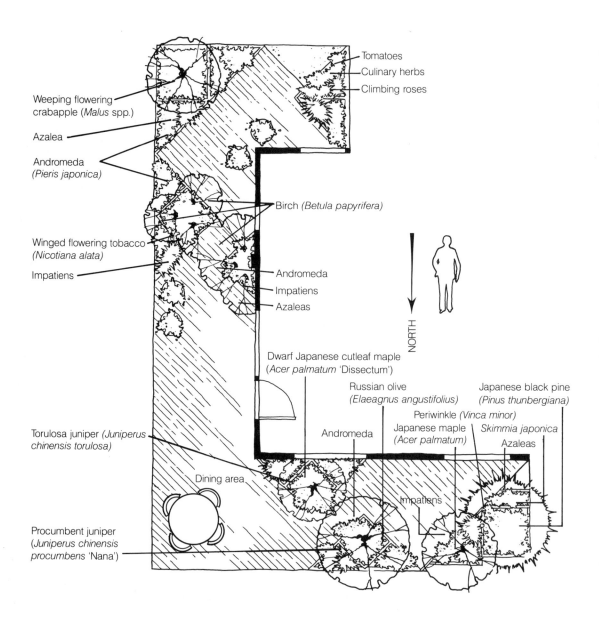

Weeping flowering crabapple (*Malus* spp.)

Azalea

Andromeda (*Pieris japonica*)

Winged flowering tobacco (*Nicotiana alata*)

Impatiens

Torulosa juniper (*Juniperus chinensis torulosa*)

Procumbent juniper (*Juniperus chinensis procumbens* 'Nana')

Tomatoes
Culinary herbs
Climbing roses

Birch (*Betula papyrifera*)

Andromeda
Impatiens
Azaleas

NORTH

Dwarf Japanese cutleaf maple (*Acer palmatum* 'Dissectum')

Russian olive (*Elaeagnus angustifolius*)

Japanese black pine (*Pinus thunbergiana*)

Periwinkle (*Vinca minor*)

Japanese maple (*Acer palmatum*)

Skimmia japonica

Azaleas

Andromeda

Dining area

Impatiens

Alternating triangular planting areas aligned with diagonal wood flooring give a feeling of greater width to an 8-foot-wide L-shaped rooftop that is 41 feet long. Within each triangular plot, the plants are grown in individual containers that facilitate moving should floor repairs be needed. Closely spaced wind-resistant species and a fence of reinforced plate glass temper the gusts.

Maurer & Maurer,
Architects;
Plant Specialists, Inc.

Plan for this garden
is shown on
opposite page.

THE CHANGING
SEASONS IN TOWN

The city garden is not
for summer only. The
same 19- by 50-foot
area is seen in its var-
ied seasonal moods.

A golden floral cascade of Warminster broom *(Cytisus praecox)* is the spring centerpiece for tulips and Kwanzan cherry trees *(Prunus serrulata* 'Kwanzan'*)*. Evergreen "bones" are provided by rhododendrons 'Cornell Pink,' 'Ramapo,' azaleas 'Ruth May' and 'Helen Curtis,' dwarf hemlock *(Tsuga canadensis* 'Nana'*)*, gold dust aucuba and Oregon holly-grape *(Mahonia aquifolium)*.
*Pamela Berdan,
Garden Design*

The Nippon or Montauk daisy *(Chrysanthemum nipponicum)* is a fail-safe first sign of autumn.

A green retreat in Brooklyn captures a Japanese mood. The grassy patch is edged with blue spruce and cinnamon and royal ferns. Slightly mounded soil around a gray birch is planted with iris *(I. japonica* and *I. germanica),* Jack-in-the-pulpit, lily-of-the-valley, English ivy and pachysandra. The homemade trellised seating area has Oriental-style louvred white walls.

Summer shade in an 18- by 30-foot yard is brightened by tubbed crabapples and a low bed planted with Christmas and lady ferns, hosta, purple impatiens and a weeping birch.

Johnny Appleseed Landscaping

In a Georgetown garden, stately purple spires of bear's-breech *(Acanthus balcanicus)* rise amidst grasses and sculpted stones. Plants include 'Big Blue' lily-turf *(Liriope muscari* 'Big Blue'), *Miscanthus sinensis* 'Gracillimus,' *M. s. purpurascens, M. floridulus* and Chinese clump bamboo *(Sina-rundinaria nitida).*

Oehme, van Sweden and Associates, Inc.

A sunny perennial and annual "border" is grown in two layers of containers, 18 inches wide and high and several feet long. The lively planting mix includes delphinium, monarda, 'Silver Mound' artemisia, cosmos, cleome, snapdragon, lavender, cupflower *(Nierembergia repens)* and dahlia.
Lisa Stamm Gardens

A hint of autumn shows on the foliage of hydrangea, crabapple, mountain ash and birch, while sweet alyssum and begonias are covered with an abundance of late summer blooms.
Johnny Appleseed Landscaping

A floriferous pink magnolia is a backdrop for tulips and a colony of rock garden residents that include purple rock-cress *(Aubrieta deltoidea)*, Siberian draba *(Draba sibirica)*, European wood anemone *(Anemone nemorosa)* and white grape hyacinths.
Pamela Berdan,
Garden Design

Hydra-like heads of cleome burst with seeds as autumn overtakes plantings of pink chrysanthemum, red-leaved coleus, silvery dusty miller, purple petunias, white sweet alyssum and rusty pink peegee hydrangea *(H. paniculata* 'Grandiflora'*)*.

Late blooming pale lilac asters *(A. frikartii)* and purple-flowered plumbago *(Ceratostigma plumbagino-ides)* are combined with *Euphorbia myrsinites* in a Portland, Oregon garden.

Laurence Farer, Landscape Architect

Fallen leaves from late blooming impatiens and a mountain ash dot the floor of a small balcony.

SOME VISITORS, WELCOME AND OTHERWISE

Crabapples are silhouetted on a winter day.

A bumblebee concentrates on a nectar harvest from monarda.

Mourning doves, always seen in pairs, rest on snowy branches.

A shallow aluminum dish holds water for wild birds.

A rose is coated with mildew.

Mottled leaves dotted with sticky spots are a symptom of lacebugs.

The caterpillar stage of the exquisite black swallowtail butterfly dines on parsley.

248

Rusty-looking, dying leaves and fine webs indicate the presence of spidermites.

Tent caterpillars, emerging from a webbed crotch, prepare to feed.

A tomato hornworm dining on a tomato plant.

A dying tomato hornworm is covered with the pupae of its natural enemy, a Brachonid wasp.

White flies feeding on the undersides of basil leaves.

Leaves of a moon-flower vine show stippling typical of ozone pollution.

Tomato leaves are flecked with browned, dead lesions from sulfur dioxide pollution.

Workmen are often the most unwelcome visitors of all.

TRAINING AND PRUNING

Clematis is trained
horizontally on wire
fencing along a railing.

A clipped hedge and
topiary yew add
formality.
Luther Greene,
Garden Design

Billowing mounds of
holly are clipped in
the Japanese
style called "cloud
pruning."
Alice Recknagel Ireys,
Landscape Architect

Not quite a maze, the
concentric rectangles
of clipped boxwood
occupy nearly all the
space in a 30- by 35-
foot yard.

Berried hollies are trained against a Georgetown picket fence.

A juniper is trained in a fan shape against a granite wall.

An espaliered fire-thorn covered with berries is an orange pattern in snow.

Winter reveals the gracefully pendulous limbs of a weeping Siberian pea tree (*Caragana arbores-cens* 'Pendula').

A weeping blue Atlas cedar *(Cedrus atlantica* 'Glauca Pendula'*)* reaches beyond the confines of a rooftop garden.
Paul Rudolph, Architect; William T. Wheeler Co., Inc.

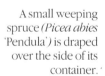

A small weeping spruce *(Picea abies* 'Pendula'*)* is draped over the side of its container.

In narrow spaces, tied branches are an alternative to pruning.

A container plant that has not been root pruned has no soil or space left.

A crabapple is root pruned.

Levels and paths are used to impose a formal order on an informally planted 18- by 50-foot yard. The bluestone walk, which begins at a bamboo-lined patio, leads past a small water garden and the mulch path of an English-style perennial border. The formal herb garden is set against a woodland backdrop.

Plan for this garden is shown on opposite page.

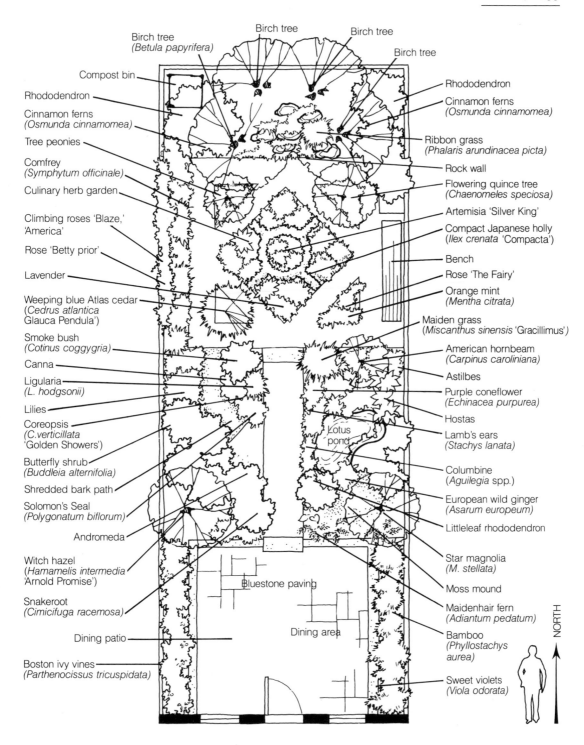

Birch tree
Birch tree
Birch tree
Birch tree
Birch tree
(Betula papyrifera)

Compost bin

Rhododendron

Cinnamon ferns
(Osmunda cinnamomea)

Tree peonies

Comfrey
(Symphytum officinale)

Culinary herb garden

Climbing roses 'Blaze,'
'America'

Rose 'Betty prior'

Lavender

Weeping blue Atlas cedar
(Cedrus atlantica
Glauca Pendula')

Smoke bush
(Cotinus coggygria)

Canna

Ligularia
(L. hodgsonii)

Lilies

Coreopsis
(C.verticillata
'Golden Showers')

Butterfly shrub
(Buddleia alternifolia)

Shredded bark path

Solomon's Seal
(Polygonatum biflorum)

Andromeda

Witch hazel
(Hamamelis intermedia
'Arnold Promise')

Snakeroot
(Cimicifuga racemosa)

Dining patio

Boston ivy vines
(Parthenocissus tricuspidata)

Rhododendron

Cinnamon ferns
(Osmunda cinnamomea)

Ribbon grass
(Phalaris arundinacea picta)

Rock wall

Flowering quince tree
(Chaenomeles speciosa)

Artemisia 'Silver King'

Compact Japanese holly
(Ilex crenata 'Compacta')

Bench

Rose 'The Fairy'

Orange mint
(Mentha citrata)

Maiden grass
(Miscanthus sinensis 'Gracillimus')

American hornbeam
(Carpinus caroliniana)

Astilbes

Purple coneflower
(Echinacea purpurea)

Hostas

Lotus
pond

Lamb's ears
(Stachys lanata)

Columbine
(Aguilegia spp.)

European wild ginger
(Asarum europeum)

Littleleaf rhododendron

Star magnolia
(M. stellata)

Moss mound

Maidenhair fern
(Adiantum pedatum)

Bluestone paving

Dining area

Bamboo
(Phyllostachys
aurea)

Sweet violets
(Viola odorata)

NORTH

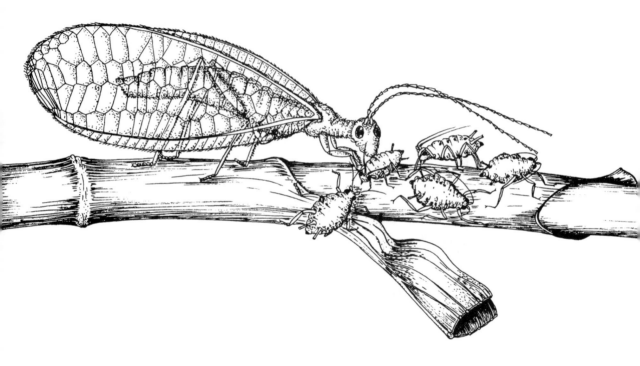

A green lacewing
feeds on aphids.

*We know, deep down in our hearts, that . . . a tablet of fertilizer
does not, by itself, produce flowers in miraculous abundance,
that a single spray will not mean complete freedom from pests,
that few plants fulfill all claims. . . . But we are eternal gamblers;
perhaps this time it will all come true.*
—Cynthia Westcott, *Are You Your Garden's Worst Pest?*, 1961

12. Not Quite Eden

In the beginning there was Eden. And in the beginning, Eden is what
every city gardener expects. I certainly did. My Paradise was to flourish
with fragrant flowers and succulent fruit, with a few melodious birds and
humming bees thrown in for ambience. As a city slicker I had no interest
in "bugs"—revolting creatures that crawl or creep. The word evoked images of cockroaches, silverfish or mosquitoes, horrid things that revel in
dirt or make mammals scratch.

*behold
the caterpillar*

So when a caterpillar was found munching the birch in my rooftop Eden,
my family was torn between apprehension and awe of this intriguing creature, which, we assumed, had arrived "on foot" (feet?), crawling up nineteen floors. When I told a country nurseryman about it, he harrumphed
in disbelief. Not at the suspected multistory hike, but at the idea that any
such wild thing could find its way to the city.

As my plants increased in number, so did the caterpillars, along with their
many beautiful and fascinating comrades whose entomological classifica-
tion was beyond my ability to place. It was soon apparent that just because I failed to see them arriving (in one stage of their life cycle or
another) it didn't mean they weren't.

And assumptions about city life notwithstanding, garden insects abound
here.

some perspective   Now before undertaking a nuclear assault on these (alleged) "enemies," it's useful to remember that insects predate humans by several *hundred million* years. Of the more than seven hundred thousand kinds of insects that scurry, jump, flit or slither about our planet, quite a few are "good guys" from our human point of view. Quite a few are beneficial predators who are adept at keeping their fellows under control. Quite a few also serve as pollinators for crops and flowers, scavengers for decaying matter, vital links in the food chain of birds, fish and animals, and sources of medicinal and commercial products.

Unfortunately, there are also quite a few with habits that gardeners don't like. And that's where Eden ends.

controlling nature   Man's desire to manipulate the natural world dates at least to 4,000 B.C., when the Chinese used fire and botanical derivatives like nicotine to rid themselves of destructive pests. Modern synthetic chemicals are more efficient. Modern synthetics have also given rise to more efficient pests, not to mention contaminated water, soil, air and food.

balancing nature   With increasing concerns about the planet, humans are beginning to accept that total control of nature has never been—and will never be—possible. The "sledgehammer approach" (as my *Times* colleague Joan Lee Faust once called it) is finally being replaced by the more realistic goal of keeping pests to *tolerable levels*—some leaves for them, and some for us.

It is, after all, irresponsible to wantonly destroy a benign or even useful majority while attempting to eliminate a destructive minority.

It's true that in a single urban plot a solid balance of nature is not readily maintained (just the right number of "good guys" to control the "bad" ones). Yet if each of us tries to disturb nature's system of checks and balances no more than is absolutely necessary, one day this collective effort will work.

innocent until   So what's a gardener to do when an unfamiliar insect appears?
proven guilty   Without a degree in entomology, how can you know if there's dirty work afoot?

The answer is *observation*. This is the only tool we amateurs have, and it's really a pretty good one.

Watch the creature carefully for a while and see what it's up to. If it seems to be minding its own business and you have no previous evidence to the contrary, guilt should not be presumed—that position, after all, is antithetical to American law.

a ferocious friend

Remember, too, you can't judge an insect friend by its looks; some important allies have a fearsome visage. Take, for example, that insectivorous monster, the praying mantis. One year, a 3-inch-long mantis settled on my tub of roses. At first my family was unsettled by its grotesque green face, ungainly limbs and truly atrocious table manners (chewing raw insects!), but by summer's end it had become an accepted and most entertaining resident. In retrospect, I can only wonder at my city children, who so casually named their peculiar "pet" *Bob*.

getting to know some "good guys"

Here's a sampling of insects that spend at least one stage of their life cycle dining exclusively on other insects (do forgive my name dropping, but I did meet more than one of them in my own garden):

❧ Antlions or Doodlebugs
The adult has long, membranous wings that it holds upright over a dark brown body that is 1½ inches long. The larva is brown or gray with pincers and eats small insects.

❧ Centipedes
Centipedes are brownish, somewhat flat and multilegged, about 1 inch long and scurry away quickly when disturbed. They eat snails and other soil insects.

❧ Flower flies or hover flies
The adult has a black body with yellow bands. It resembles a cross between a fly and bee as it hovers over flowers and feeds on nectar. The larva is a green-gray or brown worm that feeds on insects.

❧ Fiery searchers or ground beetles
These two cousins are awesome-looking nocturnal feeders, black and shiny with hints of green or violet, respectively. The larva is yellow-gray or light brown. The adult fiery searcher dines on soft-bodied larvae like cankerworms and tent caterpillars; the ground beetle prefers slugs and snails.

❧ Green lacewings
The adult has a slender, pale green, ¾-inch-long body and transparent, vertically folded wings. The larva is yellow-gray with long jaws. Both adult and larva feed on aphids and the eggs of other insects.

❧ Lady beetles or Ladybugs
The several kinds of lady beetles most easily seen are about ¼ inch long with a somewhat oval, hard body. One species is orange-red with 12 black spots, another is orange-red with few or no spots and a third is pale yellow or gray with black spots. Adults and larvae feed on many kinds of small insects.

❧ Parasitic wasps

Parasitic eggs are deposited on the bodies of insects by several species of wasps, including *Braconid, Trichogramma, Chalcid* and *Ichneumon*. As they hatch, the larvae feed on their prey. A favorite host for the *Braconid* wasp is the tomato hornworm; the *Trichogramma* wasp prefers eggs of moths.

❧ Robber flies

The adult is gray, narrow and about ¾ inch long with a hairy mouth. It makes a loud buzzing sound and feeds on flying insects. The larva is white, flat and rounded and eats soil insects.

❧ Spiders

You know what spiders look like . . . they may bite people who get in their way, but they really prefer insects.

❧ Tachnid flies

The adults are gray or brown and look like large hairy houseflies. They also scurry rapidly across leaves. The larva is gray-green and feeds within the body of many beetles and bugs.

tipping the balance of nature
Once you get to know some of your insect friends, it's possible to help tip the natural balance in your favor by adding to their numbers. Beneficial predators are now being bred for commercial sale and are even available by mail (see page 292). Instructions are also included. One supplier, for example, typically ships green lacewings in a container about the size of a pint of ice cream. While I can't imagine anyone actually counts, the company estimates that each of its packages includes some 5,000 eggs. Although it's best to place them in the garden as soon as possible, an egg container may also be refrigerated for up to a week. Predatory mites, on the other hand, are shipped alive—some 1,000 in a small ice-packed medicine vial—and these must be released immediately.

discouraging undesirables
Assuming the insects you observe in your garden are *not* really friends, there are a number of safe ways to make them feel unwelcome. One tactic, guaranteed to discourage a wide range of undesirables, is a full-force blast with your hose.

the hosing
Previously I spoke of washing plants in order to keep them clean enough to breathe—so "clean" now takes on added meaning. However, don't be discouraged to find that several hosings are needed to convince some pests they're really not wanted. The best method is a strong water stream aimed at the *undersides* of the leaves. Where needed, support weak stems, flower buds or tender growth with one hand and direct the hose with the other.

a soapy wash   If a plain water spray doesn't impress them, a soapy one will. Soap has long been an ally in the battle of the bugs, and in the nineteenth century whale oil soap was a favorite for orchards. A sudsy mix of any dishwashing liquid is useful, but insecticidal soap is best. The commercial insecticidal soap is a new addition to the modern gardener's arsenal. The product was developed by George S. Puritch, a Canadian plant physiologist, and is marketed in America primarily by Safer Inc.

Insecticidal soap is derived from a combination of potassium salts of selected fatty acids that are normally found in edible oils. For reasons not fully understood, these disrupt certain insect tissues and cause them to malfunction, and the insect dies. (Some plant species are injured by soap, so be sure to test several leaves a day ahead first; burned-looking tips or yellow or brown spotting are signs a plant cannot tolerate a soapy spray.)

horticultural oils   Horticultural oils are another prudent pest control. These oils are derived from complex mixtures of petroleum hydrocarbons that damage the insects' protective coating and interfere with breathing. Prior to the 1970s, horticultural oil sprays were used only on deciduous plants before the buds opened. They were known as "dormant" sprays since they could not be applied when the plants were in leaf; the leaf pores would be clogged and the plant would die.

Modern science has since given us more highly refined or "superior" oils. These products are lighter, less thick and evaporate more quickly and thus are safe for use on plants in leaf. These oils are sometimes called "summer oils."

repellents   Over the years, gardeners have experimented, too, with homemade mixes in the hope of keeping pests away. One widely acclaimed repellent is a blend of onions, hot peppers and garlic that has been ground well and mixed with water. (The smell also keeps neighbors away.) A less odoriferous repellent was devised for use on culinary herbs by Elizabeth Remsen Van Brunt, a founder of the New York Unit of the Herb Society of America.

Her recipe is as follows:

> *To a quart of boiling water add:*
> 4 nicotine cigarettes (paper and filter removed)
> 2 crushed garlic cloves
> 2 tablespoons household ammonia
> 2 tablespoons liquid soap
> Allow to steep several hours.
> Strain, cool and spray.
> Edible plants are safe to use the next day after a clear water rinse.

If you can't stand making a repellent, buy a readymade like hot pepper wax (from that nasty stuff in cayenne pepper) or neem oil (from neem tree seeds). Both kill on direct contact, and neem oil is also a fungicide. To avoid harming beneficial insects spray at night or when the "good guys" aren't around.

removal

Dark-eye Gladixia
Acidanthera bicolor

Another way to reclaim your territory is by "pest removal"—usually by hand. At first you may be too squeamish to pick up a slug, beetle or caterpillar, throw it on the floor and jump on it. But with time (and enough fury) you should reach this advanced level of gardening. "Search and destroy" missions also include dropping egg masses or cocoons into kerosene, undiluted liquid detergent, or a water-and-ammonia solution.

Or you might prefer to knock the beasts into a jar and donate them for "nature study" to a school. Institutions are generally grateful for such donations and rarely suspect the true reason for the altruism. Children may even be induced to do the trapping for you if offered a "bounty" for every pest caught—but keep the price low; some are tireless workers.

mechanical devices and the paper bag

Pruning away pest-infested limbs—which includes tossing out entire pest-infested plants—is another effective means of removal. The noted plant pathologist Dr. Cynthia Westcott used to advise gardeners to carry a large paper bag for the express purpose of "neatly removing afflicted remains." Also helpful are disposable devices like flypaper, sticky yellow bars, and burlap or sticky bands for encircling trees. There are also commercial traps baited with floral lure or sexual attractant (no clever philosophy here, please).

varied plantings

Many pests have definite likes and dislikes, and it's not uncommon to watch one plant being devoured leafless while its neighbor is ignored. This alone is sufficient reason to plant a good mix of species and keep to a minimum those that are continually under attack. Look for resistant plants in mail-order catalogues or ask for recommended cultivars from your state Cooperative Extension Office.

A variation on this theme is the crop rotation of farmers; you too should change the yearly location of your annual vegetables, flowers and herbs.

Integrated Pest Management

Environmental concerns have at last given rise to more sensible pest controls, and in this age of bureau-speak the "system" now espoused by professionals is called Integrated Pest Management, or IPM. Despite its fancy moniker, the basic tenets are not new. But the organized methodology and concern for the environment is, and for that, at least, we must be grateful.

The stated goal of IPM is to "keep the damage to acceptable levels" (as cited in a bulletin from Cornell University's Extension Service). A few chewed leaves, are, after all, signs of a functioning garden and can be regarded with pride. With this in mind, IPM advocates the implementation, *first,* of safe controls—like those outlined above—along with some sophisticated biological and genetic professional tinkering.

the last resort   However, when there's no longer a tolerable number of freeloaders and a major invasion is under way, pesticides are acceptable. This use of poisons *as a last resort* distinguishes the IPM approach from the once-hallowed dogma of spray-on-schedule-whether-it's-needed-or-not.

choosing your   A pesticide is any product that kills pests.
weapon   But poisons for pests are sometimes poisons for us, so the decision to use them is serious. Some pesticides are safer than others, but all must be handled with care, especially in the close quarters of town.

organics   "Organic" pesticides originate in substances found in nature and thus are mostly (but not always!) considered safer for mammals, birds, wildlife and the environment. This group includes microbial insecticides (products with disease organisms like Bacillus thuringiensis [Bt], which is lethal to specific larvae), botanical derivatives (products from plants like pyrethrum, hot pepper wax, neem oil or rotenone) and the horticultural oils noted above.

synthetics   "Chemical" pesticides are synthetic derivatives of substances created entirely by man. Chemical pesticides tend to be quicker acting than organics, typically more toxic to mammals, birds, wildlife and beneficial predators, and generally longer lasting in the leaves or soil. They are therefore more dangerous to both the gardener and the garden.

read the label   New pesticide formulations—both synthetic and organic—appear with overwhelming regularity and in extraordinary numbers. At last count, over forty thousand products were available. While a chemist or pathologist may understand the nuances of each new offering, the only way a city gardener can understand anything is to *read the label carefully.*

And don't buy anything until you do!

Never mind the miles of tempting merchandise on nursery shelves or the blithe manner in which they're sold by salesclerks who may be shockingly ignorant of the product's true potential harm.

caution, warning,
and danger

By law, the label must include some very important information. Products considered least harmful are labeled CAUTION, which means either slightly hazardous (a lethal dose is an ounce to a pint) or relatively non-hazardous (a lethal dose is more than a pint). The next most dangerous is labeled WARNING (a lethal dose is a teaspoon to a tablespoon). The most lethal products, which are best kept out of the city home completely, are labeled DANGER, and finally POISON (replete with skull and crossbones).

The label must also include the ingredients' common and trade names (not always easy to decipher), the product's specific uses (including the plants it may *harm*) and the number of days before safe harvest for edibles. First aid procedures and a poison hotline may also be listed.

a selection of pests

The following are a few of the more common insect pests you may find dining in your garden and some possible methods of control:

PEST DESCRIPTION	SYMPTOMS	POSSIBLE CONTROLS
Aphid Tiny plant lice with soft green, black or pink pear-shaped bodies. They move slowly as they suck the juice from buds and leaves.	New growth or leaves near branch ends are deformed. Buds don't open. A shiny, sticky substance coats the leaves. Clusters of aphids cover stems or leaves.	Wipe off by hand. Wash off with strong water spray. Insecticidal soap. Oil sprays (dormant or summer). Lady beetles, Lacewings. Hot pepper wax. Neem oil.
Bagworms Bagworms are the larval or worm-like stage of moths. They live and lay their eggs in an intriguing oval-shaped "bag" woven of bits of leaves and twigs.	There are numerous chewed or ripped leaves near a 1- or 2-inch-long, oval-shaped "bag" that hangs from a branch.	Snip off and burn or discard. Bt disease.
Beetles The hundreds of beetle pests (as well as friends) come in a clever assortment of colors and shapes. Included among the more infamous are the Japanese beetle (metallic green), the Colorado potato beetle (yellow with black stripes), and the flea beetle (small and black).	The white grubs or wormlike beetle larvae are found in the soil, where they chew roots. Mature beetles chew holes in leaves or flower buds. Some beetles also transmit plant diseases.	Cultivate soil in autumn to expose larvae to birds. Predatory nematodes. Hand removal. Lure traps. Commercial beetle traps. Rotenone. Hot pepper wax. Neem oil. Use resistant plants.

PEST DESCRIPTION	SYMPTOMS	POSSIBLE CONTROLS
Borers Borers are the larval stage of many different insects that feed within the stems, branches or roots of plants.	Holes are seen in the bark or stem and a waxy or sticky sawdustlike substance is on the bark or nearby. Soft-stemmed plants may suddenly wilt or collapse.	Cultivate the soil in autumn to expose eggs. Remove and destroy all infested stems of perennials or vegetables. If damage on vining plants is not extensive, slit the stem, remove borer and cover with soil to encourage new roots. In trees, probe borer holes with a flexible wire or knife to kill the borers. Wrap susceptible species with burlap layers with moth flakes in between. Braconid wasp. Tachinid fly. Woodpeckers, vireos and other birds.
Caterpillars Caterpillars are the larval or worm-like stages of moths and butterflies and come in an equally exotic range of colors, shapes and sizes. Some are smooth, others have tufts of hair (which may produce allergic reactions).	Leaves or buds are chewed. Caterpillars often blend smoothly into their surroundings but can be seen if you look carefully.	Wash off with strong water spray. Manually remove cocoons and caterpillars (wear gloves to avoid possible allergic reactions). Parasitic wasps. Bt disease. Sticky barrier band. Pyrethrin. Rotenone. Hot pepper wax. Neem oil.
Cutworms Cutworms sever plants near or below the soil surface or climb to eat upper stems, leaves or buds.	Plants are cut off at or near soil line. Dig the soil around plant to confirm that cutworms—fleshy, hairless caterpillars that curl up when disturbed—are present.	Wrap aluminum foil or paper collars around seedlings as barriers. Bt disease. Neem oil.
Lacebugs These green, brown or yellow-gray insects hold their lacy wings in a horizontal position (they should not be confused with beneficial lacewings, whose wings are held vertically).	Broad-leaved evergreens in particular may be mottled or speckled with somewhat rusty-looking patches. The damage resembles that inflicted by mites and leafhoppers but is differentiated by the hard, black, sticky droplets found on the undersides of leaves.	Insecticidal soap (especially on underside of leaves). Ornamentals only: systemic insecticide. Hot pepper wax. Neem oil.

PEST DESCRIPTION	SYMPTOMS	POSSIBLE CONTROLS

Leafhoppers and Treehoppers

These truly fascinating-looking insects hold their green, brown, red or sometimes brightly banded, wedge-shaped wings in a tentlike roof above them. They jump away quickly when disturbed.

Leaves are stunted, stippled or deformed, sometimes browned on the edges and curled.
Some leafhoppers also transmit plant diseases.

Wash off with strong water spray.
Insecticidal soap.
Summer oil spray.
Hot pepper wax.
Neem oil.

Leaf Miner

These extremely tiny maggots, as the name implies, "mine" tunnels inside leaves.

Leaves have serpentine browned or dead areas or blisters. A hand magnifier reveals a hollow area between leaf surfaces.

Cultivate the soil in autumn to expose eggs to frost and birds.
Remove and destroy infected leaves of crop plants and edibles.
If damage on ornamentals is severe and repeated yearly, apply a systemic insecticide in early spring.
Neem oil.

Scales

Scales are immobile round or oval-shaped reddish, purple-brown, black, gray, pink or white insects that are hard to see since they blend well with the leaf or stem.
Soft scales have a waxy or cottony covering.

Hard or armored scales have a tough outer shell when mature.

Scales feed by piercing and sucking and secrete a toxic substance that kills the leaves and branches.
Leaves may crinkle, yellow, brown and drop. Tree bark may split and fall away. Branches may appear malformed and "bumpy." Sooty mold is often present on the "honeydew" secretions of scales.

Scrape off with fingernail or brush.
Insecticidal soap (during crawler stage).
Parasitic wasps.
Lady beetles.
Oil sprays (dormant and summer).
Neem oil.

Ornamentals only: systemic insecticide.

Slugs and Snails

These are soil-dwelling creatures with long bodies. Snails have a shell; slugs do not. Both are night feeders that hide by day in damp places under pots, debris or rocks.

Leaves have holes or ragged or ripped edges. Silvery, winding trails coat the leaves or nearby floor.

Remove by hand.
Crush underfoot.
Cover soil with roughly-ground eggshells, ashes, sand or diatomaceous earth.
Trap in shallow saucers of beer or dry yeast mixed with water that is sunk to soil level.
Around ornamentals only: commercial slug bait.
Reduce hiding places by removing boards, rocks, etc. from area of susceptible plants.
Iron phosphate blends (marketed under names like Sluggo and Escar Go!).

PEST DESCRIPTION	SYMPTOMS	POSSIBLE CONTROLS

Spider Mites and Mites

There are many species of these tiny pests, which are related to spiders. Use a hand lens to look for webs; the mites appear as tiny dots or moving spots.

Leaves are pale and stippled with yellow or rusty brown spots. Fine webs cover needles or leaf undersides. Early stages are not easily noticed.

Wash off with strong water spray.
Insecticidal soap.
Lacewings.
Lady beetles.
Predatory mites.
Oil sprays (dormant and summer).
Miticide.
Hot pepper wax.
Neem oil.

Tomato Hornworm

This large, 2–4-inch-long, pale green caterpillar has white and black markings and a reddish "horn" on its rear.

Tomato leaves disappear from the plant and large dark green droppings are found at the base.

Hand removal.
Braconid parasitic wasps (the white pupae may be seen protruding from the hornworm's body).
Neem oil.

Webworms and Tent Caterpillars

These are the larval form of several moths. The caterpillars develop in masses within silky webs.

Silky webs enclose bunches of leaves or small branches or the entire crotch of a large branch. Adjacent leaves are skeletonized.

Wash off with forceful hosing.
Prune out nest and inhabitants.
Neem oil.
Bt disease.
Ornamentals only: systemic insecticide.

White Flies

These tiny white flies cluster on the undersides of leaves. They are tropical pests that survive winter indoors. The larvae are scalelike.

Plants are wilted, stunted or dying and covered with a shiny sticky substance, or "honeydew." A sooty black mold may grow on this covering. A white cloud appears when the plant is shaken or moved.

Wash off with forceful hosing.
Insecticidal soap.
Cultivate the soil to expose overwintering eggs to frost and birds.
Flypaper.
Sticky yellow bars.
Inspect undersides of leaves of new annuals for white flies or their eggs and avoid purchasing infected plants.
Hot pepper wax.
Neem oil.

Winter Jasmine
Jasminum nudiflorum

pesticide application Whatever pesticide you choose—organic or synthetic—treat only the plant under attack, and don't apply to plants that are wilted or stressed from lack of water. The label provides instructions on the proper amount or dilution and the proper method of application, and woe to the gardener who does not follow these directions to the letter. Improper use of *any* pesticide can be injurious not only to the plant but to you, your children, neighbors, passersby or pets.

Only the attacking insects may emerge unscathed.

and formulation Some pesticides are powders designed to be dusted directly onto the leaves. Others are granules that must be worked full strength into the soil. Some are sold in pressurized cans or siphon action bottles (a few of which are designed to be used upside down). A majority are designed to be diluted in water before application.

If your garden is tiny or you have no tall trees, a hand-pumped quart-size plastic bottle should suffice for distributing water-soluble sprays.

For larger shrubs and small trees, a "trombone"-type sprayer is better and can direct water-soluble mixes to at least 15 feet.

The least efficient sprayer and the one most difficult to control in a small city space is the "hose-end" siphon sprayer, which depends on even water pressure to ensure proper distribution and dilution.

Apply liquid sprays early in the morning when temperatures are above 45F° and a freeze is not expected within 24 hours; or early in the morning when temperatures are unlikely to rise above 80F°. Coat the plant thoroughly, just to the point of runoff.

storing and mixing Finding a place to store and prepare your pesticides and accompanying paraphernalia does take some planning. Outside is best except for bottles or cans that need protection from frost. *Nothing* should be in your kitchen—no matter how careful you think you may be.

safety first When using pesticides, I am guided by the principles formulated for commercial nurserymen:

- ❧ Wear gloves, long sleeves, hat and long pants (some nurserymen also wear a nose mask).
- ❧ Afterward, change all clothes including underwear and wash hands, arms and face with soap and water.
- ❧ Never eat, drink or smoke during preparation or application.

🍃 Store the products in their original containers, in a dry place, and out of reach of children and pets.

🍃 If any symptoms of illness occur during or shortly after, a physician should be called immediately and the product and its label should be shown.

🍃 Mix only enough spray to do the job, and use it all.

Tomato hornworm

don't blame the insects Pity the poor insects—blamed for plant problems even when they are innocent. Take the case of leaves that develop a white-stippled appearance. Maybe it's lacebug or spider mite, you guess (feeling very smug since stippling is typical of either).

air pollutants What a nasty surprise to discover that stippling may also indicate a plant's response to ozone air pollution. Ozone pollution is a kind of photochemical smog from automobile exhaust. Plant problems typically develop during periods of air stagnation like those that occur in early or

ozone midsummer. The stippling may vary from light to dark depending on the plant. Light or whitish spots, for example, appear on the leaves of nasturtium, cucumbers, parsley or roses. Dark patterns—purple or brownish black—may discolor the leaves of green beans or grape plants. Unfortunately, leaf color changes like this also appear with normal aging or may indicate a phosphorus deficiency.

According to Dr. Ann F. Rhoads, a plant pathologist at the Morris Arboretum of the University of Pennsylvania, ozone is only one of several pollutants whose symptoms mimic other garden problems.

Even knowledgeable gardeners may be fooled.

sulfur dioxide Unlike ozone pollution, sulfur dioxide and hydrogen fluoride pollution tend to be localized with a single point of origin. My own introduction to sulfur dioxide damage came courtesy of a building furnace across the street where apparently high-sulfur fossil fuel was being burned. When the winds shifted, my garden was enveloped in a shroud of smoke— and within 24 hours my tomato plants responded with irregular, light brown areas of dead tissue between the veins of the leaf (symptoms much like those of windburn, leaf miners, certain fungus diseases and water stress).

The leaves looked a mess, but I'm happy to say the tomato fruit was fine and also safe to eat.

dirty soil Soil pollutants, however, pose more serious problems for edibles and may be present in areas adjacent to heavy vehicular traffic. You can

Root crops:
Radish, Beet and Carrot

alleviate the problems to some degree by planting your vegetables, fruit or herbs as far back from the traffic as possible and by adding a barrier hedge to help filter the fallout. You may succeed in neutralizing the contaminants in the soil by working in quantities of humus or decayed organic matter and by raising the pH closer to 7.

You may also have to limit the kinds of plants you grow; tests have shown that lead content is highest in leafy crops like lettuce and basil, moderately so in root crops like radishes and lowest in fruiting plants like tomatoes, beans and squash.

In any case, a professional soil analysis is essential.

While there's not much each of us gardeners, alone, can do to protect our plants from pollution, together we can work for passage of stricter laws. For if the day comes when garden plants are no longer able to survive, neither will gardeners.

nonpathogenic problems　There are several other environmental or nonpathogenic causes that lead to plant decline or death. Incorrect watering is probably the most serious. And this is so important that I have devoted all of Chapter 9 to water. (I have no scientific statistics but have long suspected inadequate moisture to be *the* major cause of loss of container plants on balconies and terraces.)

There may also be soil deficiencies or incorrect pH, and this is covered in Chapter 6.

Closely related is the overenthusiastic use of fertilizers, pesticides or both. You can prevent this by *reading* that label.

And finally, it is just possible you have the wrong plant for your place—one that's not at all suited to your sun, wind, area or seasonal temperatures. The remedy is a change to a more compatible species.

plant diseases　And then there are plant diseases.

It's easy to forget that plants are living beings and get sick sometimes—just like people, dogs and tropical fish. Major causes of plant ailments include bacteria, fungi and viruses. Although some diseases have no cure, quite a few can be eliminated or at least controlled by one of the many broad-spectrum over-the-counter "medicines."

But, you may wonder, without a degree in pathology how will you know your plants are sick? Well, without a degree in medicine, how do parents know that their children are sick? Here again the answer is *observation:* make a habit of looking closely at your plants (or "admiring," if you prefer). If you know what they're like when they're healthy and happy, you'll know when they're not.

noninsect problems　The following list may help you detect and cope with some of the noninsect problems you may encounter:

SYMPTOMS AND/OR TYPICAL NAME	POSSIBLE CAUSE	TREATMENT
Blossom End Rot Vegetables have water-soaked or sunken brown spots on the opposite end from the stem.	Fluctuations in soil moisture.	Maintain even soil moisture with proper watering and mulching.
	Calcium deficiency.	Add ground egg shells, oyster shells, wood ashes, ground limestone or other calcium-rich nutrients to soil. Avoid high-nitrogen fertilizers. Maintain pH of 6–6.5.

SYMPTOMS AND/OR TYPICAL NAME	POSSIBLE CAUSE	TREATMENT
Chlorosis Leaves are small and pale, with yellowish marks between veins.	Nutrient deficiency, usually nitrogen.	Apply high-nitrogen fertilizer.
	Lack of available iron because of incorrect pH.	Analyze soil and adjust to proper pH for plant species.
	Trace elements are inadequate.	Add well-decomposed organic matter to soil. Use fertilizer that includes trace elements.
	Insufficient oxygen around roots.	Amend soil with perlite or sand to alleviate compaction and increase drainage.
Fire Blight Blossoms or young twig endings and leaves wither and die. Bark is water-soaked, then darkens and dries. Affects rose-family members such as crabapples, pears and cotoneasters.	Various bacterial diseases.	Prune and destroy infected twigs or cut away infected areas (sterilize tools in household bleach). Spray with copper sulfate. Use resistant cultivars or species.
Leaf Spot Spots or holes in leaves resembling irregular polka dots.	Various bacterial or fungal diseases, usually aggravated by dampness.	Remove and destroy fallen leaves and infected portions. Avoid wetting leaves in evening. Prune to improve air circulation. Use fungicidal soap. Neem oil.
Mildews Whitish coating on leaves or buds.	Powdery mildew thrives with warm days and cool nights in either humid or dry weather.	Remove badly infected leaves and prune to increase air circulation. Spray with an antidesiccant. Clean surrounding area well in autumn. Use fungicide spray. Neem oil. Use a baking soda spray (Mix ¼ cup of warm water, 1½ teaspoons baking soda and 1 tablespoon vegetable oil. Blend into 1½ gallons of water and spray.
	Downy mildew is small white cottony growths on leaf surfaces. It thrives in cool, moist weather.	Avoid nighttime watering. Clean surrounding area well in autumn. Use fungicide spray. Plant resistant cultivars or species.

SYMPTOMS AND/OR TYPICAL NAME	POSSIBLE CAUSE	TREATMENT
Scorch Edges or tips of leaves appear dried or burned.	Insufficient watering.	Increase frequency and/or quantity of water. Increase organic content of soil for better water retention.
	Sun and/or wind too strong for species.	Transplant to more protected spot. Replant with more tolerant species.
	Potassium deficiency.	Add greensand marl or other high-potassium fertilizer.
	Fertilizer burn from overfeeding with chemical fertilizer.	Read labels carefully before fertilizing. Flood soil with water to dilute excess chemicals.
Wilt Leaves droop, branch endings are limp.	Too little water reaching ends.	Increase frequency and/or quantity of water. Add more organic material to soil to improve moisture retention.
	Insufficient top pruning to compensate for root loss.	Prune newly transplanted plants or those that were recently root-pruned.
	Various fungal or bacterial diseases.	Remove afflicted twigs (use household bleach to disinfect tools).
	Various root problems including nematodes or disease.	Check roots for rot, lumps or disease. Remove plant and discard as much of surrounding soil as possible. Replant area with species from a different plant family. See page 236.
Leaf Problems (misc.) Lower leaves become yellowed or purplish, and/or curl backwards and droop. There are few flowers and fruiting is poor.	Phosphorus deficiency. Pot bound roots or insufficient roots.	Apply high-phosphorus fertilizer. If symptoms are accompanied by lush leaf growth, discontinue use of nitrogen fertilizer.
Yellowed leaves and spindly growth with poor flowering.	Insufficient sun.	Transplant to better light conditions or use shade-tolerant species.
Unusually vigorous growth with dark leaves but poor flowering or fruit set.	Too much nitrogen.	Reduce use of nitrogen fertilizers and read labels for proper application.

getting professional help   Studying this section (or even several specialized books) will not guarantee you'll be able to cure or even recognize every plant problem any more than memorizing first aid makes you a doctor. At some point, preferably before things get overly desperate, it may be best to seek professional help.

botanical institutions or societies   You might begin by joining a local botanical garden, arboretum or horticultural society. The dues are a small enough price to pay for the many services provided, not the least of which are plant identification and diagnosis of plant diseases and pests.

the Cooperative Extension System   Then there's the Cooperative Extension System. This national resource, which dates from 1914, has traditionally helped farmers but now also ministers to needs of city folk. The extension is part of the United States Department of Agriculture and works with county governments and state land grant colleges. To locate your extension agent, either call your state land grant college (in New York, for example, it's Cornell, in New Jersey it's Rutgers) or look in your telephone directory's state government listings under headings such as "Extension service" or "Agricultural agent."

helping the helper   If one of these organizations has a telephone "hotline," a verbal description may suffice. Otherwise, submit a sample for diagnosis. Follow the cutting and packing procedures for plant identification (page 124) and add a brief summary of the problem including:

- How long you have been aware of the symptoms and the season they first appeared.
- The extent of the problem for different plant parts.
- Other plants that display similar symptoms.
- Recent fertilizing and/or watering procedures.

persistently troublesome plants   Adapting my grandmother's saying about children—"little plants, little problems; big plants, big problems"—is not to imply that the size of plant necessarily alters the seriousness of the problem. But it does make life easier in the case of a young or small specimen of a commonly grown species.
The best cure for persistently troubled plants is the trash can.

the birds and bees   The casual observer may assume that no "real" birds or bees reside in town (pigeons and yellow jackets don't count). While impediments like skyscrapers, television towers and shiny windows do take a toll, chickadees and sparrows catch insects and sing and honeybees can be found foraging for nectar among stamens and pistils. Both bird and bee are sure to be attracted to the oasis they see from on high.

And if your goal is a "real" garden, you will not try to keep them away.

supplementing nature   The birds will arrive looking for a safe spot to rest as well as insects, seeds, fruit and water. Since small gardens are limited in their natural food supply, caring gardeners can provide something extra, especially in winter. But this doesn't mean tossing out bread scraps—which is a good way to welcome cockroaches, pigeons and rats.

the feeders   Proper wild bird feeders vary from the inexpensive "bells" sold at supermarkets or dime stores to some highly decorative accessories. These are found primarily at large garden centers or in mail-order catalogues, but also check pet shops, the zoo or a botanical garden.

Choose a feeder that's easy to install and easy to fill. Since it's particularly important to avoid attracting pigeons (which carry disease and bully smaller birds), select a feeder with a dowel-stick-shaped perch; pigeons must stand flat while eating. Also, locate the feeder so that spilled seed falls onto a heavily planted area, not paving. Then cover any bare soil underneath with a deep, rough mulch such as bark chips or evergreen boughs.

Most feeders hold loose seed. Black thistle, peanut hearts, fine cracked corn and sunflower seed are particularly enjoyed by chickadees, cardinals, titmice, nuthatches and the many species of finches and sparrows. Beef suet, begged from your butcher and hung in a bag of mesh, is also a welcome addition for many winter residents (in my garden, it's a magnet for handsome redheaded woodpeckers).

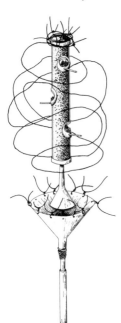

A wild bird feeder "pigeon-proofed" with wire coat hangers and funnels

Fresh water is important for wild birds too, for bathing as well as drinking, especially when the weather hovers around freezing. Elaborate birdbaths make fine garden ornaments, but all birds really require is a shallow dish that won't crack in the cold. Don't be shocked to see birds also rubbing themselves against soil. These abrasive "dust baths" are believed to be a way they eliminate the parasites that lodge among their feathers. If the birds' vigorous winter dust baths expose shallow-planted perennials or bulbs, cover the bare patches with mulch.

berries for people   Any collection of plants that produces fruit, berries or seeds or gives shelter to insects will attract birds. But problems arise if you want to enjoy this bounty yourself, as I discovered one autumn when every bright orange berry disappeared from my firethorn. The secret is to keep the feeders well stocked and the plants covered with deterrents like wind chimes or hanging pieces of shiny aluminum foil. Netting— and timely harvesting of edible fruit—may also be needed.

ongoing pleasure and care
Wild birds prefer dining and drinking in a sunny, wind-sheltered spot within flitting distance of the protective limbs of a bushy shrub. For maximum enjoyment (for humans) the feeder should also be where it can be viewed from indoors. There is enormous pleasure in hearing and observing the wild birds that are sure to visit your garden. But where winters are cold, bird feeding is also a responsibility.
If you start, you mustn't stop.

the busy bees
Once you realize that birds expect to share your city space, you'll accept that bees will too. Hard-working bumblebees and honeybees forage in flowers for nectar and sugars (and simultaneously help spread pollen). The most active period for busy bees is the same as for busy workers: nine to five. And like many workers, bees often pause for a midday break. On dark, cold or rainy days they too prefer to stay home.
City folk may find it hard to believe that bumblebees and honeybees are gentle creatures, entirely different from the ill-tempered hornets, yellow jackets and wasps. Unless you're on top of their hive or try to swat or crush them, the possibility of being stung by a honeybee or bumblebee is remote. It's only your plants they're after.
But even knowing that, you may be disconcerted by their presence. To guarantee their lack of interest in you while you're working in your garden, wear light-colored clothing, avoid sudden moves and don't wear perfume or powder.

squirrels
Squirrels are another matter.
They can be fun to watch, but not when they dig up your bulbs, attack fresh flowers or make off with newly ripened fruit. My own solution for the few squirrels I've had was to trap them in a raccoon-size Havahart trap (a clever invention that catches animals unharmed and alive) and release them at some good distance, on the far side of a very busy thoroughfare. If there are too many to trap, other ways to thwart their having their way with your garden is to plant bulbs fairly deep and disguise the area with a heavy mulch to make it appear undisturbed. Tulips and crocus are favorite winter fare, but allium family members and daffodils do not seem to appeal.

If they also go after your bird feeders, try thwarting them by placing the feeder on a tall pole that is beyond jumping distance of a tree or fence—at least about 6 feet away.

Coping with all aspects of nature isn't always easy. And sometimes even plants can be downright dangerous.

poisonous plants Poison ivy and poison oak, for example, are notoriously toxic and no sane person knowingly plants or touches them. However, some of the most attractive and rewarding garden plants also have parts that are toxic to varying degrees if eaten or chewed.

City children must be taught that random garden pickings must not be put in their mouths.

not just any berry It's not wise to assume that a berry or stem is acceptable for a human to munch on just because a cat, squirrel or bird does. Children have to be taught that only *specific* portions of *specific* plants are safe—the berries from the blueberry shrub only, for example, and not just any berry that's blue, or the tomato *fruit* or rhubarb *stem* only, and not the leaves.

symptoms of plant poisoning Symptoms of plant poisoning vary considerably but may include drowsiness, stomach pain, vomiting or diarrhea. Some toxic portions may also affect the nervous system and heart. If you suspect plant poisoning, immediately call your doctor or a poison control center. Describe the plant or plant parts you suspect and bring them along if you need to go for treatment.

plants with some toxic part Here's a sampling of plants with some portion (stems, leaves, flowers, berries, seeds or roots) that have been known to cause serious or fatal illness when eaten or chewed:

Autumn crocus	Daffodils	Jack-in-the-pulpit	Oleander
Azalea	English ivy	Lantana	Peach trees
Bittersweet	Euphorbia	Larkspur	Rhododendron
Caladium	Foxglove	Lily-of-the-valley	Skunk cabbage
Cherry trees	Holly	Mountain laurel	Yew
Crocus			

But don't allow the idea of danger to affect your selection of garden plants. There are so many potentially toxic portions that if you really want to eliminate hazards altogether you won't have a garden. A little prudence is needed.

After all, if Adam had just been *careful,* we might still be in Eden.

Ginkgo
Ginkgo biloba

*Many worthwhile projects are abandoned because the energy of
a gardener in August does not match his aspirations of the pre-
ceding April.*
—Frederick McGourty, Jr., Brooklyn Botanic Garden Record
Handbook: "Gardening with Wildflowers," July 1979

13. The City Gardener's Almanac: A Seasonal Summary

Early Spring

Reassess and bring up to date your original cardboard copy of your garden plan. If you haven't made one, do it now.

If spring drizzles are sparse, water everything. Give special attention to
street trees and woody plants in containers.

Hose soot off evergreens. Douse those near heavy vehicular traffic with a
water solution of mild dishwashing detergent.

When nighttime temperatures show signs of remaining above freezing,
begin removing decorative boughs and winter mulches.

Press down clumps of perennials that have been pushed up by winter
heaving.

If you didn't do it in autumn, repair, clean or repaint garden furnishings,
including balcony or terrace railings, latticework, awnings, fences, containers and window boxes. Build anew where needed.

Transplant woody species that no longer fit their alloted space.

Prune summer-blooming shrubs back to the strongest signs of life.

If you didn't loosen and fertilize your garden in autumn, do it as soon as
the soil is no longer soggy wet and sticky.

Fill window boxes and empty containers with soil for new plants.

If you didn't do some root pruning of container shrubs and trees in autumn, do it now.

Plant spinach, radishes, peas and other cool-weather crops now.

Test your soil pH with a kit or meter, or send a sample for professional testing.

Appraise your houseplants and eliminate those that warrant discarding. Groom and prune survivors and repot those in need of larger quarters.

Apply dormant oil sprays to deciduous plants that have had problems with insects or disease. Spray only if nighttime temperatures no longer drop below freezing and days remain above 45F°.

Late Spring

Don't get impatient about moving houseplants and homegrown seedlings outdoors; wait until nighttime temperatures stabilize above 65F°.

Keep houseplants outside in a sheltered spot for several days until they become acclimated to the sun and wind.

Divide emerging perennials that are getting crowded. Donate extras to community groups, schools or other city institutions.

Throw out garden plants that are obviously weak or show no signs of life. Use the space for species you've never grown before.

Plant dahlias, cannas, gladiolus and other summer-flowering bulbs and tubers.

Prune winter-killed limbs of trees and shrubs.

Scrub your birdbath and fill it with fresh water daily.

Garden ponds that have turned murky brown should now be cleaned and refilled with fresh water. Wait 2 days or use a dechlorinator before adding fish or plants.

Be ruthless about eliminating seedlings of ailanthus, striped maple, mimosa or any others you don't want in your garden.

Plant vine crops like cucumbers, squash or beans. To save space, train them up a wire fence or a trellis. When all danger of frost is past, add warm-weather crops like tomatoes, peppers and eggplants.

The planting season is in full swing now; take it easy if you've not left your office desk for a while.

Log in new plant purchases on a photocopy of your garden plan.

Early Summer

Water newly planted species and recently divided perennials regularly if there is insufficient rain.

Nip off the faded flowers of rhododendron, lilac and other spring bloomers for good bud set for next year.

Yard gardeners with at least 5 hours of sun can encourage spring bulbs to rebloom next year by cutting flower stalks and allowing the leaves to brown and die naturally (if the leaves look messy, bunch them together with a rubber band).

Where growing conditions are not ideal (e.g., extreme shade or limited space), dig up and discard spring bulbs. Plan to reorder and replant in autumn.

It's never too late to add another window box—or improve the one you have.

Remove the spent blooms of early perennials.

Fertilize with a water-soluble high-phosphorus fertilizer (i.e., 5-10-5 or equivalent) annual flowers, summer bloomers like roses and butterfly shrub, and annual veggies like tomatoes and cukes.

Don't apply pesticides or fertilizers when dog day temperatures hover near 85F°.

Deadhead annuals regularly to encourage new blooms.

Order autumn flowering bulbs for planting in late summer.

Wield your pruning shears now and get spring blooming shrubs and trees back in control. They'll soon begin setting their buds for next year.

Stake tall or leggy flowers before they flop or fall. Use plastic ties and natural bamboo or pruned twigs of sturdy shrubs.

Late Summer

Maiden Pink
Dianthus deltoides

Don't procrastinate on spring bulb orders for autumn planting. Use a photocopy of your garden plan for planning.

Keep up with fruit and vegetable harvest—overripe produce tastes awful, is less nutritious and attracts pests.

Continue fertilizing summer annuals and autumn bloomers with a water-soluble high-phosphorus fertilizer (i.e., 5-10-5 or equivalent).

Stop fertilizing trees and shrubs. Prune only to remove dead twigs.

Keep insect pests and soot under control with a weekly hosing of top and underleaf surfaces.

Take advantage of this quiet time in nurseries to land some bargains. Avoid bare-root plants or those with health problems.

Your vacation may be the end of your garden. Find a sympathetic friend to water your plants while you're away.

Fill in empty spaces with transplants of late-blooming species like Michaelmas daisies, Japanese anemones or cool-weather veggies like broccoli, spinach or lettuce.

Keep plants well watered through dry spells. Plants on sunny or windy rooftops may need twice-daily watering.

Save and recycle household water as much as possible.

For winter color indoors, cut and dry garden flowers like astilbe, baby's breath, tansy, cockscomb, globe thistle and hydrangea. Tie them with a rubber band and tack them upside down to a wall to dry.

Make your own potpourri by harvesting flowers and fragrant herbs. Spread them on a cookie sheet or paper towel to dry, then pile them into a deep salad bowl and blend. Add a drop of perfumed essential oil like lavender, or a spice like cinnamon bark and cloves. Add a tablespoon of powdered orris root as a fixative.

Early Autumn	Be ruthless about eliminating the plants you abhor; use your space for maximum pleasure and plan to try something new next year.
	Continue planting woody species and hardy perennials in yards. Keep new plantings well watered if there is no rain.
	Harvest and dry or freeze culinary herbs—don't be lazy about labeling.
	Dig up dahlias, caladium, canna and other summer bulbs and keep them in a cool dry spot if you have a storage room indoors. Otherwise treat them as annuals; reorder anew next year.
	Get your houseplants back indoors before the furnace is activated. But first get them clean and pest free by covering the soil with a damp paper towel and turning them upside-down in a soapy water bath.
	Encourage hardy species to enter dormancy by reducing the frequency of waterings.
	Last chance this year to thin and divide perennials that are crowded and straggly. Share those you can't use with a community group or neighbor.
	Add spring-flowering bulbs to yards and large containers and around street trees.
	Don't save seeds from flowers and vegetables that are hybrids—many will not breed true next year.
	Stop pruning woody species.
	Start a small compost pile with fallen leaves from areas beneath healthy plants.
Late Autumn	Take a pH test of the soil around plants that have done poorly.
	After most deciduous leaves have dropped, replenish soil nutrients of terrace tubs, yards and street tree pits.
	Lightly root prune mature container trees, shrubs and vines if you did not do so last spring.
	Add winter mulches and decorative evergreens as the cold weather settles in.
	Wrap and protect your awning for winter.
	Remember to water rooftop plants and street trees if there are weeks with no rain.

Dormant oil sprays can be applied to deciduous species as long as daytime temperatures remain above 45F° and there is no nighttime frost.

Repair, clean or repaint balcony or terrace railings, lattices and fences as well as garden furniture, containers and window boxes.

Secure climbers and vines with string or plastic ties to prevent their flapping with the wind.

Before storing soil tools, clean, sharpen and wipe them with an oily cloth. Take pruning shears to a hardware store for sharpening.

Winter	Mulch perennials and small shrubs after the ground has frozen.

Keep feeders stocked for birds and set out shallow pans of water.

Use discarded Christmas tree branches as a winter mulch and to enliven bare window boxes.

Begin application procedure for street tree-planting permit.

Lightly thin spring-flowering shrubs and trees in late winter to have cut branches bloom in vases indoors.

Prune the upper limbs and twigs of trees and shrubs that were root pruned in autumn.

Remember to water container trees and shrubs outdoors if snow or rain is minimal. Evergreens in exposed locations are particularly vulnerable.

Pile fresh snow around street trees for a meltdown contribution.

Don't de-ice around your street tree or front garden with salt compounds. Use sand, sawdust, wood ashes or urea fertilizers.

Hire an arborist to thin or cable large yard trees for better control and more summer light.

Use this peaceful time for undramatic activities such as restocking soil supplies like peat moss and cow manure.

Bring your original cardboard copy of your garden plan up to date. If you haven't yet made one, do it now.

Peruse catalogues and look for species that are right for you, but check your garden plan to see if they fit. Even if you have no room, catalogue shopping is a good way to learn.

Place orders for summer-flowering bulbs and mark their locations on a photocopy of your garden plan.

This is flower show season; plan a pilgrimage to as many exhibits as you can get to.

Hardy cyclamen
Cyclamen sp.

Camellia
Camellia japonica

Any garden demands as much of its maker as he has to give. But
I do not need to tell you, if you are a gardener, that no other
undertaking will give as great a return for the amount of effort
put into it.
—Elizabeth Lawrence (circa 1950), *Gardening for Love,* 1987

Afterword

Elizabeth Scholtz
Director Emeritus, Brooklyn Botanic Garden

Here we are, fifteen years later. Since I wrote the Foreword to her first
work, *The Terrace Gardener's Handbook,* Linda Yang has relocated from
her high-rise rooftop terrace to a city backyard, where in a 19-by-50-foot
space she has created a birch "forest" (four birches), a "pond" (4½-foot
diameter), a rock garden (maybe twenty rocks), a perennial "border"
(about 5 feet long), a bamboo "grove" (five clumps) and a formal herb
garden—all on an admittedly Lilliputian scale and in the part shade that
prevails in city backyards.

Armed with this decade and a half of experience, she has been able to update and considerably expand this successor to her first book. She has
widened not only her own territorial boundaries but also her geographi-
cal horizons, having surveyed some of the problems and solutions of gardeners in other parts of the country.

In this same decade and a half, gardening in the Big Apple has grown;
New York City has acquired its own horticultural branch of the Extension
Service; many groups have been formed to aid aspiring city "beautifiers";
radio and television programs on gardening proliferate; and there is even
an organization to satisfy the needs of the increasing numbers of professionals in the urban gardening milieu. Brooklyn Botanic Garden, along

with its many sister institutions and horticultural societies in cities from coast to coast, has continued to expand its educational offerings of courses, symposia and other programs for increasingly well-informed gardeners.

It has been a pleasure to study this delightful new comprehensive account that is the product of an enthusiastic tiller of the urban soil. To paraphrase my original Foreword, she has written this book in the hope that what has proved successful for her will be useful to those facing similar problems and situations when trying to garden in limited space and containers. Here again, her photographs prove that it is possible to grow a wide variety of beautiful plants in town. I am proud too of my colleague here at BBG, Dr. Stephen K-M. Tim, whose exquisite line drawings in this book are the result of an artist's soul and botanist's eye.

Like its predecessor, this book will be most useful to all those who face the challenge of bringing the green world into their lives despite the restricted confines and attendant demands of an urban habitat.

Filling mail orders at the Burpee Company, Philadelphia. Circa 1890 *Courtesy, W. Atlee Burpee & Co.*

Oh gentle reader, forgive me if you are "sleepy" or bored or an-
noyed. The tired catalog-writer has emptied his "sack of adjectives
at your feet."
—Will Tillotson, "Roses of Yesterday," 1955 Catalogue

Where to Find What by Mail

Nothing beats armchair shopping. Certainly, when I started writing this book, I would never have believed it possible to further enhance the concept of "gardening by mail." But it seems the Internet has managed to do just that. Now, virtually anything a gardener might need is a finger flick away. And with increasing numbers of suppliers jumping into this business, it seems that more and more enticing garden accoutrements—plants as well as non-plants—are being purchased without first being seen "for real."

The following pages contain a mere sampling of the thousands of such suppliers, large and small, that city gardeners will find useful. Some of these purveyors I've dealt with myself. Others I know only by reputation. In any case, a mention here should not be construed as endorsement; an omission bears no sinister implication.

In an effort to save space (and eliminate repetition) I've listed merchants only once, although a good bit of overlap exists. Some tool suppliers, for example, also offer furniture, while some plant suppliers also sell "good" insects, and so on. Such overlaps will be evident once you actually start perusing the catalogues.

finding suppliers Advertisements for mail-order suppliers are much in evidence in magazines, local newspapers and Internet pop-ups that seasonally adorn the computer screen. Extensive compilations of sources may also be found in such specialty horticultural periodicals as the remarkable and long-lived *Avant Gardener* (P.O. Box 489, New York, NY 10028), publications of local botanical gardens and source books (like Barbara J. Barton's classic *Gardening By Mail*) published regularly enough to keep gardeners in touch. The Mail Order Gardening Association, founded in 1934, has many scores of members and offers its directory for a $2 fee. You can write them at P.O. Box 2129, Columbia, MD 21045 or visit their Web site: www.mailordergardening.com.

smart shopping   I believe what I can see and touch. But I also know temptations in catalogues and online advertisements are hard to resist. So it's essential to use some smart shopping precautions, not the least of which is taking time to read every bit of fine print and regard with skepticism unusually low prices or outrageous claims. If it seems too good to be true, it probably is. In any case, wide variations in price—and quality—from one company to another should be expected.

As you will quickly discover, not everything is spelled out in the catalogue text, so sometimes it's important to contact suppliers—the hardgoods especially—for detailed information, such as whether the merchandise is in stock, when and how will it be shipped, and—most important—whether there is there a "free-trial, money-back, no-questions asked" time slot.

Once you've made a decision, fill out the order blank carefully, print clearly (and proofread what you're e-mailing), keep a record of what you've bought and a copy of electronic forms or receipts and use a credit card or check, which makes withholding payments easier should there be a problem.

sources of   Among the larger items you are likely to need are such furnishings as
garden furnishings   chairs, benches, tables and plant containers. Catalogue offerings of furnishings invariably appear to be more interesting than what can be found locally. But with only a picture to work from, you must take time first to consider the actual size of the object (will it really fit your allotted space?), the actual material (in a photograph, painted plastic looks like painted wood), details of assembly and shipping (how much hammering and nailing you will really have to contend with), and the company's policy on returns (you just might hate what you see when you really see it and it would be a shame to have to pay).

Several sources of garden furnishings and containers follow:

Adirondack Designs
350 Cypress Street
Fort Bragg, CA 95437
(800) 222-0343
www.adirondackdesign.com

BenchSmith
429 Easton Road
Warrington, PA 18976
(800) 482-3327
www.benchsmith.com

Charleston Battery Bench, Inc.
191 King Street
Charleston, SC 29401
(843) 722-3842
www.birlant.com

Country Casual
9085 Comprint Court
Gaithersburg, MD 20877
(800) 284-8325
www.countrycasual.com

Florentine Craftsmen
46-24 28th Street
Long Island City, NY 11101
(800) 876-3567
www.florentinecraftsmen.com

Gardener's Eden
17 Riverside Street
Nashua, NH 03062
(800) 822-9600

Kinsman Company
P.O. Box 428
Pipersville, PA 18947
(800) 733-4146
www.kinsmangarden.com

Rosenwach/Sitecraft
40-25 Crescent Street
Long Island City, NY 11101
(718) 729-4900
www.site-craft.com

Smith & Hawken
4 Hamilton Landing
Novato, CA 94949
(800) 776-3336
www.smithandhawken.com

Walpole Woodworkers
P.O. Box 151
Walpole, MA 02081
(800) 343-6948
www.walpolewoodworkers.com

garden ornaments Once major furnishings are in place you can relax and peruse catalogues with such other interesting garden ornaments as statuary, fountains, birdhouses and feeders, sundials and the like. Here are several sources:

Audubon Workshop
5200 Schenley Place
Lawrenceburg, IN 47025
(812) 537-3583
www.audubonworkshop.com

Duncraft, Inc.
102 Fisherville Road
Concord, NH 03303
(800) 593-5656
www.duncraft.com

Kenneth Lynch & Sons Inc.
P.O. Box 488
Wilton, CT 06897
(203) 762-8363
www.klynchandsons.com

Wind & Weather
250 North Main Street
Fort Bragg, CA 95437
(800) 922-9463
www.windandweather.com

gazebos Some mail order companies specialize in truly unusual items, and one of the most intriguing is the gazebo. Detailed directions are included with these prefabricated kits, so if you're handy, you can assemble a gazebo yourself (or hire someone with talent to do so). While only basic woodworking tools are needed, a rudimentary knowledge of construction techniques is advisable, as is a minimum of two helpers. Don't forget to check to see if a local building permit is required *before* placing your order.

The following manufacture gazebos (and various other large garden structures) in kit form:

Bowbends
P.O. Box 900
Bolton, MA 01740
(800) 518-6471
www.bowbends.com

The Garden Concepts Collection
P.O. Box 241233
Memphis, TN 38124
(901) 756-1649
www.gardenconcepts.net

Dalton Pavilions, Inc.
20 Commerce Drive
Telford, PA 18969
(215) 721- 1492
www.daltonpavilions.com

Vixen Hill Gazebos
Main Street
Elverson, PA 19520
(800) 423-2766
www.vixenhill.com

tools and other essential gadgets There's no planting without spade and fork, and there's no maintaining without shears and hose. Most local garden centers offer some tools but mail-order suppliers, such as those listed here, have a far greater array to choose from:

Charley's Greenhouse Supply
17979 State Route 536
Mount Vernon, WA 98273
(800) 322-4707
www.charleysgreenhouse.com

Gardener's Supply Co.
128 Intervale Road
Burlington, VT 05401
(888) 833-1412
www.gardeners.com

Kinsman Co, Inc.
P.O. Box 428
Pipersville, PA 18947
(800) 733-4146
www.kinsmangarden.com

A.M. Leonard, Inc.
P.O. Box 816
Piqua, OH 45356
(800) 543-8955
www.amleo.com

Walt Nicke Co.
P.O. Box 433
Topsfield, MA 01983
(978) 887-3388
www.gardentalk.com

The Urban Farmer
2833 Vincente Street
San Francisco, CA 94116
(415) 661-2204
www.urbanfarmerstore.com

soil tests What's happening beneath the soil is ever a mystery, but professionals can help—either before or after planting—and soil analyses may also be handled by mail. Soil samples should be collected and marked as suggested on page 143. They may then be sent to your State Cooperative Extension Office (look in your phone book for location) or to one of the following companies (call for specific directions).

Integrated Fertility Management
1422 North Miller Street
Wenatchee, WA 98801
(800) 332-3179
www.agricology.com

Peaceful Valley Farm Supply
P.O. Box 2209
Grass Valley, CA 95945
(888) 784-1722
www.groworganic.com
(also natural controls and fertilizers)

natural controls and fertilizers The safest weapon in the battle of the bugs and diseases are weapons provided by nature herself. Beneficial predators, disease controls and organic fertilizers, which help inspire healthy soil, are available from the following suppliers:

Gardens Alive!
5100 Schenley Place
Lawrenceburg, IN 47025
(812) 537-8650
www.gardens-alive.com

Harmony Farm Supply
P.O. Box 460
Graton, CA 95444
(707) 823-9125
www.harmonyfarm.com

Nature's Control
P.O. Box 35
Medford, OR 97501
(541) 899-8318
www.naturescontrol.com

Rincon Vitova
P.O. Box 1555
Ventura, CA 93002
(800) 248-BUGS
www.rinconvitova.com

Territorial Seed Company
P.O. Box 158
Cottage Grove, OR 97424
(541) 942-9547
www.territorial-seed.com

Worm's Way
7850 North Highway 37
Bloomington, IN 47404
(800) 316-1261
www.wormsway.com

garden plants And then there are mail-order plants. I must confess first that I'm a big believer in local suppliers of plants. But no neighborhood garden center or regional nursery can possibly offer every plant that might be of interest. So this is where a countrywide selection of sources is essential.

Avoid disappointment with sold-out species by ordering early in the season and listing possible substitutes and alternate delivery dates. Some mail-order nurseries strive for a broad selection of plants, while others focus only on those the owners themselves are drawn to, and their catalogues are filled with anecdotes or personal comments stating their reasons.

But while we gardeners in town enjoy our ecstasy of armchair dreaming, we must also remember that mail-order catalogues are costly to print and just as costly to mail. As a result, many suppliers must now demand a nominal fee. Often this is deductible from the price of a first order, but it's up to you to remember to do so.

Here's a sampling—more or less by specialty—of mail-order suppliers and some of the plants they focus on primarily, but not necessarily exclusively:

seeds, perennials
(may include
annuals),
ornamental shrubs
and trees

Bluestone Perennials
7211 Middle Ridge Road
Madison, OH 44057
(800)-852-5243
www.bluestoneperennials.com
(perennials)

Camellia Forest Nursery
9701 Carrie Road
Chapel Hill, NC 27516
(919) 968-0504
www.camforest.com
(shrubs and trees)

Fairweather Gardens
P.O. Box 330
Greenwich, NJ 08323
(856) 451-6261
www.fairweathergardens.com
(perennials, shrubs and trees)

ForestFarm
990 Tetherow Road
Williams, OR 97544
(541) 846-7269
www.forestfarm.com
(perennials, shrubs and trees)

Gardenimport
P.O. Box 760
Thornhill, Ontario
L3T 4A5
(905) 731-1950
www.gardenimport.com
(perennials, shrubs)

Greer Gardens
1280 Goodpasture Island Road
Eugene, OR 97401
(541) 686-8266
www.greergardens.com
(shrubs and trees)

Greenlee Nursery
241 E. Franklin Avenue
Pomona, CA 91766
(909) 629-9045
(ornamental grasses)

Heronswood Nursery Ltd.
7530 NE 288th Street
Kingston, WA 98346
(360) 297-4172
www.heronswood.com
(perennials, shrubs and trees)

Klehm's Song Sparrow
  Perennial Farm
13101 East Rye Road
Avalon, WI 53505
(800) 553-3715
www.songsparrow.com
(perennials)

Limerock Ornamental Grasses
70 Sawmill Road
Port Matilda, PA 16870
(814) 692-2272
www.limerockgrasses.com
(ornamental grasses)

New England Wildflower Society
180 Hemenway Road
Framingham, MA 01701
(508) 877-7630
www.newfs.org
(seeds)

Niche Gardens
1111 Dawson Road
Chapel Hill, NC 27516
(919) 967-0078
www.nichegardens.com
(perennials, shrubs and trees)

Park's Countryside Gardens
1 Parkton Avenue
Greenwood, SC 29647
(800) 213-0493
www.countrysidegardens.com
(seeds)

The Perennial Gardens
13139, 224th Street
Maple Ridge, B. C.
V4R 2P6
(604) 467-4218
www.perennialgardener.com
(perennials)

Pinetree Garden Seeds
P.O. Box 300
New Gloucester, ME 04260
(207) 926-3400
www.superseeds.com
(seeds)

Plant Delights Nursery, Inc.
9241 Sauls Road
Raleigh, NC 27603
(919) 772-4794
www.plantdel.com
(perennials)

Select Seeds—Antique Flowers
180 Stickney Hill Road
Union, CT 06076
(860) 684-9310
www.selectseeds.com
(seeds)

Siskiyou Rare Plant Nursery
2825 Cummings Road
Medford, OR 97501
(541) 772-6846
www.siskiyourareplantnursery.com
(perennials)

roses   **Corn Hill Nursery**
2700 Route 890
Corn Hill, N.B.
E4Z 1M2
(506) 756-3635
www.cornhillnursery.com

Heirloom Roses
24062 NE Riverside Drive
St. Paul, OR 97137
(503) 538-1576
www.heirloomroses.com

Stokes Seeds
P.O. Box 10
St. Catharines, ON
L2R 6R6
(905) 688-4300
www.stokeseeds.com
(seeds)

Wayside Gardens
1 Garden Lane
Hodges, SC 29695
(800) 845-1124
www.waysidegardens.com
(perennials, shrubs and trees)

We-Du Nurseries
2055 Polly Spout Road
Marion, NC 28752
(828) 738-8300
www.we-du.com
(perennials)

White Flower Farm
P.O. Box 50
Litchfield, CT 06759
(800) 503-9624
www.whiteflowerfarm.com
(perennials, shrubs and trees)

Jackson & Perkins Co.
1 Rose Lane
Medford, OR 97501
(800) 292-4769
www.jacksonandperkins.com

Nor'East Miniature Roses
P.O. Box 307
Rowley, MA 01969
(800) 426-6485
www.noreast-miniroses.com

the edible landscape

Burpee Seeds & Plants
300 Park Avenue
Warminster, PA 18974
(800) 888-1447
www.burpee.com
(veggies and herbs)

The Cook's Garden
P.O. Box 5010
Hodges, SC 29653
(800) 457-9703
www.cooksgarden.com
(veggies and herbs)

Edible Landscaping
P.O. Box 77
Afton, VA 22920
(800) 524-4156
www.ediblelandscaping.com
(fruiting shrubs and trees)

Indiana Berry & Plant Co.
5218 W 500 South
Huntingburg, IN 47542
(800) 295-2226
www.inberry.com
(fruiting shrubs and trees)

J.E. Miller Nurseries
5060 West Lake Road
Canandaigua, NY 14424
(800) 836-9630
www.millernurseries.com
(fruiting shrubs and trees)

The Rosemary House
120 South Market Street
Mechanicsburg, PA 17055
(717) 697-5111
www.therosemaryhouse.com
(herbs)

bulbs

Brent and Becky's Bulbs
7900 Daffodil Lane
Gloucester, VA 23061
(804) 693-3966
www.brentandbeckysbulbs.com

Sandy Mush Herb Nursery
316 Surrett Cove Road
Leicester, NC 28748
(828) 683-2014
(herbs)

Seeds of Change
P.O. Box 15700
Santa Fe, NM 87506
(888) 762-7333
www.seedsofchange.com
(organic veggies)

Seed Savers Exchange
3076 North Winn Road
Decorah, IA 52101
www.seedsavers.org
(heirloom veggies)

Shepherd's Garden Seeds
30 Irene Street
Torrington, CT 06790
(860) 482-3638
www.shepherdseeds.com
(veggies and herbs)

Tomato Growers Supply Co.
P.O. Box 2237
Fort Meyers, FL 33902
(888) 478-7333
www.tomatogrowers.com
(veggies)

Well-Sweep Herb Farm
205 Mt. Bethel Road
Port Murray, NJ 07865
(908) 852-5390
www.wellsweep.com
(herbs)

Dominion Seed House
Box 2500
Georgetown, Ontario L7G 5L6
(905) 873-3037
www.dominion-seed-house.com

Dutch Gardens
P.O. Box 2037
Lakewood, NJ 08701
(800) 818-3861
www.dutchgardens.com

John Scheepers, Inc.
23 Tulip Drive
Bantam, CT 06750
(860) 567-0838
www.johnscheepers.com

Kelly's Plant World
10266 E. Princeton
Sanger, CA 93657
(559) 294-7676

tropicals and houseplants

Glasshouse Works
P.O. Box 97
Stewart, OH 45778
(800) 837-2142
www.rareplants.com

Logee's Greenhouses, Ltd.
141 North Street
Danielson, CT 06239
(888) 330-8038
www.logees.com

water plants, fish and aquatic supplies

Lilypons Water Gardens
P.O. Box 10
Buckeystown, MD 21717
(800) 999-5459
www.lilypons.com

S. Scherer & Sons
140 Waterside Avenue
Northport, NY 11768
(631) 261-7432

McClure & Zimmerman
P.O. Box 368
Friesland, WI 53935
(800) 883-6998
www.mzbulb.com

Old House Gardens-Heirloom Bulbs
536-W Third Street
Ann Arbor, MI 48103
(734) 995-1486
www.oldhousegardens.com

Van Bourgondien
P.O. Box 1000
Babylon, NY 11702
(800) 622-9997
www.dutchbulbs.com

Shady Hill Gardens
821 Walnut Street
Batavia, IL 60510
(630) 879-5665
www.shadyhill.com

Stokes Tropicals
P.O. Box 9868
New Iberia, LA 70562
(800) 624-9706
www.stokestropicals.com

Van Ness Water Gardens
2460 North Euclid Avenue
Upland, CA 91784
(800) 205-2425
www.vnwg.com

Waterford Gardens
74 E. Allendale Road
Saddle River, NJ 07458
(201) 327-0721
www.waterfordgardens.com

Chinese Witch Hazel
'Arnold Promise'
Hamamelis intermedia
'Arnold Promise'

If you get one viewpoint, one suggestion, one idea out of a book, it's paid for itself.
—Elisabeth Woodburn, 1988 (Antiquarian Garden Book Dealer)

Selected Bibliography

Dirty fingernails alone do not a gardener make. Countless published works—old and new—have educated and inspired me. Here are a few that were also useful for preparing this book.

Books and Occasional Publications

Bailey, Libery Hyde, and Ethel Zoe (Staff of the L. H. Bailey Hortorium, Cornell University). *Hortus Third.* New York: Macmillan Publishing Co. Inc., 1976.

Bartels, Andreas. *Gardening with Dwarf Trees and Shrubs.* Portland, Ore.: Timber Press, 1986.

Barton, Barbara J. *Gardening by Mail.* Boston: Houghton Mifflin, 1993.

Carr, Anna. *Rodale's Color Handbook of Garden Insects.* Emmaus, Pennsylvania: Rodale Press, 1979.

Clausen, Ruth Rogers, and Nicolas H. Ekstrom. *Perennials for American Gardens.* New York: Random House, 1989.

Crowe, Sylvia. *Garden Design.* New York: Hearthside Press Inc., 1959.

Dirr, Michael A. *Manual of Woody Landscape Plants: Their Identification, Ornamental Characteristics, Culture, Propagation and Uses.* Champaign, Illinois: Stipes Publishing Co., 1983.

Duryea, Minga Pope. *Gardens in and About Town.* New York: E. P. Dutton and Co., 1923.

Everett, T. H. *The New York Botanical Garden Illustrated Encyclopedia of Horticulture*. New York: Garland Publishing, Inc., 1981.

Foster, F. Gordon. *Ferns to Know and Grow*. Portland, Ore.: Timber Press, 1984.

Fox, Helen M. *Gardening with Herbs*. New York: Macmillan Publishing Co. Inc., 1933.

Frederick, Wm. H. Jr. *100 Great Garden Plants*. Portland, Ore.: Timber Press, 1986.

Goldsmith, Carolyn. *Compost; A Cosmic View with Practical Suggestions*. New York: Harper Colophon Books, 1973.

Harper, Pamela, and Frederick McGourty. *Perennials: How to Select, Grow and Enjoy*. Tucson: H P Books, Inc., 1985

Hill, Lewis. *Pruning Simplified*. Pownal: Storey Communications, Inc., 1986.

Hockaday, Joan (photographs by Henry Bowles). *The Gardens of San Francisco*. Portland, Ore.: Timber Press, 1988.

Hunt, Peter (editor). *The Book of Garden Ornament*. London: J. M. Dent & Sons Ltd., 1974.

Hunter, Beatrice T. *Gardening Without Poisons*. Boston: Houghton Mifflin Co., 1970.

Jellicoe, Geoffrey and Susan. *The Landscape of Man*. New York: Van Nostrand Reinhold Co., 1975.

Johnson, Hugh. *The Principles of Gardening*. New York: Simon & Schuster, 1984.

Kellogg, Charles E. *Our Garden Soils*. New York: Macmillan Publishing Co., 1952.

Krussmann, Gerd (revised and translated by Michael E. Epp). *Pocket Guide to Choosing Woody Ornamentals*. Beaverton, Ore.: Timber Press, 1982.

Lloyd, Christopher. *The Well-Chosen Garden*. New York: Harper & Row, 1984.

Maccubbin, Robert P., and Peter Martin (editors). *British and American Gardens in the Eighteenth Century*. Williamsburg: The Colonial Williamsburg Foundation, 1984.

McLean, Teresa. *Medieval English Gardens*. New York: Viking Press, 1980.

Meyer, Mary Hockenberry, and Robert G. Mower. *Ornamental Grasses for the Home and Garden*. Ithaca: Information Bulletin 64, Cornell Cooperative Extension, 1986.

Morse, H. K. *Gardening in the Shade*. New York: Charles Scribner's Sons, 1939.

Organic Gardening Staff (editors). *The Encyclopedia of Organic Gardening*. Emmaus, Pennsylvania: Rodale Press, 1978.

Pirone, Pascal P. *Diseases and Pests of Ornamental Plants*. New York: Ronald Press, 1970.

Poor, Janet Meakin (editor). *Plants That Merit Attention. Volume 1: Trees*. Portland, Ore.: Timber Press, 1984.

Safe Pest Management Around the Home. Ithaca: Information Bulletin 74, Cornell Cooperative Extension, 1989.

Schenk, George. *The Complete Shade Gardener*. Boston: Houghton Mifflin Co., 1984.

Scott-James, Anne, and Osbert Lancaster. *The Pleasure Garden*. Ipswich, England: Gambit, 1977.

Smith, Edward C. *The Vegetable Gardener's Bible*. Pownal: Storey Books, 2000.

Smith, Michael D. (editor). *The Ortho Problem Solver*. San Francisco: Ortho Information Services, 1982.

Steffek, Edwin F. *The Pruning Manual.* New York: Van Nostrand Reinhold Co., 1969.

Taylor, Norman. *Taylor's Encyclopedia of Gardening.* Boston: Houghton Mifflin Co., 1961.

Truex, Philip. *The City Gardener.* New York: Alfred A. Knopf, 1964.

Van Gelderen, D. M., and J.R.P. van Hoey Smith. *Conifers.* Portland, Oregon: Timber Press, 186.

Verey, Rosemary. *Classic Garden Design.* New York: Congdon & Weed, Inc., 1984.

Westcott, Cynthia. *The Gardener's Bug Book.* New York: Doubleday & Co., 1964.

Wilkinson, Elizabeth, and Majorie Henderson. *The House of Boughs.* New York: Viking Penguin Inc., 1985.

Wyman, Donald. *Dwarf Shrubs:* New York: Macmillan Publishing Co., 1974.

———. *Wyman's Gardening Encyclopedia.* New York: Macmillan Publishing Co., 1986.

Zion, R.L. *Trees for Architecture and the Landscape.* New York: Reinhold Book Corp., 1968.

———. *Garden Projects.* New York: Arco Publishing, Inc., 1985.

Periodicals

Allen Lacy's Homeground. Linwood, New Jersey: Allen Lacy.

The American Gardener. Mt. Vernon, Virginia: American Horticultural Society.

The Avant Gardener. New York: Horticultural Data Processors.

Canadian Gardening. Markham, Ontario, Canada: Avid Media, Inc.

Country Living Gardener. New York: Hearst Communications.

Fine Gardening. Newtown, Connecticut: The Taunton Press, Inc.

Flower and Garden. New York: KC Publishing.

Garden Design. New York: World Publications.

Green Scene. Philadelphia: The Pennsylvania Horticultural Society.

The Herb Companion. Loveland, Colorado: Herb Companion Press.

Horticulture. Boston: Primedia.

OG (Organic Gardening). Emmaus, Pennsylvania: Rodale Press Inc.

Plants and Gardens News: Brooklyn Botanic Garden Record. Brooklyn, New York: Brooklyn Botanic Garden.

Elephant's-ear, Taro
Colocasia esculenta

With Gratitude

The following garden owners, de-signers and landscapers have gen-erously shared with me their ideas or allowed me to photograph their gardens for inclusion here:

Mr. and Mrs. Manuel R. Angulo
Trevor Ashbee
Mrs. Paul Page Austin
Susan and Ned Babbitt
William E. Barnes, Jr.
Pamela Berdan
Bob Berg and David Remnek;
     Farm & Garden Nursery Inc.
Raf Borello
James C. Blair
Bill Blass
Gwen and John Burgee
Philip Chandler
Monte Clinton
A. Billie Cohen
Mr. and Mrs. William J. Conklin
Keith Corlett
Jay Crawford
Judge Charles and Elizabeth K.
     Crookham
Page Dickey
Ken Druse
Tim Du Val, Plant Specialists Inc.
Mr. and Mrs. Arne Ekstrom
Nicolas H. Ekstrom
Carol Franklin, Andropogon
     Associates
Laurence and Maryvonee Ferar
Dr. Robert M. Giller
Maro A. Goldstone
Sondra Gilman Gonzales-Falla
Dimitri and Basil Gravanis,
     Dimitri's Gardens Ltd.
Luther Greene
Prof. Merton C. and Dr. Elizabeth
     ten Grotenhuis-Flemings
Patti Hagan
Edmund M. Hastings
Philip L. Herman
Joan Hockaday
Alice Recknagel Ireys, Landscape
     Architect

David L. Jeffries, Johnny
     Appleseed Landscaping
Mr. and Mrs. Michael Klebanoff
Maryssa La Rose, Eclectic Garden
     by Design
Robert Lester
Kathe Tanous and Bob Levenson
Mr. and Mrs. Robert F. Little
Patricia and Francis Mason
John Mayer
Jeff Mendoza
Julie Moir Messervy
Lynden B. Miller
Ann McPhail
Mr. And Mrs. Paul Mellon
Stewart Mott
David Murbach
Nobuko and Takamichi Nakajima
Shiro Nakane
Victor Nelson
Signe Nielsen, Landscape
     Architect
Mr. and Mrs. Waldemar Nielsen
Wingate Paine
Monroe E. Pinckard
David A. Protell, Chelsea Garden
     Center, Inc.
Mary Gehr Ray
James and Joanne Quan
     Reynolds
Kenneth and Ellen Roman
Carole and Alex Rosenberg
Paul Rudolph
Ruth and Marvin Sachs
Lalitte and Howell Scott
Dorothy and Herbert Silberman
Irene and Sidney B. Silverman
Irene Zambelli Silverman
Joseph Sirola
Lisa Stamm
Daniel D. Stewart
Barbara Stonecipher
Beverly and John Fox Sullivan
Steven and Mary Green Sweig
Lawrence B. Thomas
Nancy E. Turnbull
James van Sweden, Oehme, van
     Sweden & Associates Inc.

Sara and Gene Vogel
Ann Marie and Joseph Vingo
Shep and Myra Waldman
Donald J. Walsh
Andrea Marks and David
     Warmflash
Earl D. and Gina Ingoglia Weiner
Halsted Welles
William T. Wheeler
Nadine Zamichow
Josephine Zeitlin

Photograph Credits

Although most of the garden pho-tographs in this book were taken by me, friends have contributed pictures as follows:

William Aldrich, page 105 bot-tom; Henry Bowles (courtesy Joan Hockaday), pages 97 bot-tom, 164 bottom; Trevor Cole, page 108; Keith Corlett, page 22 top; Ken Druse, page 20 top; Nicolas H. Ekstrom, pages 99 top, 167 bottom; Jean-Pierre Godeau (courtesy Jacques Barret), page 25 top; Peter Land, page 104 top; Michael McKinley (courtesy Andropogon Associates), page 15; (courtesy Oehme, van Sweden Associates) page 174; Ann McPhail, page 98 bottom; Julie Moir Messervy, page 107 top; Shiro Nakane, page 166; Kenneth Roman, page 241 bottom, 248 third row right; Ann F. Rhoads, page 247 third row right, 248 top right, 248 sec-ond row right; George Taloumis, page 160 top, 247 bottom, 248 top left, 248 third row left; James van Sweden, page 243; Donald J. Walsh, page 28 bottom; Josephine Zeitlin, page 23.

Every gardener's life begins with an act of seduction, whether it comes at age 10 or age 50.
—Allen Lacy, 1987 (garden columnist and author)

Index

About the Author

Linda Yang, former garden columnist for *The New York Times,* writes about city gardening from a lifetime of dirty fingernails that, she admits, includes "quite a few trials and more than one error." Originally trained as an architect at the University of Pennsylvania, she has chosen to walk a garden path instead, and for more than three decades her garden articles and photographs have appeared in numerous periodicals. She presently tills one-fortieth of an acre behind a New York City townhouse five blocks east of Rockefeller Center, where she resides with her husband, John, and cat, Cleome hassleriana.

Also by Linda Yang:

The Terrace Gardener's Handbook
Plants for Problem Places
Topiaries & Espaliers